> In a sense, I'd forgotten my main motivations for becoming a chef: bringing people together and making them happy through food.

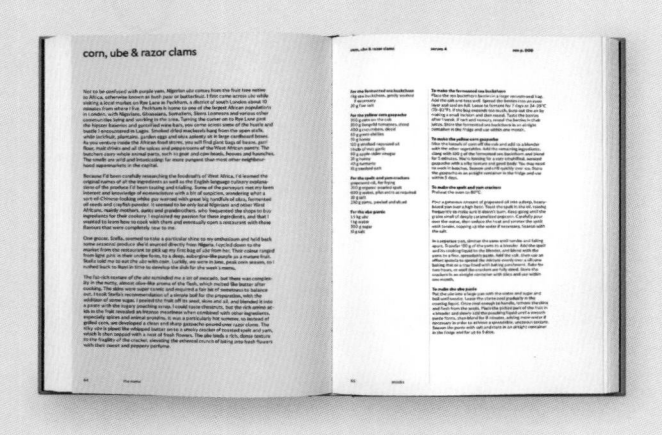

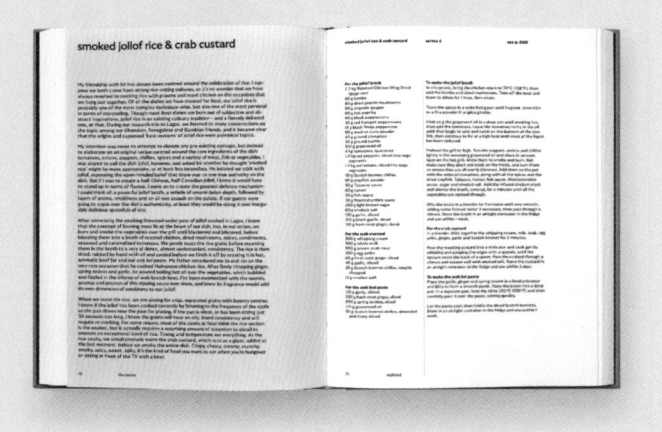

The two-Michelin-starred restaurant Ikoyi is one of the most original restaurants of its time.

-

The brainchild of acclaimed chef Jeremy Chan, who is behind the restaurant's applauded and unique tasting menu, and childhood friend Iré Hassan-Odukale, Ikoyi is visited and admired by diners from all over the world. It debuted on the 2022 Worlds 50 Best Restaurants list.

In this stunning cookbook, Chan shares more than 80 recipes that show how he achieves his signature bold heat. Peppered throughout the recipes are stories about the producers and spices that lie at the core of Chan's inspiration – as well as his own journey of how he came to be a chef and a culinary innovator, pushing boundaries at the forefront of the gastronomic landscape.

Jeremy's eloquent writing and stunning recipes are accompanied by original ethereal atmospheric photography.

Ikoyi

Jeremy Chan

Ikoyi

A Journey through
Bold Heat with Recipes

introduction

origins

I was born in Stockport, England, in 1987. My mother is Canadian and my father is Chinese. For the first eight years of my life, we lived in Hong Kong, where I went to a local international primary school with kids from all over the world. This time in Hong Kong was definitely a fundamental period in my life in terms of building memories: the towering skyscrapers, the neon lights and the pungent smells emanating from the crowded markets all remained entrenched in my mind.

The Chinese have a very strong food culture that I feel privileged to be connected to in such a profound way. Every Sunday, we would gather with family and friends and feast on dim sum; noodles, drunken shrimp, jellyfish and chicken feet are only a handful of the delicacies that I soon became deeply obsessed with. In Chinese culture, food dominates conversation and the daily routine, and the cuisine is much more complex than in many Western cultures. The number of dishes at the lunch table can be vast, as can the spectrum of taste and textures found in the dishes themselves. My father was always quite strict with us in terms of eating – he insisted that we try everything. I was slightly scared of his penetrating stare, but I look back now and am grateful that I was pushed to keep an open mind.

We moved to the northwest of the UK, near Manchester, when I was eight years old. Later, I spent my high-school days in Winchester. Since my parents are from two very different places, I was lucky enough to experience both of their worlds. I spent most summers in Canada with my mother's family, enjoying their relaxed maritime way of life in New Brunswick on the east coast. Where the Chinese experience had expanded my horizon of flavour, Canadian cuisine brought me back down to earth. I found Chinese food mentally stimulating, but there was something grounding about hot dogs with relish and tuna melts made by my aunt using store-bought American cheese and soft white bread. In the end, both food cultures have had an equally important part to play in my formation as a chef.

After four years of college at Princeton, I moved to Madrid to pursue a career as an analyst for a renewable energy private equity firm. This decision was not necessarily steered by my heart; rather, it appeared to be the most practical choice given the direction my peers were going in, and there was also quite a bit of not-so-subtle pressure from my father. It was during my years in Spain that I realized I had been in love with food for a long time. Although on the face of it, Spanish cuisine is very different to what I had eaten in Hong Kong growing up, the communal way of eating, the conversation, the sharing of dishes and the celebration of ingredients are all very much at the heart of both cultures.

Since I had moved to Madrid alone, I didn't really know anyone. I spent my days off roaming the local markets to buy ingredients, or walking around the busy neighbourhoods lined with bars, chock-full of Spaniards sipping cold beers. At my work desk, I began to fantasize more and more about ingredients and cooking, fetishizing the idea of slow-roasting a chicken to perfect doneness, or researching the best type of red wine to use in a stew. I would race to complete my work by early afternoon so I could spend time on my food research. There was a particular part of banking culture the Spanish called *calentar la silla*, or 'keeping the seat warm', which entailed staying late at work – even when there was no work left to do – simply to gratify one's boss or to keep up with colleague rivalry. This was one aspect of the culture that was definitely not for me. I felt like a caged beast, counting down the seconds until I could leave. As soon as the clock struck eight, the earliest 'acceptable' time to go home, I would explode off the edge of my seat, walking briskly – but within the limits of socially acceptable speed – towards the elevator. As I left the building, I would often sprint into the cold night, my jacket and tie flapping behind me. There was something in me, a monstrous energy I was doing my best to suppress. During those two years at the bank, I became a kind of autodidact, reading and learning from all the great chefs through books. I remember seeing the first *Noma* cookbook, its unfamiliar but beautiful aesthetics grabbing my attention, and devouring many other works, including cookbooks written by Harold McGee and Thomas Keller. At the time, I genuinely believed I had it in me to open a world-class restaurant, because I could recall every single detail and recipe from each book I read. But that was a conceited attitude soon to be proved wrong.

I gained my first real kitchen experience at Hibiscus in London in 2012. Claude Bosi was kind enough to let me enter his kitchen after receiving a few of my impassioned letters. Claude was, and still is, one of the leading names in modern French cuisine. At the time, he had a reputation for running a rigorous environment. I arrived on my first day wearing a pair of jeans and old sneakers. With no knife, shoes or chef whites in hand, I spent the day in one of the cook's used jackets, sliding around with my grip-less shoes. I'd never experienced such early starts or such long days. I was up at 5.45 a.m. to be at work before 7 a.m., and often finished near midnight. I soon realized that working in a top kitchen requires both the hardy resilience of a manual labourer and the stamina of an endurance athlete. One does not simply walk in at that level without experiencing severe mental and physical strain. Removing peas from their pods and skins for four hours, hand-cutting boiled pig skin, scouring the scorching hot plancha, my body felt slow and timid, lacking the aggressive dexterity of the other young cooks. Some of them made fun of me because of my previous job, teasing me that this would only be a brief stint before I fell back into finance, but I didn't pay them much attention. I deeply appreciated the fact that, regardless of résumé, education or background, if your hands didn't move fast enough or you couldn't accurately julienne leeks, you simply weren't good enough. In a kitchen, there is nowhere to hide: raw ability and attitude eventually triumph.

In a kitchen, there is nowhere to hide: raw ability and attitude eventually triumph.

While many of the chefs preferred to keep their heads down, 'pushing on', this was one tenet of kitchen culture I did not abide by. Instead, I asked a lot of questions, walking from station to station and interrogating the chefs on every aspect of their function – 'How long do you cook the pork? What percentage of salt do you use in a brine? How do you smoke in hay? What's the recipe for that peach tart? Who supplies your beef?' and so on – until I felt they had reached the threshold of their patience. I wrote everything down, and still own that same notebook today. It was my earliest practical guide to cooking. It didn't matter how little time I had spent in a kitchen; no one could stop me from learning and accumulating vast amounts of knowledge at an almost manic pace. It was as if I had been set loose in a world without restrictions, where knowledge was key. Yes, we had to stay late, but there was always something to do. I was doing far more than just keeping the seat warm. My limitless energy had finally met an equally limitless outlet.

Over the next four years, I worked in a number of different restaurants. It was rare that I stayed in any one kitchen for more than three months, because I was out the door as soon as I had the knowledge I felt I needed. I definitely felt the scorn of a few chefs who considered my trajectory neither conventional nor worthy of respect. I was told time and again that in order to become a real chef, I had to commit to a job for at least two years and develop my skills under a mentor. I never saw any of the chefs I worked for as mentors, not just because I had limited contact with them, but also because my tenure was usually so short. I felt more like an observer, gathering and evaluating information like an anthropologist embedding himself in his field work.

I continued to burn through kitchens, gradually becoming accustomed to the speed and brutality of kitchen life. As well as my fascination with the techniques and creativity of the chefs, I also developed an obsession with the physicality of the work: prepping vegetables and executing orders offered a temporary release for some of my repressed energy. However, this did not satisfy my deeper urges to create my own vision.

I was fortunate enough to have the opportunity to move to Copenhagen for several months to intern at one of the most exciting restaurants in the world: Noma. My time there really opened my eyes to the possibilities within food. I greatly appreciated René Redzepi's relentless approach to working with produce from the Scandinavian terroir in a totally innovative way. He was the first chef I had heard speaking of roasting carrots as if they were meat and treating animal cuts as supporting acts to the plant kingdom. Noma was equipped with a team of cooks from all over the globe, and it felt special to be surrounded by individuals of all different backgrounds and beliefs. There was an exceptional kind of energy emanating in that old seafaring warehouse. We worked long, 100-hour weeks, and I met some remarkable people, some of whom would later become collaborators.

After three months, I moved back to London to take on a job at Dinner by Heston Blumenthal. It was there that I really learned about grafting. The restaurant served up to 300 guests per day with a two-Michelin-star level of detail. I have great respect for the culture of discipline and consistency at Dinner. Everything, from a single potato chip to a spoonful of mushroom ketchup, was checked by at least one sous chef before making it to the next stage of preparation. To achieve this surgical precision at such high volumes required an exceptionally organized system. As before, I observed, analysed and retained all aspects of how this restaurant functioned, keeping visual records of the checklists, temperature controls and recipe peculiarities.

Thinking of my future, I decided it would be best for my career if I stayed in this kitchen for at least two years. But one day, during my eleventh month of work, I went in as usual and began setting up the fish section. It was 7.30 a.m. Suddenly, an immense sadness washed over me, and I no longer felt the will to do anything. I dropped the herbs I had been picking and walked out the door. I deeply missed my family. It was as if the years of pressure and constant energy release all came to a head that morning. Since the moment I had started cooking, I had felt, deep down, that I had something extraordinary to prove to myself and to my family. I'd burned my bridges with nothing to fall back on, embarking on a risky path at a late point in the game. This burden also gave me immense drive to succeed and was probably the reason I learned so quickly. But I'd left very little room for my own life and the emotional space required to connect with others. In a sense, I'd forgotten my main motivations for becoming a chef: bringing people together and making them happy through food. I never wanted to cook again. I spent the next few months unsure of what I was going to do, pondering my future in my basement flat – until I got a call from my childhood friend Iré Hassan-Odukale, asking if I was interested in opening a restaurant together.

Although we must respect the growing, sourcing and innate properties of ingredients, it is how we employ them that communicates who we are.

opening

It was a cold October day in 2016 as I prepped away in the basement kitchen of Iré's family home. Like me, Iré had recently left a career in finance to pursue his passion for hospitality. We had met more than fifteen years ago through mutual friends, and had become close when we'd both moved to London in our twenties. Iré's idea for the restaurant was for him to look after our guests and manage the business while I focused on the cooking. We had just agreed to cook dinner for sixty guests at a gallery in east London. It was as much a test of whether or not people liked our food as it was a chance to understand whether or not we were indeed capable of being in hospitality.

The day began with us collecting produce from around London and arranging everything in neat piles across the dining table. As the octopus baked in his mother's small oven, I blitzed mountains of papaya in the small blender Iré's younger sister usually used for her breakfast smoothies. I'd read interesting articles about a digestive enzyme found in papaya; although normally used as an anti-inflammatory remedy, this enzyme could also act as a tenderizer, softening the protein strands in tougher cuts of meat. I had two whole sides of goat resting on the freezing garden bench outside, and I needed to quickly process the fruit with salt and aromatics so I could apply the resulting cure to the meat for a full 48 hours. I'd never cooked goat, nor had I used papaya in this way before, but I decided to brave this risky experiment, taking the gamble that it would produce something sublime.

On the second prep day, 10 kilos (22 pounds) of wild salmon arrived through the back door, and I began to sweat anxiously, wondering whether I could pull this off. As members of Iré's family came and went, I rushed to scale the giant, slimy salmon bodies that slid around on the small marble countertop. The tiny cutting board, fit for a supermarket onion, wobbled precariously as I continued to break the fillets down into respectable tranches; a portion of them was already cured and chilling in the frosty garden. With little space in the family kitchen, I was lucky to have the wintry garden to serve as a kind of 'walk-out' fridge. I just hoped the foxes wouldn't eat my goat.

With sixty mouths to feed and five courses promised, I somehow had to produce 300 plates of food in a small domestic kitchen on the opposite side of the city to the event's location. My hands ached from crushing and squeezing fresh tamarind, which was now reducing into a tart, slick, dark purple glaze for the fish. Peanuts toasted over the open flames in a basket on the stove as I walked in and out of the sliding back door to burn plantain leaves over the barbecue. I reeked of the smoke. The tea-like aroma of the smouldering leaves seemed to fill the inside of my head as much as my hair. I entered a delirium of anxiety and exhaustion.

I had visited the gallery before agreeing to do the dinner. We were so taken with the idea of cooking in such a beautiful space that we hadn't noticed the fact that the building and its kitchen were not particularly suitable for an ambitious culinary event. But I was truly inspired, and my menu would not be held back. We'd spent days in the British Library researching the produce of Sub-Saharan West Africa, amassing lists of all the possible ingredients we might use, from seeds and peppercorns to plants, exotic fruits and fermented beans. I was confronted with a wealth of new flavours accented by fiery chillies, piquant umami and rich starches. While it felt like I was learning a new culinary language, there was strong undercurrent of familiarity, particularly in terms of the intensity of these spices and the burning sensation they inflicted, which reminded me of certain dishes of my childhood, eaten in Hong Kong and mainland China.

As I developed the menu for the event, I drew inspiration from my instinctive reactions to these flavours, rather than considering the traditional usage in their regular context. Iré had told me of a rich stew he'd eaten growing up, *miyan taushe*, a northern Nigerian soup of pumpkin and goat seasoned with palm oil, peppers, crayfish and peanuts. I'd never eaten such a combination of ingredients, but the idea sparked the potential for a deeply powerful dish that would both be comforting and stir my guests to their core. I dreamed of slowly extracting the sweetness of winter pumpkin into a rich broth, imbued with the collagen of meltingly soft goat, and the perfume of roasted shellfish and rich, buttery peanuts.

I'd read about the synergistic effects of combining the amino acids of fish and meat proteins, inosinic and glutamic acids, to create a kind of 'super umami'. Layering this bonding of flavours with mellow pumpkin and savoury nuts could only lead to disturbingly delicious results. I was captivated by the idea of pushing the sensation to its limit. Could something be *too* delicious?

I began with a base of very slowly caramelized onions, peppers, garlic and crushed Scotch bonnet chillies cooked down into a delicately aromatic paste. Earlier, I had butchered the goat and slow-roasted its bones and residual flesh, releasing these animal flavours into a stock left to bubble the night before. The goat meat, now marinated for two days in the papaya cure, was already tender. I grilled the pieces before adding them to the vegetables. Heads of giant prawns (shrimp) kissed the flames before their brains oozed out of their golden pink shells into the goat broth. I took a handful of the peppercorns and nutmegs I'd received from Iré's family friend, who'd brought them back from Nigeria. Toasted and blitzed to a fine powder, they smelled like a burning forest of eucalyptus and resin. I threw these into the broth after taking note of their weight, then strained the stock into the large pot, along with the smoky goat meat, diced pumpkin, a few large spoonfuls of home-made roasted-nut butter and the concentrated, sweet meat of the prawn tails, which I'd left to brown throughout the day.

This was no *miyan taushe*, but my own creation was born from an obsession with amplifying each cooking process to create a distinctive layer of flavours. The dish embodied what I found to be the most exciting aspect of cooking: rather than being a natural process expressing the intrinsic quality of single ingredients, it instead reveals the inexplicable otherness in combining them. Cooking is by no means a natural phenomenon, since it's not a process that could exist without human intervention. Although we must respect the growing, sourcing and innate properties of ingredients, it is how we employ them that communicates who we are. I could tell from the complexity of this dish that my form of culinary expression wasn't going to be straightforward.

With the stew simmering away, releasing a persistent pungency throughout the house, I proved the dough for one of the sweet servings and sifted the ash of the charred plantain leaves on to pillows of meringue, lined like army ranks across the silicone baking sheets on the dinner table. My knees ached from standing for the past few days; my thoughts were overcrowded by the hundreds of notes covering my prep sheet. I pulled the giant 60-litre pot off the small stove at around 3 a.m. and plunged it into the snow outside, nature's 'blast-chiller'. I fell asleep in the small bedroom adjacent to the kitchen. Everything from the walls to the sheets smelled of boiled crustaceans and the cheesy decay of aged meat, as if the house and all its contents had fused to the thick aromas emanating from that mysterious cauldron.

I woke up to the thought of the monumental tasks for the day ahead, and completely lost my appetite. I had barely eaten for the past few days, as my senses were so overloaded. I warmed up some of the stew but found I could no longer smell anything. I brought a spoonful of the dark orange ragout into my mouth and could only feel its texture. I'd lost my sense of taste. The strangeness of the meat, shellfish and tender pumpkin, and the fat coating my ineffectual taste buds, caused me to believe the stew had gone off. The event was to begin in four hours, and I hadn't even begun to pack up all my preparations. There was no time to stop this disaster from unfolding. I gathered every small container I could find, displacing the family's own food into bowls so I could stow all my garnishes, salts, powders, oils and condiments.

I checked my list and assessed the stacks of equipment and prep ready to load into Iré's car, a multitude of vivid concoctions. Several times, I had to turn back for yet one more product, the proving dough or a serrated knife, simple but essential parts of the evening's event that I almost forgot in my panic. We managed to fit everything into the car, the boot stuffed to the hilt, including the giant pot of stew wrapped in cling film. Surely the car could take no more. I squeezed one last plastic container of dried berry salt between a roll of pastry bags and the water bath, fearing it would cause the suspension to collapse. With all the rented plates, cookware, induction burners, crockery, food and drink crammed in, we steered the rocking car out of the drive and headed through central London.

From the moment we arrived at the venue, everything blurred together. We hustled in a fury to set up the dining room, bar and kitchen, which was situated two flights of stairs below the main room, followed by a 30-metre (100-foot) walk. The kitchen itself was no more than a large cupboard, windowless and without an extractor fan or kitchen appliances, save for a small sink. I stacked the plates for each serving in six rows of ten along a large fold-out table in front of the kitchen entrance, with all the garnishes waiting at hand. For some reason, I had until now blocked out the memory that the stew had tasted off, or like nothing at all, and it dawned on me that I should probably ask Iré to try it before we served it to sixty guests. 'Seems good to me,' he said, coolly, in his usual nonchalant manner, and reassured me that it was not rotten as I had believed. I lamented my reveries about papaya tenderization.

Friends and family were by our side to help us with the event. Everyone chipped in, whether by running plates, taking photos or handling the drinks station. The collective support from those closest to us gave way to a militarized procession of plates I fired out with my friend Mervyn. Some new acquaintances, friends of friends, stood on the side to place a simple sorrel leaf on top of each quenelle of brown-butter yam, or apply a swift dusting of peppered sugar to the coconut mousse. In just under two hours, we had fed the entire room. The stew of goat, pumpkin and baked octopus turned out to be the thunderbolt of depth I had been hoping for. Although our cooking has evolved since then, some of the guests that evening still talk of that stew today. While I was beginning to believe in my ability to conceptualize new flavours and develop my own cooking style, the idea of Ikoyi as a restaurant was still far from being fully formed.

A few months before the pop-up at the gallery, Iré and I had decided to meet for coffee to plan how we would open the restaurant, approaching it like some kind of thought experiment. We sat in Monmouth Coffee in Covent Garden and simply put together a document that included every hypothetical 'to do' we could imagine relating to starting our own business. We could have been trying to build a boat and we would have been just as in the dark. We developed a pragmatic method: gather all the information we could from within our sphere of knowledge and common sense, and then pose the remaining questions to industry professionals and technical experts. Nothing could be left out and everything would be recorded in writing. We built that list with an intended timeline of six months. Little did we know it would take us over two years to open Ikoyi.

The list turned out to be an immeasurably long and difficult exercise, as we moved between brand design and menu development, financial modelling and landlord pitches. When we first turned our attention to searching for a property, we naively thought it would be as simple as an online search followed by cold-calling the various agents managing commercial property across London. How wrong we were. Without a big name behind us or any kind of track record, no one would even return our calls. We would see online listings as well as signage while walking the streets of our favourite neighbourhoods, but by the time we managed to get in touch with someone, the property was either already under offer or completely off the market. It turned out there were even more unlisted properties, only shown to the most reputable restaurateurs with big backing or Michelin stars. We put together a landlord pack, a 50-page document with everything from financial projections and interior design ideas to our analysis of the restaurant market and the conceivable success of our unique business within it. I'd spent so much time in front of the computer expanding on our

While I was beginning to believe in my ability to conceptualize new flavours and develop my own cooking style, the idea of Ikoyi as a restaurant was still far from being fully formed.

beloved restaurant idea that it began to feel like I was back in finance, modelling an investment. Although we'd produced an impressive pack, the whole thing seemed like an elaborate act; we seemed to be fashioning what was essentially a compelling marketing brochure. But this was London, and we'd accepted that the complex flavours of powerful ingredients weren't going to grant us access to this city. Instead, we would have to rely on our brand and its identity.

Iré and I were keen to explore his heritage and food culture from a more historical perspective as we refined the restaurant concept. Given that he was born and raised for most of his life in Nigeria, with some roots in Sierra Leone, we concentrated on Sub-Saharan West Africa as the focal point for our ingredients research. We learned about the therapeutic properties of peppercorns in aiding digestion and the benefits of increased access to amino acids via *dawadawa*, a fermented locust bean paste used to saturate dishes with savoury flavours. We read about the use of pounded starches, steamed bean cakes and ground seeds as thickening agents in soups and stews, and we learned about the nose-to-tail style of cooking with brain, feet and offal. There were native peppercorns, such as grains of paradise, which release cardamon-like flavours, as well as Scotch bonnet chillies, introduced from Central America and now a common feature throughout all regional cuisines. It was clear that West African cuisine contained many global influences, from the Arab world to Europe, intertwining them with indigenous plants, pulses (legumes) and vegetables. While many native grains existed, the Portuguese brought Asiatic rice to West Africa in the sixteenth century, and this foreign species became a dominant feature in the rice dishes through all the countries in the region from the Gambia to Nigeria. The more I studied the history of the cuisine, the less clear it became what it meant for something to be truly authentic.

Rather than focusing on individual cuisines, we kept looking for broader patterns and influences throughout West Africa, hoping to capture a wider net of possible ingredients and styles that could inform our restaurant concept. We didn't want to label our food Nigerian, as this would limit our creative scope; nor did we want to employ the term 'West African' as a category, since many of the ingredients we would be using were sourced locally. I was inspired by the culinary equivalencies between the African fermented locust bean, *iru*, and its Chinese counterpart, *douchi*, the black fermented soybean, and also Japanese miso. Here was a commonality transcending the colonial exchange of ingredients – an amino paste as the foundation of umami in cultures with no previous interaction. With origins dating back to 300 BC, misos are a Japanese culinary staple and emblematic of a sophisticated gastronomic culture. Indeed, many Western chefs now make their own misos, inspired by the Japanese method. The varied uses for the locust bean sparked my imagination further. The locust bean's aroma, which is sour and almost cheesy, is ten times more potent than miso and belies a profound savoury taste used to season a sauce or stew. The medicinal benefits, however, outlast the applications for flavour, as the salted, preservative qualities of the locust bean provide access to rich protein in areas without refrigeration in tropical heat. Human beings and their diverse cultures appeared to be linked by the quest for savouriness. Whether or not umami is something that has enabled us to survive or meets a kind of societal enjoyment, it is obviously part of a deeper human need. I wanted to explore the question of West African umami further and figure out a way of harnessing it in my own cooking.

I couldn't stop thinking of West African food culture as the totality of many parts, be they the wild cultivated grains or the produce of the New World and the Indian Ocean. The global interconnectedness of West Africa finally led us to the idea of 'Jollof Cuisine'. Jollof rice is probably one of the most famous dishes of West Africa. It's a one-pot serving of rice cooked in a spicy broth of tomatoes, chillies, peppers, garlic, ginger, onions and stock. Some cultures add different cuts of meat, fish or vegetables, as well as seasoning salt, and herbs and spices such as thyme, cayenne pepper, nutmeg and curry leaves. There are as many variations of the dish as there are countries that claim their version tastes the best. Although etymologically the term *jollof* can be traced back to the fourteenth-century Wolof Empire that ruled the Senegambian region, historians remark that the dish travelled throughout the region via the commercial centres of the Mali empire and the colonial effects of the French oil industry in central Senegal, where traditional grass staples were replaced by South East Asian rice. While deeply rooted in West African food culture, this indigenous dish is made of ingredients brought in from the global food trade. With all the regional variations, we began to perceive the term 'jollof' as synonymous with the idea of interpretation. While our discovery of the umami commonality between East Asia and West Africa was a trigger for our culinary development, Jollof Cuisine would be the argument for our cooking style, rooted in West African ingredients but open to global influences. Jollof Cuisine was our way to employ the techniques of international gastronomy and weave together a menu based on ingredient interpretation. There was also something poetic in this idea behind the restaurant, reflecting the bond between two friends from mixed backgrounds that blended Nigerian, Chinese, Sierra Leonean and Canadian origins.

Our carefully curated narrative now had a name, and with Jollof Cuisine, several landlords began to invite us to pitch in person for their prime locations in Soho, Marylebone and Mayfair. For our first meeting, we entered the cavernous, corporate entrance of a major developer. Startled by the blindingly bright luminescent ceiling, we approached the long desk, behind which sat three security receptionists signing in visitors. The guard muttered our names to someone through his headset, then ushered us to sit on the faux leather islands by the entrance. There seemed to be very little human activity in this building that supposedly housed hundreds of employees. Everyone must have been hiding behind the thick swivelling doors and walls that were panelled with silver and faint green, the trademark colours of the estate. We sat contemplating the potential outcome of the meeting, conversing and laughing nervously about how strange this all felt to us. Soon a figure emerged from one of the panels, the company secretary, and she warmly invited us into the meeting. Iré had printed our presentations into bound booklets, one for each executive sitting on the other side of the giant boardroom table. I had prepared snacks for our interviewers to sample: a fleeting taste of the concept we'd carefully crafted. We passionately discussed the idea behind Jollof Cuisine, explaining our credentials, financial proposition and the market potential for our concept within their portfolio.

As compelling as the story we were telling was, we couldn't help but feel like travelling salesmen, carting around our pamphlets and box of tricks to entice the unwilling. Our assessors munched on the snacks, and the room filled with the crackling sounds of paper and mouths inhaling fried dough. We watched the smoked chocolate ooze from the sides of their lips on to the napkins we had provided. There was a palpable incongruity between the lovingly made treats and the gazes strategically devoid of emotion in that sterile white room. We left the meeting with an initial burst of adrenaline, followed by a slow descent into disappointment when only weeks later we came to learn that we were no longer in the running.

We marched in and out of proposal meetings armed with tasters and potential wines for our list. As the rejections kept coming, we started to feel like a mobile snack bar for hungry and thirsty property directors. Perhaps we were paranoid, but we sometimes wondered whether the mid-afternoon and end-of-week timings of these meetings had been chosen as opportune moments for the prospective landlord to entertain our food and beverage pitches. That certainly seemed to be the case on one occasion, when an interviewer asked if she could take home a bottle of Albariño we had brought with us, and proceeded to bury it in her handbag.

We were so far off from what we were hoping to achieve. In a desperate attempt to lure landlords to a space where we could cook, we succeeded in our convincing an important central London real estate company to dine in the comfort of Iré's parents' basement kitchen. It didn't seem like a strange idea at the time, but in hindsight it was a very intimate and vulnerable setting for a business meeting. The act of accepting someone into your home creates a very personal dynamic, which we'd hoped would work in our favour. During the tasting, Iré's father, Oye, appeared out of the blue, probably coming downstairs to make himself a cup of tea. He burst in casually, quite surprised at what was going on. The awkward interaction made our presentation feel slightly less professional, but I respected Oye for telling the landlord that she should most definitely give us the site because we were hardworking boys. After dozens of courses, cocktails and wines, the party thanked us and departed. In the end, we didn't get the site. After a year and a half of searching, we were still without any prospects. Over thirty landlords had either rejected our applications or neglected to respond, or gazumped us with a better offer from another operator.

We received an invitation to cater for 1:54, the contemporary African art fair at Somerset House, a former royal residence and centre for cultural enterprise. Somewhat close to the end of our tether, we took the opportunity to align ourselves with a known establishment that would hopefully further reassure a potential landlord of our credibility. The event space was a labyrinth of open rooms, sprawling over the floors of the neo-classical mansion. It was a refreshingly welcome change to be working among so much art. Burning hues of hot oranges, shades of dark, cracked earth and patchworks of textured canvases surrounded us. Our menu focused on cocktails, along with smaller, spicy bites that would go well with alcohol and a few sweet dishes. We seemed to be drawn to putting ourselves in stressful situations, since once again there was no on-site kitchen. I'd been working on the recipe for the treats we had offered at proposal meetings: fried sourdough, slowly fermented to create ultra-crisp, slightly chewy and savoury doughnuts.

I smoked lashings of melted dark (semisweet) chocolate, which I later combined with burned cream, brown sugar and *suya*, a barbecue marinade commonly used for meat. The warmed, savoury ganache would be the filling injected into the sourdough puffs. The projected footfall was in the hundreds for each of the five days ahead. I proved and rolled the dough in Iré's flat in Vauxhall from four to seven in the morning so that I could begin frying soon after, just in time to transport the finished products to the event by midday. Every inch of his tiny kitchen, from the tables to the tops of the cabinets six inches from the ceiling, was covered in trays holding the proving dough, which was gradually doubling in size. I'd turned off the heating to slow down fermentation and made sure to block out the morning sun, which put some of the dough out of sync in accelerating the rise. Each ball weighed exactly 45 grams. By the time I'd finished rolling, the first batch had been proving for three hours and were ready to fry. Six hours after I'd started, 300 fist-sized clouds lay before me, their sugar glimmering like frost in the morning light. After a full day of serving, we'd return to the flat, numbed by the whirlwind of the day's activity, quickly passing out before rising early to begin all over again.

Midway through the week, we'd been asked to stay into the evening to cater for some private clients. They'd requested more savoury servings. I'd been experimenting with plantain, and wanted to test out my fried plantain with raspberry salt and smoked Scotch bonnet emulsion. The vast room where the event was due to take place looked out on to a terrace with a central view into the courtyard. I'd snuck my deep-fat fryer through the back security entrance, as I knew the building management certainly wouldn't have approved of us using it in the allocated room, which had once been occupied by a past queen of England. I opened the large glass doors to create a fresh draft. I hoped the smell of caramelizing plantain sugars and atomized fryer oil would go unnoticed long enough for me to evade security. There appeared to be a side door inside the room, semi-hidden to the left, flanking the exit on to the terrace. Inside, there were jumbles of wires and electrical boxes with flashing red, green and blue dotted lights. It was a complex circuit board of controls, which happened to be regulating the lighting in the courtyard. I noticed several available power outlets and a large unoccupied table. Could this be my satellite kitchen? It took me less than a second to decide it was the right thing to do, and I quickly set up my fryer. Half an hour later, I was grinning with delight, and as the large sash window sucked wafts of smoke out into the courtyard, I contemplated the insolence of frying plantains next to the bedroom of seventeenth-century royals. The glowing, red-dusted shards of crispy plantain soon infiltrated the large room, and we proudly observed as the piercing forms of the sharply cut fruit turned heads, burned mouths and ignited taste buds. The shock effect of the fiery snack had caught the guests' attention. We went on to befriend and collaborate with other institutions and galleries that had heard about us through this residency. As our audience grew, we moved closer to finding a home for the restaurant.

Our friends at Carousel, a restaurant space featuring a roster of international and emerging guest chefs, kindly let us use their spare dining area to create a pop-up restaurant for a tasting we had secured with The Crown Estate, a major UK landholder belonging to the British monarch. From servings of grilled Cornish mackerel with tiger-nut milk and ice plants, to confit feather blade of beef *suya* and curry-leaf ice cream,

we delivered an onslaught of contrasting, mouth-watering tastes, offering combinations of spices our guests had never tried before. Without another business to our name, we conveyed our abilities through our cuisine. One month later, we secured the premises: bang in the centre of London Piccadilly, in a new development, St James's Market. Funnily enough, it was the first site we had applied for and been rejected from. Here we were with the keys, two years later. From that moment on, we were finally able to drop the sales-man act. We began designing our restaurant and worked to finalize the menu for the opening.

When we were coming up with a name for the restaurant, we knew that we needed to reflect the sense of interpreta-tion at the heart of our cooking style. Iré mentioned that his birthplace was called Ikoyi, and I replied, 'That sounds kind of Japanese.' The idea that the word 'Ikoyi' could yield mul-tiple impressions was intriguing to us. There was a certain cultural and linguistic ambiguity in the name, yet it still represented a sense of home, at least for one of us. When I sketched out a logo, we were hooked. The sound – 'ee-koi-ee' – felt instinctively warm and unpretentious. The way the image looked on paper was alluring and impactful. We knew we had to create a symbol for the restaurant with a strong identity. The sharp lines and simple symmetry of the logo's geometry would embody our vision for clean and angular cuisine. Even though Ikoyi was the name of the place, we didn't want to be defined by its existing meaning.

Our design brief challenged prospective interior architects, as we wanted to reflect our respective heritages while excluding any obvious signs to cultural origin. The desire to be uncategorizable makes it difficult to come up with that clever one-liner branding summary. The industry wants you to choose a label, like 'modern African', 'West African', 'con-temporary Nigerian interpretation of British produce', and so on, but just saying those words felt corny and fake. What is an African restaurant supposed to look like, anyway? There were moments during the first meetings when we seemed to be on a very different page to potential designers. We were shown photos of African children running through puddles scattered in a dusty grassland, smiling mothers in traditional dress holding their babies wrapped up in canopies, and men bearing spears. As I flipped through a mood board for the staff uniforms, I cringed at the thought of our future waiters dressed in baggy jerseys with collages of guns inspired by Boko Haram warriors. Throughout the process, we seemed to be constantly fighting against the pigeonholing effects of the 'new African food trend'. Although it was challenging to explain our conceptual goals, our aesthetic vision for the restaurant was fairly simple. We liked the idea that the restaurant could make anyone feel welcome and at home, regardless of where they came from.

In the end, we worked with Studio Ashby, a successful firm run by a mutual friend, Sophie, and lead designer Fiona. I'm sure they found it frustrating to work with us, as we pushed back and challenged every creative decision they put forward. Iré and I were fastidious about every single detail being original to our restaurant, and spent much of our time cross-referencing suggested patterns, textures and colour palettes with existing restaurants in order to ensure that our choices were unique. I paid most attention to the lighting, as I wanted our dishes to be totally on display at the table, brought to life like actors on stage at the theatre.

I fought hard to incorporate the conical pendant lighting, which was hung at a very precise height to make sure that meat juices and matte vegetable textures would be the focal point of the dining experience. It was important for there to be a tremendous amount of detail in the design features, from the lines running around the perimeter of the room to the geometric pieces of wood buried into the tabletops. But we wanted the emphasis to be on the interaction between our guests and the food that was to be presented before them. The service would be like the surroundings: warm but discreet. Despite our many small negotiations, Sophie and Fiona finally delivered the design pack for our first restau-rant, and it completely succeeded in translating our vision.

Pushing back on colours and wood styles proved to be less perplexing than the kitchen design. There was barely enough space for a small cooking hob, let alone a commercial kitchen. But what was initially a major constraint eventually became the ideal environment for our cooking style. With only one standing fridge and no walk-in, our kitchen seemed more fit for a small tapas restaurant. From the first day, we adapted our menu to the limitations of the space and what we calcu-lated as consistently achievable. We made sure desserts were ingredient-driven, with no more than three elements; we removed garnishes, and incorporated a spectrum of tastes into a single sauce. We achieved a system of constant micro-stock rotation, whereby every vegetable, from the last four cabbage-flower shoots to the two remaining beetroots, would find their way into à la minute elements for a dish. The benefits in terms of freshness and immediacy gained by working out of a small fridge and kitchen far outweigh a larger operation when it comes to detailed, precise cooking. With the whole team connected by no more than a metre and the vantage point of the pass in the centre of it all, nothing would go unnoticed, and we could truly convey the idiosyncratic, personal details in our dishes. With daily deliveries of farm produce and line-caught fish, we never had the luxury of stacking crates of ingredients within a large cold store. The small kitchen cultivated an obsessive attitude to breaking down produce upon its arrival with extreme urgency. The exploitation of the hyper-fresh quality of our raw materials – the true crunch of turnips plucked from the ground that very same day, or the buttery yet dense texture of an Orkney Scallop steamed just out of its shell – became our way of expressing flavour.

Our first few opening services were a far cry from the state of efficient calm that later permeated Ikoyi. On the morning of 17 July 2017, our team finalized the preparations for our very first service. With no prior experience of running a kitchen, restaurant or team, I had to make it up as I went along, relying on common sense and what I had observed from other chefs. I'd not fully grasped scale when it came to ordering ingre-dients, which was a major concern that morning, as twelve kilos of whole spinach had arrived and were sitting next to a giant pile of shellfish, raw chicken, plantains and cassava. It was the middle of summer and approaching 38°C (100°F) in the kitchen, as the air-conditioning system was still not fully commissioned in time for the opening. Waves of customers began to arrive early for their bookings, and the restaurant filled up like a sweltering tin of sardines. People flowed in and out like a strong tide, flooding our bar and coming as far as the pass of our open kitchen. I thought they'd engulf us. I gazed at the dense print of long text on the cheques, noting that nearly every table had ordered the entire menu, multiples of the same dish and a portion of rice each. The chefs battled the crashing swell of orders heroically, their faces puce, dripping with sweat and contorting with tension. Every time I opened the standing fridge, the gastronorm fit to burst with spinach would explode over, littering the floor with bruised leaves. There were only twelve of us when we opened, and many of the team members were as new to the industry as we were.

We served ribs of Manx Loaghtan sheep marinated in roasted kelp with a relish of fermented Scotch bonnets; slow-poached chicken with a caramelized benne sauce made with young, unhulled sesame; and oysters glazed in tamarind and fermented cassava. Our first version of jollof rice had one or two more Scotch bonnets in the recipe, and set mouths on fire. We smoked the rice with wobbling lobes of bone marrow melting over the grains in dark ceramic bowls. Frozen buttermilk and hibiscus-marinated papaya cooled everyone down at the end. Meanwhile, Iré handled the room of guests who seemed to come from every corner of the globe, each reacting very differently to the experience. Some were hot and angry; others were very jolly and embraced the heat and flavours. Perhaps overambitious in our seating capacity, we managed to cook for over 90 people those first few days, which meant three seatings in our 30-cover restaurant. I look back on that period with some embarrassment at the heavy-handedness with which I sauced a dish or left unclean lines in my butchery. While I lacked finesse, I do miss the raw flavours of the opening menu: a truly spicy, pain-inducing and polarizing cuisine. My relationship with spice has developed a lot since then. At the time, I was concerned mainly with heat, whereas now our menu weaves together a range of articulations of spice, some subtle, others more peppery and aromatic, interacting with ingredients rather than masking them.

Critics from *The Times*, *Evening Standard*, *Guardian* and *Telegraph* wrote very positive reviews of Ikoyi. Although their glowing words meant the restaurant was busy, the narrative of West African cuisine we'd been trying to avoid took hold and we polarized our diners once again. The tagline 'Central London's first Nigerian restaurant' meant Ikoyi was fully booked with guests from the Nigerian diaspora living in London. And nearly every dish was sent back to the kitchen. Angry faces stared at me furiously, wondering why servings of raw fish were being lauded as authentic representations of Nigerian cuisine. I laughed and cried at the lengthy, hateful one-star reviews quickly building up on websites: some of the fondest notes left by our esteemed guests were that we should get rid of 'that Chinese cook' and hire a real African chef, and claims that we'd served them rotten leftovers. At the opposite end, we witnessed the phenomenon of a cult following. It seemed the entire readership of *Sunday Times*' food critic Giles Coren made the pilgrimage to London from the home counties to get their 'first real taste of African cuisine'. Our customer base suddenly transformed, going from an entirely Black audience to one made up of white, mid-60s middle-class women from Berkshire and Kent, who ordered only the dishes mentioned in the favourable review. Everything became so complicated and political when we only wanted to serve tasty food. We continued to fight for our ideal of a de-culturalized cuisine and persevered in serving food free from attachments and prejudgements.

After several months, the excitement began to die down. Perhaps the perception was that we were a one-off gimmick, and the media now drew the masses to feast on a new concept. I watched the bookings drop from 90 to 40 to the low teens, then to single digits only half a year after opening. The lethargic and excruciatingly long services meant sending staff members home early on nights when only two covers were booked for 9 p.m. Many had told us opening a restaurant would be hard, but we didn't expect to swing so dramatically in and out of favour with the city. We loved our restaurant space, but it didn't help to be hidden within a side street of an unknown development. As I relentlessly pursued creative integrity, I started to realize that my resistance to fitting within a box could have been the cause of our downfall. I don't know how we survived the first year. Our takings were so insignificant that Iré and I began to live a hand-to-mouth existence. The closer we came to the point of closing, the harder I pushed for original flavour combinations. Very gradually we started to receive chefs from London who were eager to try our food. I had mixed feelings of embarrassment and gratitude as one of my idols, Araki San of Michelin three-star The Araki, came to eat in our empty restaurant with his wife and a friend. I watched him very carefully as he bit into our braised octopus with coffee sauce. His eyes closed and he groaned with appreciation. '*Oishii*' (delicious!), he proclaimed under his breath.

As costs were very tricky, we decided to get rid of our à la carte menu and serve only a blind tasting menu made up of pristine ingredients from our beef farmers, fishermen and local growers. We ordered for the number of guests dining with us, eliminating wastage and allowing us to cook with the exact contents of our fridges. With such an uncompromising focus on ingredient-led and spice-based cooking, word started to spread, and chefs from Europe and beyond began to eat with us regularly. The *Michelin Guide* recognized our fervent approach to working with hyper-local produce and awarded us our first star, calling us 'one of the most innovative and original restaurants to open in the capital in recent times'.

bold heat

I always wanted to stay true to our love of spice, since it was part of both my own DNA and Iré's. If you grow up eating intensely spiced cuisine, your palate adjusts to this heightened, sometimes pain-inducing flavour. A love of spice and a way of life accustomed to eating it is sort of like being addicted to the strongest drugs – once you've had the good stuff, everything else seems weak. The menu at Ikoyi is a journey in bold heat, taking you through many levels of complexity and layering of spice through infusion, aromas and emulsions. I wanted to create a menu with relentless flavour that would always leave the guests' mouths tingling, whether through the zing of a white peppercorn or the candied tobacco resin of smoked chillies. Could spice not be subtle, varied and nuanced in its own way? Bold heat also entailed a sense of defiance. I wanted to wake up mouths right from the start – a lingering burning sensation that would send signals of what was to come.

Early tasters of our dishes tried to convince me to tone things down, fearing that the heat would put off the local British audience. There is something inherently risky in serving heavily spiced cuisine in a restaurant with a tasting menu. I wanted to disrupt this context and instil a stronger sense of my personality into the dining experience. Open-mindedness to other cultures and cuisines means perceiving their ingredients for what they are. If the Scotch bonnet is ferociously spicy, why should we shield this part of its nature? Ata rodo chillies entered almost every dish Iré made me try in his hometown, and it made me wonder whether our own menu could reflect the same use of this chilli. As the world imposed preconceptions on to Ikoyi, I wanted to make sure we retained our own identity. Why should we be timid and lower the heat levels to create more conventional food?

There was always a link between heat and flavour in the food I grew up eating, such as steamed dumplings of scallop, pork and scallion with a side of XO sauce, a spicy Cantonese condiment of chopped dried shellfish, chillies, garlic and ham; or lo mein, shrimp egg noodles with wontons drowned in hot chilli and sesame oil and chicken broth. I used to watch in awe as my father spooned great teaspoons of chilli condiments into his soup, and often remarked on how the clear liquid would fade into a thick darkness once it reached the depth of flavour and spice to which he was accustomed. At the end, I'd measure the clarity of my bowl of remnant liquid against his, and wonder if my own soup would become this dark as I grew older. In this regard, spice seemed to me a kind of rite of passage, a testament to character and one's ability to appreciate strong flavours. Little did I know these subconscious musings would become the driving force behind a restaurant later in life.

During college, while I was routinely eating hot pot with my friend Dao, I came to the conscious realization that my ideal experience of deliciousness involved chillies and peppercorns. Dao was born in Sichuan, but his parents had emigrated to the United States when he was young. We became friends in college thanks to a shared sense of humour, the Chinese connection and a love of very spicy food. Neither of us were particularly bowled over by what was on offer in the school canteen: wispy, dry salads; fries; nondescript Parmesan bakes; and overboiled frozen vegetables. Luckily, Dao's parents lived a short walk from campus, and I was fortunate enough to be invited for dinner regularly and experience his father's cooking. Sometimes I would go alone, and other times we'd bring one other spice afficionado, our Vietnamese friend Thu, and perhaps an American, too, to initiate into our small ritual.

Dao's family always greeted us with big smiles, welcoming us into their small kitchen, which was directly in front of the entrance to the house. As I removed my shoes, I was already drawn in by the steam of the bubbling pot of broth set over the burner. We walked through into the dining room, where every inch of a large table was covered, leaving almost no room for us to sit, with a smorgasbord of meat, fish, shellfish and vegetables. Thinly sliced lamb, pork, beef, tripe, sea bass, squid, clams, tiger prawns, tofu, mushrooms, sprouts, cabbage and winter melon were only some of the provisions ready to be devoured. Before we began the meal, we'd each grab a bowl of steamed rice and another smaller dish for a dipping sauce of our own liking. I threw condiments of chilli paste, mashed garlic, ginger, sugar, coriander (cilantro) leaves into my bowl, adding generous glugs of roasted sesame oil and black rice vinegar into the mix. I still think of the smell of this blend when I'm cooking: a sweet, aromatic, sour, spicy and nutty mixture. I felt privileged to be accepted into this small family unit that so loved flavour.

Two broths sat inside the large pot, divided by a central wall to allow differing heat levels. The broth on the left was milkier in colour, sweet from emulsified chicken fat and scented with the gentle herbs and aromatics with which it was infused before serving. The broth to the right was also opaque at the base, but covered in a crimson oil littered with bobbling chillies: some long, some round, like savoury cherries rehydrating in the fat-split soup.

'You should probably eat from the right-hand side, if you can handle it!'

I got the impression that having the capacity to tolerate the heat was the mark of being daring, a risk-taker.

There was a rebellious ferocity in Dao's father's eyes as he giggled wildly at the prospect of me burning my mouth. 'Eat one of these,' he said, as he dropped a small green peppercorn into my hand. I'd never seen such a fresh-looking Sichuan peppercorn. He told me he'd brought this one from back home.

The difference is
that chilli heat
is the pain that
cries wolf.

As I bit into the peppercorn, I could feel the voltage of the citrus berry buzzing like a low humming current, as if I were licking an electric fence. The neurological confusion was disturbing. My nerve endings had never encountered this intensity of peppercorn.

'These will lead you into Pandora,' Dao's father whispered into my ear, before challenging me to an arm wrestle over a beer. I think he was referring to the technicolour universe in the movie *Avatar*.

In truth, I couldn't handle the heat, but that didn't stop me from continuing. The boiling hot chillies made my body sweat and inflate, while the numbing effects of the peppercorns left me with the sensation of having been punched in the face. I knew that I was uncomfortable, but my mouth wouldn't stop watering from the powerful effects of all the different ingredients, the soup and the dipping sauce. I realized that pain forms as much a part of the human sensory experience as pleasure, and in this moment, I was unable to discern between the two. I walked hazily back to campus, euphoria lingering for several hours, high off the peppercorns, the catharsis of sweating, and the endorphins that were released after an evening of tensing my body. If someone were to ask me what my most intense food experiences were, eating hot pot with Dao's family would be the first to come to mind. I loved the way this kind of heat turned eating to an elevated sensory experience, where taste and smell gave way to more complex bodily sensations, such as pain. I was fascinated by the multidimensional aspect of this kind of meal: the tastes of the condiments, the sour, the bitter and the sweet, all working as accompaniments to this great heat.

This way of thinking about food as something beyond taste deeply affected my way of cooking. I wanted to share this intimate story of spice that spanned my lifetime. In almost all the recipes at Ikoyi, we employ spice through varieties of fresh or dried chillies, perfumed dry ingredients and peppercorns. Whenever I have worked in other kitchens under other chefs, I've been taught to use spices sparingly, hidden well enough to complement other ingredients rather than stand out on their own. But the bold heat of Ikoyi's recipes means using the bitter, burning aspects of peppercorns at the forefront of the recipe, almost to the point of harshness. In a glaze of chicken jus and tamarind, nearly three per cent of the weight is made up of Penja peppercorns. Just when you think the hot sensation is too much, there is comfort to be found in the tartness of the tamarind, while the chicken fat and brown butter from the jus mellow out the burn.

Figuring out why we crave pain in spice as a major sense of flavour begins with an understanding of our bodies' relationship to heat. Dangerously hot temperatures and capsaicin, the active component in chilli peppers, both activate an important gene encoding a receptor. The sensation of heat we experience when eating chillies is real to the brain: as far as it can tell, the mouth really is burning. But this is a feeling, not a taste or smell, and it is communicated to the brain through the same nerves that govern the sense of touch. If capsaicin and other elements picked up by the receptor send warnings of imminent danger through the sensation of pain, why do we actively enjoy this sensation? It's not like we take equal pleasure in holding our hands over an open flame. The difference is that chilli heat is the pain that cries wolf.

Bold heat is the essence of my experiences of spice, and the menu at Ikoyi shares those pivotal moments that have shaped my cuisine and informed my creativity. Bold heat is the backbone of our dishes.

forget everything you know: creating new reference points

One evening at the restaurant, a few years after we had opened, a guest came up to me and said, 'It was a delicious meal, but there were no reference points.' He was dining with his wife at the time, and he mentioned somewhat proudly that he was also a chef. I felt he had accurately expressed the creative objectives of our cooking. Ikoyi is not about representing single traditions or mixing and matching easily identifiable concepts. Most restaurants cook within a theme. A modern British restaurant with Basque influences will offer locally sourced grilled meats and seafood, baked cheesecakes and galettes, in the same way a 'fusion' Japanese and Latin American restaurant serves sashimi with serrano chillies and lime, or spiced chicken with a ponzu dipping sauce. We tend to feel self-satisfied and in control when we can describe the derivation of an ingredient or accurately pinpoint a particular style of cookery. It denotes a certain level of experience and taste, impressing friends and dinner dates. I seek to strip the guest of that experience and go beyond for something more original. If we are always on the hunt for accessible familiarity, will we ever be open to the truly unfamiliar? I prefer for there to be both the sense of the familiar and of the unknown.

Since I was very young, my father pushed me to keep an open mind. He would become furious at me for being fussy and not trying new things. Perhaps he was trying to teach me not to be wasteful, but I think the real purpose of his method was to make sure I would approach life with an objective lens – always questioning, always listening to others' points of view, always trying new things.

I used to have a severe phobia of mushrooms. Their slimy, gilled appearance and strange aromas led me to believe they were all poisonous. One particular evening, we were eating lo mein with soup, dumplings and those wretched mushrooms for dinner. I remember my father wouldn't allow me to leave the dinner table until I had finished my entire bowl. It was a tortuous experience to say the least: as I furtively carved the alien fungus into miniscule pieces, I pushed through to the end in tears to finish my dinner.

Today, despite – or perhaps because – of this experience, mushrooms are among my favourite ingredients, and I use them throughout my kitchen for their texture and flavour-optimizing characteristics. In fact, as an adult, there is almost nothing that I do not like to eat. The experience of my phobias being forced out of me resulted in my desire to see the beauty in everything. Some cultures may look on this way of childrearing as cruel, but what I know now is that this learning phase at a young age is a critical stage of one's development as a human being. However traumatic it may have been, I wouldn't have the capacities I do today without this kind of parenting.

When I apply my creative process to ingredients, I deliberately remove them from their cultural context and traditional usage. Just as I came to perceive mushrooms as innocuous organic matter with flavour, I also began to look at all the produce in my kitchen from a totally objective standpoint, almost as if in a vacuum. Without any context, one can look at ingredients as if they were alien artefacts – beautiful, strange, elegant and sensual. In forgetting everything I know with respect to food, I relate to ingredients purely through their potential for flavour and their untapped dimensions for aesthetic expression.

Forgetting everything I know helps me access visual and psychological associations that arise from the depths of memory – all that I have perceived and attached to the subconscious throughout my lifetime. Without having to think about the historical and cultural context of an ingredient, I'm free to draw inspiration from different mediums, such as a Ridley Scott film or a Mark Rothko painting. I can watch a cartoon and use its overly exaggerated, simplistic depictions of food in my own kitchen. Like cartoon artists, I often strive to make produce appear even plumper, shinier and more alive than it does in its natural state. My aim is to express the very essence of the animal or vegetable, rendering it even more *itself* than it was before it landed on the plate. That moment in childhood when I opened my mind to the peculiarity of mushrooms has inspired me to come up with infinite interpretations of ingredients, which form the menu at Ikoyi.

the birth & death of a concept

Throughout our journey to create Ikoyi, we've always had trouble giving a name to the kind of restaurant Ikoyi is and what cuisine it most represents. At the start, when people used to ask me what kind of food we cooked, I'd say, 'Tasty food, good ingredients with some cool spices.' I tried to keep words like 'alienation' and mentions of Ridley Scott out of the definition, and instead aimed to go with the raw, simple explanation of our food. I was hesitant to call the restaurant West African or Nigerian, because in creating the menu, I was delving into my own pool of references, ideas and interpretations. I'm neither a West African chef nor someone with a close familiarity with the area's food culture, so there would be no integrity in claiming this kind of authenticity. The concept of Jollof Cuisine had been our key branding strategy when it came to opening the gates to the property market, but it was too limiting a classification for what we were actually looking to achieve. The connection to a specific region remained too strong. Iré's idea was to present me with materials from his heritage, but to leave the cooking entirely to me. As I've explained, rather than taking pre-existing traditions and feebly attempting to 'elevate' them, we sought to be concept-less, focusing our attention on the ingredients themselves and what these meant to us on their own account. Colour, texture, shape and smell would be the catalysts for creativity.

Iré and I decided it would be sensible to travel to Nigeria on a research trip all the same. The journey would better acquaint me with the flavours of his upbringing and the ingredients I'd read about. So in 2016, we spent two days driving up, down and across expansive Lagos, traversing the interminably long Third Mainland Bridge. We saw level housing as far as the eye could see through Ikeja, and fishermen casting their nets alongside the floating houses of Makoko. The oil crisis left us in traffic jams so slow it could take us up to four hours to reach a different pocket of the city. Huge, bustling Lagos reverberated like a throttling engine, a giant beehive of human beings moving, working, hustling. I felt somewhat vulnerable and struggled to locate myself amongst the strangeness of names I'd never seen before and the absence of landmarks and other urban reference points.

We ate elephantine Nigerian tiger prawns as long as my forearm, and in the Ikoyi neighbourhood we had goat pepper soup, the spiciest dish I have ever consumed. There was a strong initial savoury taste akin to dipping your finger into instant ramen powder, an indulgently comforting kind of salty, followed by jaw-aching spice, my pores fruitlessly bursting open for breath in the humid evening air. Underlying the heat were delicate peppercorns, their medicinal scent of menthol and smoked leather clearing my passages as the scorching soup entered my throat. Iré's aunt had a small restaurant and served us Nigerian-style jollof rice tossed with shrimps and diced carrots, with hot servings of stewed chicken on the side. The long grains of rice were denser than the rice I was accustomed to, but my addiction to the heat of *ata rodo* chillies grew stronger, and any dishes without these Scotch bonnets seemed dull.

We tried indigenous, unpolished *ofada* rice, pearly and aromatic like nutty barley. We ate it with *amayase*, an intense stew of green bell peppers, locust beans, tripe, palm oil and ground crayfish. We crammed four to five meals into each day, as we had such limited time in the city. I could not miss out on my first taste of *egusi*, a soup in which ground gourd seeds are used as a thickening nutty base, iron-rich and slightly bitter, paired with native varieties of sorrel and spinach. I watched the giant African snail boil into a tender band of wiry meat; its texture, like some kind of oceanic cartilage, reminded me of molluscs, and harmonized with the crunches of peppers and onions in a roasted *asun* stir-fry.

The restaurant we wanted to create would be as much a part of my story as Iré's, and the trip had been fundamental in familiarizing me with a whole new set of ingredients and spices I had never seen or tasted before. The window into Iré's own food culture made clear there were certain primal qualities to these flavours, especially the salivation-inducing aspect of the chillies in the pepper soup, which had strong commonalities with the Cantonese broths of meat, fish and hot chilli oil I'd grown up eating. What most captured my imagination were the aromatics of the Nigerian peppercorns and spices – *uziza*, *uda* and *ehuru* – which brought me back to the first time I bit into a Sichuan peppercorn or smelled over-infused, dark oolong tea. But this was not my food culture, and I did not want to be the chef to tell the story of Nigerian cuisine in London. The notion of trying to modernize and popularize a food I had not grown up eating made me feel dishonest and uncomfortable. In the end, the trip had pushed me further away from the concept of a Nigerian restaurant.

What had always drawn both Iré and me to cooking in London was the ability to source organic raw materials from local producers while simultaneously having access to many international ingredients. Considering that I didn't want to make Nigerian food, I'd have to reinterpret the arsenal of spices and seasonings associated with West Africa outside of their traditional context. I developed the idea of being an ingredient explorer, interpreting food such as grains of paradise stripped of their original usage. Exploring this concept, I infused the citrussy tang of this rich peppercorn into a caramelized jam of ripe strawberries. Removing preconceptions had unlocked limitless creative potential. New friends I'd made in Lagos and Iré's family members gave us access to local spices, which were to form the original backbone of the restaurant menu.

With everything that inspired me, from the fiery umami of West African spices to the landscape of British produce and seasonality, I couldn't hold back the instinct to cook in this de-culturalized way. I wanted to be guided by what immediately connected to the deepest aspect of my imagination, and not the categories and attributes of a specific concept. In opening Ikoyi, I felt like I had to precisely define the meaning of my work and the concept behind it. I wanted to kill the concept and contradict this desire, leaving space for association, uncertainty and interpretation.

What had always drawn both Iré and me to cooking in London was the ability to source organic raw materials from local producers...

the setting: a cow foot in piccadilly

It's 6.30 am in the summer of 2021. I wake up briskly and my legs, knees and back are aching from the long week. I've had a bad night's sleep, as the adrenaline from yesterday's service kept me up late. My phone is already buzzing; I'm exchanging texts with butchers, farmers, fishermen and logistics companies who are flying shellfish down for the next day. There is something manic about waking up and moving straight into a furious exchange of data and timings. I message one of my chefs, asking that the team keep the recently delivered aged rib of Angus beef aside, as I'd like to inspect it before we break it down. I scan the bookings and make notes of all the regulars and friends eating with us that day. I'm quite stressed about the fact that three different tables of chefs are having lunch with us, and they will all be arriving at midday, which isn't far off. I've kept aside some pristine scallops for them from last night, but I'm worried these won't shine as brightly as I'd like them to. I think through the 15 servings I'd like to put on the menu, filtering through my memory of what was left in our standing fridge last night and anticipating the farm deliveries that will reach the kitchen in the next hour. I suddenly realize we also have a delivery of 100 oysters and a whole sheep from Cornwall. The adrenaline kicks back in and I jump out of bed. After a swift coffee, I'm out the door in less than 10 minutes.

It's about five miles to cycle from south London to Ikoyi. Every morning, I zip through Walworth Road from Camberwell to the centre of the city, weaving through the long and narrow street humming with the frantic energy of commuters beginning their day. I pass by the colossal roundabout at Elephant and Castle amid buses, cars, hundreds of cyclists, art students and workers. There is an intensity on everyone's faces as they all brace for the day ahead, an expression that says: 'Don't touch me and don't get in my way.' I realize I am not the only one bursting with adrenaline. I pick up the pace to escape the weight of the slog and finally make it over Waterloo Bridge, while dodging the behemoth buses and lorries over the intersection.

As I make my final passage down The Strand over Trafalgar Square, everything is suddenly calmer. The buskers, street performers and jugglers are setting up shop in front of the National Gallery and Nelson's Column. A few tourists sip coffees and wander around an art installation. I finally reach Haymarket, turning left on to Jermyn Street and into St James's Market. Despite all the commotion of Londoners entering and exiting the city centre, there is a strange serenity within the belly of the beast...

As this book goes to press, Ikoyi is about to move to The Strand, but it originally nestled in a side street, hidden among the commercial giants sandwiched between Haymarket and Regent Street on either side, with Piccadilly and Pall Mall above and below. When envisaging a place to open a restaurant, Piccadilly Circus wasn't the first location to come to mind. My earliest memories of London relate to Piccadilly: its iconic garish neon signs, the the Shaftesbury Memorial Fountain statue statue and the sense that this was it, the beating heart of the modern world. Piccadilly is much the same today. Throngs of tour groups still congregate in front of the shining symbols of capitalism to have their picture taken. It really is a circus. For all the idiosyncratic variety available in London, I'm still surprised at Piccadilly's ability to pull crowds to a place full of the kind of global branding that can be found in any other modern capital. Perhaps the energy I felt as a child is still there for those new to the city. Like most other Londoners, I am probably jaded to its effects.

London is a stratified city, split into boroughs and neighbourhoods with a multitude of peoples of all different backgrounds, classes and ethnicities. Choosing where to live, hang out or open a business reveals in which community one feels most comfortable. East London has garnered a reputation for the younger, hip and liberal generation, while west London seems to be more posh, residential and conservative. North and south London, while very different and separated geographically, both harbour eclectic mixes of all cultures, incomes and tastes. Granted, these are very broad generalizations, but it's undeniable that these distinct communities make London a complex yet stimulating environment in which to live.

In St James, I always thought of Ikoyi as a kind of satellite floating in the middle of it all. Some may have interpreted our location as a desire for commercial success, but in reality we didn't quite fit into our environs. I didn't see Ikoyi in the global centre of Piccadilly, but rather in a neutral zone, detached from associations with specific neighbourhoods and buried within a corporate development. With the long open window spanning the length of the restaurant, our diners truly gazed on to the real London, the good and the bad. The aristocratic heritage of St James glowed quietly in the evening light, but things could quickly devolve into scenes of drunken debauchery as revellers turned down the passage towards the restaurant.

At one point, we served a dish called Cow Foot. One of our chefs, Lasi, had spoken of a stew of braised beef hoof and okra he liked to eat with his family in Gambia, and so we decided to play with the idea of feet on the menu. We braised young calf feet and shins overnight in Guinness and dark stock until they broke down. The tendons and skin went into the blender to form a milkshake-textured paste, into which we set the shredded shin meat. The reduced stock, rich with beef flavour, loosened out the base as we poured it into a large gastronorm. We finished the dish with fresh lemon thyme, lemon zest and pickled shallots to lift the opulent melee. Then we carved the solidified beef matter into small cubes and rolled them in light breading before deep-frying them and finishing them with a purple salt of dried beetroot and Penja peppercorn. The tart and crispy bites went out into the dining room on the polished, boiled bones that had been released during the cooking process. Some guests frowned, while others rejoiced at the somewhat macabre spectacle of eating cow foot straight off a calf bone. Cow Foot was decidedly divisive.

Part of me enjoyed the disruptive nature of the dish, but it was still ultimately homely comfort food. I was amused by the incongruous image of our guests chewing cow flesh off the femurs with the regal backdrop of St James's behind them.

the menu

the recipes

We serve a blind tasting menu at Ikoyi, a sequence of fifteen to twenty servings contingent on the seasonality of fresh produce from our growers, farmers and fishermen, as well as what inspires us most in the moment. When we opened the restaurant, we initially served an à la carte menu. To the majority of our guests, the menu read a bit like the song titles on an album or even a foreign language. Random combinations of ingredients, unusual-sounding names and a minimalist, discreet wording pattern. I was always insistent that a menu should only reveal the three key ingredients or ideas, as these were the concepts I wanted to imbed in the dining experience. Because we use so many kinds of ingredients and techniques, if we were to list them all, the explanatory prose would only confound our guests further. To make matters more difficult, our servers struggled to explain the flavours and ideas succinctly, even after tasting the dishes themselves.

I thought about the experience of looking at art, allowing its beauty or ugliness to wash over you, experiencing the true feelings of delight or disgust emanating from your subjective gaze upon a work. Quite often, I find the explanatory critique accompanying art ambiguous and pretentious. It disrupts one's natural reaction to the subject matter by injecting confusing, wordy ideas. I find art criticism even more troubling when it comes to more abstract art, which often transcends definitions. To be clear, I don't consider what we do at Ikoyi to be the same as art. But the relationship between the critic and art and other media made me realize that the best way for us to serve our food at the restaurant might be to just drop the plate with a brief introduction and then walk away. The blind tasting menu precludes the need for an awkward a priori discussion of what's to come. As we describe the dish for the first time, we are no longer talking of an abstract idea, but are explaining the colours, shapes and smells right in front of us. The menu is therefore a kind of surprise, each course to be revealed after the next.

Throughout my conversations with our various suppliers, I'll agree to take delivery of many varying quantities of prized produce, available only momentarily and often in smaller amounts. These conversations do not involve a great deal of planning, but rather encourage spur-of-the-moment inspiration: a few kilos of hand-dived scallops from Devon, a small bush of sea buckthorn berries on its way out, the last gai lan broccoli tops in late spring. We devise our menu following a basic structure. Snacks, followed by servings of fish, vegetables, a plantain serving, improvised dishes, a meat serving, our smoked rice and several sweet servings. We also have a pantry of spices, hyper-smooth, umami-rich sauces, seasoning powders, home-made misos, nut butters and pickles, all of which act as the foundations. In taking delivery of such wide-ranging bounty, we plan that day's menus using the incoming ingredients within this paradigm.

Since the menu could be different for each table, my cooks require a great deal of culinary dexterity. It is normal for us to be serving up to five different kinds of fish going to different tables for their fish serving. For instance, the first table of four could take the two red mullets, the following sixteen covers the octopus and the remaining twelve the trout and john dory. At the end of the day, there will never be a single portion left. Things become more difficult when there are differing quantities of meat in house, as well as new improvised dishes being tested. There have been nights when up to eight menus are being served simultaneously, with grouse, lobster, sweetbreads, whole roasted daikon, cabbages, ribs of beef, sweetbreads, scallops, clams, fried chicken and turbot heads all going out at the same time. While there is a lot of pressure on the cooks in these moments, I genuinely believe the food we serve tastes better thanks to this tension. The panic-inducing agility and mental alertness needed to cook menus made up of changing seasonal produce creates great flavour and energy. Our dynamic menu reflects the passion we have as chefs for exceptional produce and our ability to use it in its optimal condition, allowing our guests to let our creations wash over them.

I have presented the recipes in this book exactly as they are written in the kitchen folder at Ikoyi. Each recipe will produce four portions of the dish, which is probably more than is required for a meal at home. I appreciate that many of these ingredients will be difficult or at times impossible to procure, but that challenge represents what it's like to run a restaurant like Ikoyi, with a kitchen comprised of a complex network of supplier and producer relationships. My hope is that these recipes will inspire you to learn more about produce: where it comes from, the stories of its suppliers, and how it can be used in daring but innovative ways. The cooking instructions are to the point, and I have chosen not to include historical information about ingredients, as I prefer to view them in a contextless vacuum. It is, of course, up to you to use your common sense and intuition to adapt them, especially if the recipes are to be recreated in a home kitchen without professional cooking equipment. I hope that instead of feeling pressured to recreate a dish in its entirety, you are inspired by specific components, such as emulsions, sauces or marinades. In other words, I hope you see each recipe as a beginning.

snacks

Although we call them snacks, our first servings are probably more substantial than the traditional amuse-bouche. I think of the term 'snack' as something you could eat between meals with a glass of wine or before dinner with cocktails. Dainty bites don't really do it for me. I like to eat food I can tuck into: generous, plentiful and at least two mouthfuls. Our snacks reflect this ethos. Since these are the first dishes on the menu, I also believe they need to be impactful, arresting the attention of our guests and heightening their excitement for what's to come. In some cases, we make exceptions and serve certain snacks later in the meal if we feel they fit better there within the sequence of produce. It's important that we also don't take ourselves too seriously and focus on what matters: playfulness, generosity and uncompromising flavour. Plump and explosively juicy oysters, spoonfuls of caviar with okra-infused martinis, fresh slices of chilled melon and sour emulsions of smoked chillies ignite the palate and create a sense of celebration.

steamed oyster from maorach beag,
agbalumo & hot sauce

see p. 60

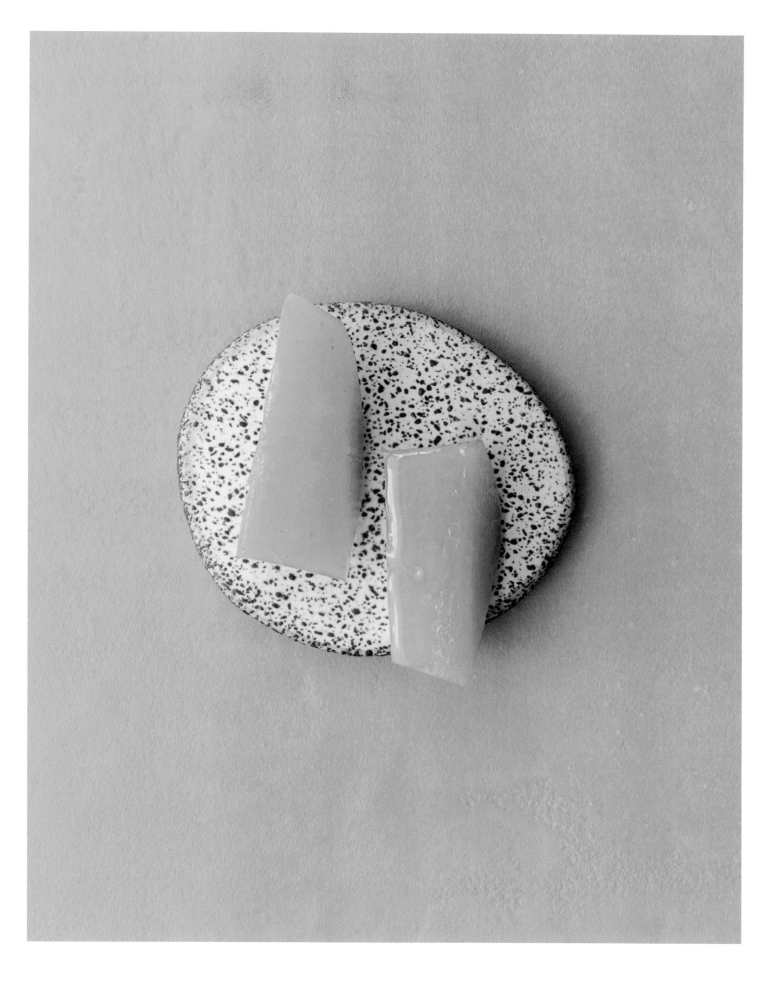

51   **melon from mantua &**
         peppercorn tea **see p. 62**

corn, ube & razor clams   **see p. 64**

fermented rice, pink peppercorn &
raw squid   see p. 70

54   **cassava terrine, calf brain & morel**   see p. 67

langoustine moin moin **see p. 72**

blue poppyseed waffle, smoked honey
butter & daikon ganache

56

see p. 75

lobster, red currants &
strawberry vinegar jelly

see p. 78

58   **crab & roasted malted barley bread**   **see p. 80**

59

octopus fried in wild rice &
yeasted béarnaise

see p. 83

steamed oyster from maorach beag, agbalumo & hot sauce

When contemplating new ways of serving produce at Ikoyi, I look back on my most memorable mouthfeel experiences. Great mouthfeel is achieved by paying close attention to the sensation of texture and the vehicles of flavour. It often relates to something carnal within us, a sensual burst of epidermal layers releasing warm broths, fat-rich and tender proteins, or something crunchy and sweet. When we thought about putting oysters on the menu, it was a prime moment for us to focus on intensifying mouthfeel. I'd decided to work with Maorach Beag, a small farm in the highlands of Scotland that was rearing native and rock oysters in the pristine waters of Loch Broom. While the natives had a delicate, metallic finish, I was more impressed with the creaminess of the rock oysters, which had a sweet, meaty taste and grassy cucumber finish. Eaten raw, the oysters were tender, their melted flesh giving way almost too easily. I wanted our guests to bite into our oysters and for there to be a light crunch, followed by a pop and explosion of sweet salinity.

We experimented by placing the oysters over the middle rack of the grill and taking them off when just opened. While this method worked well in terms of cooking the oysters in their own juices, I found the grill imparted little to no flavour to the meat. Steaming the oysters was the best solution, as the heat penetrating the shell gently warmed up the juices inside, poaching the oyster and firming up its flesh. Once cool, we shucked the oysters and left them to marinate in a bath of their chilled, strained broth and some fragrant elderflower oil, which balanced out the saltiness and gave the oysters a glistening, pearl-like sheen. We kept the oil frozen so that we could apply it like a gel, giving the oyster a cold and refreshing aspect. I loved how they plumped up after cooking, taking on a more defined shape, rounded like baby squid.

We serve the oysters with a generous spoonful of aged kaluga caviar, herb jelly, our hot sauce and a few slices of agbalumo. These intensely tart, cherry-like fruits give a sweet and sour finish to the dish and cleanse the palate of the rich, savoury oyster and caviar.

**steamed oyster from maorach beag,
agbalumo & hot sauce**

serves 4

pictured on p.50

For the elderflower oil
500 g locally foraged elderflower –
   choose young, tender branches
350 g grapeseed oil

For the marigold jelly
75 g honey
300 g chardonnay vinegar
80 g Mexican marigolds
1.05 g agar agar

To finish
4 rock oysters
Ikoyi Hot Sauce (page 234), to taste
8 × 2 mm (1/16 in)-thick slices of
   agbalumo
40 g N25 kaluga caviar

To make the elderflower oil
Carefully rinse the elderflower, being sure to handle the
flowers gently so they don't fall apart. Leave to dry for 1 hour,
then vacuum seal with the grapeseed oil. Cook sous-vide for
15 minutes at 88°C (190°F). Cool to room temperature and
leave to infuse for 2 days before straining. Store the oil in an
airtight container in the freezer and use within 6 months.

To make the marigold jelly
In a saucepan, bring the honey and vinegar to the boil, then
take off the heat. Allow the liquid to cool to 70°C (158°F),
then add the marigolds. Leave to infuse for at least 1 hour.
Strain the liquid and mix in the agar agar with a hand-
blender. Bring the liquid back to the boil for 2 minutes, then
strain once more into a shallow container. Leave to set for
3 hours. Store the jelly in an airtight container in the fridge
and use within 3 days.

To finish
Preheat the oven to 100°C/210°F/Gas Mark ¼.

Make 4 small nests with foil. Rest an oyster on each one and
place into a flat gastronorm or baking dish. Wrap tightly with
cling film and steam in the oven for 1 minute 20 seconds–2
minutes. Remove from the oven and let the oysters continue
to cook in the residual heat.

Once cool enough to handle, gently open the oysters. They
will be open already, so there's no need to shuck them. Place
them back in the oven if necessary, but if they still don't open
after several minutes, then discard. Place the oysters, turned
over, into a shallow container. Strain the juices from the shells
over the oysters and then generously spoon over a tablespoon
of the chilled elderflower oil.

Place an oyster in the base of a small, chilled ceramic bowl,
folding the dark lip of the oyster underneath its body. Use
a thin-rimmed teaspoon to slice a layer of Mexican marigold
jelly and place it on top of the oyster, along with a dollop of
hot sauce, followed by 2 agbalumo slices, 1 large teaspoon
of the caviar and finally a few more drops of extra-cold
elderflower oil. Repeat with the remaining oysters and serve.

melon from mantua &
peppercorn tea

The beauty of a perfectly ripe, sweet and acidic slice of fruit is that it can wake you up with a sense of renewal before you eat, refresh your palate after a rich, spicy dish, or even leave you with a cold burst of sugar at the end of the meal. Growing up in Hong Kong, I used to eat a lot of exotic fruit, and I have particularly fond memories of giant plates of longan, cantaloupe and watermelon arriving at the table at the end of our family lunches, the arrangement of fruit so vast one would have thought we hadn't eaten yet. I remember how particular my Chinese side of the family was when selecting the fruit, always double-checking the level of sweetness with the waiter before ordering. Those melons were indeed sweet; they had a sort of artificial melon taste, closer to the synthetic taste of melon fabricated for candies. Ever since then, I've been obsessed with the way the natural flavour of fruit can be so defined that it reminds us of our artificial imitation, the attempt to crystalize taste into artificiality. Even though we were able to finish a whole watermelon after a long lunch of dim sum, I don't think human beings need to eat that much fruit. At Ikoyi, we tend to serve fruit at the beginning of the meal, especially during the summer. At the end of a long day in mid-July, London can be quite hot and stuffy. It's a great pleasure to cool your palate with an unctuous slice of melon glowing radioactively under the dimly lit lamps.

Serving a single slice of fruit is actually not as easy as it seems. It's sort of like looking at a painting of a can of beans: some might say it's too simple, or think 'I could do that.' For us, the challenge lies not only in finding the right grower, but also in the handling of the fruit between the kitchen and the dining room. We use melons from Mantua in northern Italy, which are thinned up to just five melons per vine and minimally watered to guarantee that natural sugars pervade. After a month of maturation, the melons are transported in an insulated blanket of wet wool, to keep them cool and whole.

It's important to take a position on what 'perfect ripeness' is and to stick to this. We serve the melons only when they are ripe to the point of just holding their shape but almost falling apart. The skin should feel creamy and not dry, while the underside should have a slightly giving springiness. These physical indications mark my idea of perfect ripeness.

The Sun Sweet melon alone is so sweet that, at times, you have the feeling of eating a full teaspoon of caster (superfine) sugar, like the melon is trying to transform into confectionery. We season the melons by marinating them in a savoury spiced tea accented with locally grown chamomile and glazed with semi-frozen almond oil. I like to think of the great sushi masters when slicing this fruit – why should we not take the same care with our melon as Saito San does with aged tuna? I find that respect and precision in preparing the melon greatly enhances the aesthetic; the smallest motions and decisive angles can transform its presence from humble fruit to an incandescent form of architecture. We use an ultra-sharp slicer to carve long, triangular wedges out of the melon, flattening off the seeded flesh and the back end. We use a smaller boning knife to round the underside, removing a small layer so the melon can sit flat. Once the melons have been compressed in their tea, they're blast-chilled to -12°C (10°F) for a few minutes to get them extra cold before serving. The freezing and slight thawing process also helps to break down the flesh by the time it arrives with the guest. The resulting mouthfeel is at first dense, but the fruit's meat then shreds apart to allow the cold, aromatic juice to flow.

For the peppercorn tea
15 g ehuru
25 g black peppercorns
25 g green Sichuan peppercorns
15 g cubeb peppercorns
666 g caster (superfine) sugar
1.333 kg filtered water
200 g fresh chamomile, washed and
 roughly chopped
150 g maple verjus

For the fruit
1 very sweet Sun Sweet melon
Fresh Almond Oil (see Nut & Seed
 Oils, page 232), for glazing

To make the peppercorn tea
Toast the spices in a wide frying pan until fragrant, then blitz roughly in a spice grinder.

In a large saucepan, bring the sugar and water to the boil, then take off the heat. Add the spices and chopped chamomile and pour into a deep container. Wrap the container with cling film and leave to infuse for 2 hours, or until the tea is very dark and aromatic. Pass through a muslin cloth-lined chinois and season with the verjus. Store the tea in an airtight container in the fridge and use within 3 days.

To prepare the fruit and assemble
Slice the melon into 8 equal-sized pieces. If the melon is extra-large, you may be able to slice again into a further 8 pieces. Scoop out the seeds and flatten off each wedge of melon, carefully carving the skin of the base to retain a smooth shape. Flatten the bottom of the melon and then square off its back end.

Place the melon slices in an even layer on a gastronorm and pour over the tea. Compress on full pressure in a vacuum-pack machine and repeat 5 times.

Just before serving the melons place the tray into a blast-chiller or freezer set to -12°C (10°F) for 3 minutes. Transfer to a plate and glaze with the almond oil. It's important the melons go straight to the guests so they can be eaten in their most refreshing state.

corn, ube & razor clams

Not to be confused with purple yam, Nigerian *ube* comes from the fruit tree native to Africa, otherwise known as bush pear or butterfruit. I first came across ube while visiting a local market on Rye Lane in Peckham, a district of south London about ten minutes from where I live. Peckham is home to one of the largest African populations in London with Nigerians, Ghanaians, Somalians, Sierra Leoneans and various other communities living and working in the area. Turning the corner on to Rye Lane past the hipster bakeries and gentrified wine bars, you come across some of the hustle and bustle I encountered in Lagos. Smoked dried mackerels hang from the open stalls, while jackfruit, plantains, garden eggs and okra aplenty sit in large cardboard boxes. As you venture inside the African food stores, you will find giant bags of beans, garri flour, malt drinks and all the spices and peppercorns of the West African pantry. The butchers carry whole animal parts, such as goat and cow heads, hooves and haunches. The smells are wild and intoxicating: far more pungent than most other neighbourhood supermarkets in the capital.

Because I'd been carefully researching the foodstuffs of West Africa, I'd learned the original names of all the ingredients as well as the English language culinary explanations of the produce I'd been tasting and trialling. Some of the purveyors met my keen interest and knowledge of nomenclature with a bit of suspicion, wondering what a sort-of-Chinese-looking white guy wanted with great big handfuls of okra, fermented oil seeds and crayfish powder. It seemed to be only local Nigerians and other West Africans, mainly mothers, aunts and grandmothers, who frequented the shops to buy ingredients for their cookery. I explained my passion for these ingredients, and that I wanted to learn how to cook with them and eventually open a restaurant with these flavours that were completely new to me.

One grocer, Stella, seemed to take a particular shine to my enthusiasm and held back some seasonal produce she'd sourced directly from Nigeria. I cycled down to the market to pick up my first bag of ube from her. Their colour ranged from light pink in their unripe form, to a deep purple as a mature fruit. Stella told me to eat the ube with corn. Luckily, we were in June, peak corn season, so I rushed back to Ikoyi in time to develop the dish for the week's menu.

The fat-rich texture of the ube reminded me a lot of avocado, but there was complexity in the nutty, almost olive-like aroma of the flesh, which melted like butter after cooking. The skins were super tannic and required a fair bit of sweetness to balance out. I took Stella's recommendation of a simple boil for the preparation, with the addition of some sugar. I peeled the fruit off its seed, skins and all, and blended it into a paste with the sugary poaching syrup. I could taste chestnuts, but the rich amino acids in the fruit revealed an intense meatiness when combined with other ingredients, especially spices and animal proteins. It was a particularly hot summer, so instead of grilled corn, we developed a clean and sharp gazpacho poured over razor clams. The silky ube is piped like whipped butter on to a smoky cracker of toasted spelt and yam, which is then topped with a nest of fresh flowers. The ube lends a rich, dense texture to the fragility of the cracker, elevating the ethereal crunch of biting into fresh flowers with their sweet and peppery perfume.

For the fermented sea buckthorn
1 kg sea buckthorn berries, gently
    washed if necessary
20 g fine salt

For the yellow corn gazpacho
500 g corn on the cob
500 g Sungold tomatoes, diced
400 g cucumbers, diced
60 g green chillies
50 g honey
120 g smoked rapeseed (canola) oil
1 bulb of wet garlic
90 g apple cider vinegar
20 g honey
40 g turmeric
10 g smoked salt

For the spelt and yam crackers
grapeseed oil, for frying
200 g organic pearled spelt
600 g filtered water, plus extra as
    required
20 g salt
250 g yams, peeled and sliced

For the ube purée
1.5 kg ube
1 kg filtered water
300 g caster sugar
15 g salt

To make the fermented sea buckthorn
Place the sea buckthorn berries in a large vacuum-seal bag. Add the salt and toss well. Spread the berries into an even layer and seal on full. Leave to ferment for 7 days at 24–28°C (75–82°F). If the bag expands too much, 'burp' out the air by making a small incision and then reseal. Taste the berries after 1 week. If tart and savoury, reseal the berries in their juices. Store the fermented sea buckthorn in an airtight container in the fridge and use within 1 month.

To make the yellow corn gazpacho
Slice the kernels of corn off the cob and add to a blender with the other vegetables. Add the remaining ingredients, along with 100 g of the fermented sea buckthorn, and blend for 5 minutes. You're looking for a very emulsified, aerated gazpacho with a silky texture and good body. You may need to blend it in batches. Season and chill quickly over ice. Store the gazpacho in an airtight container in the fridge and use within 3 days.

To make the spelt and yam crackers
Preheat the oven to 80°C/175°F.

Pour a generous amount of grapeseed oil into a deep, heavy-based pan over a high heat. Toast the spelt in the oil, tossing frequently to make sure it doesn't burn. Keep going until the grains smell of deeply caramelized popcorn. Carefully pour over the water, then reduce the heat and simmer the spelt until tender, topping up the water if necessary. Season with the salt.

In a separate pan, simmer the yams until tender and falling apart. Transfer 150 g of the yams to a blender. Add the spelt and its cooking liquid to the blender, and blend with the yams to a fine, spreadable paste. Use an offset spatula to spread the mixture evenly over a silicone baking mat or a tray lined with baking parchment. Bake for 2 hours, or until cracked and fully dried. Store the crackers in an airtight container with silica and use within 1 month.

To make the ube purée
Put the ube into a large pan with the water and sugar and boil until tender. Leave the ube to cool gradually in the cooking liquid. Once cool enough to handle, remove the skins and flesh from the seeds. Place the picked part of the fruit in a blender and slowly add the poaching liquid until a smooth purée forms, then blend for 8 minutes, adding more water if necessary, in order to achieve a spreadable, unctuous texture. Season the purée with the salt and store in an airtight container in the fridge for up to 5 days.

    continued overleaf

For the razor clams
2 kg razor clams
grapeseed oil, for frying
500 g filtered water
60 g Roasted Garlic Oil (page 232)
iced water

To finish
Green Oil (page 232)
borage and marigold flowers
House Pickle (page 230)
smoked salt

To cook the razor clams
Soak the clams in salted water for 1 hour, then rinse well under cold running water for 15 minutes.

Using a small paring knife, carefully release the clams from their shells, slicing out the main body away from its stomach and other organs. Reserve the bodies on a dry cloth.

Heat a wide-based frying pan over a high heat and pour in enough grapeseed oil to cover the base of the pan. Add the shells and leftover pieces of clam to the pan, shaking to ensure the shells cover the pan evenly. Pour over the measured water, then reduce the heat to low and simmer for 20 minutes. Strain to remove the shells and solids, then reduce the stock to 150 g.

Preheat a water bath to 56°C (133°F). Separate the clam bodies into 3 vacuum-seal bags, adding 50 g of the clam stock and 20 g of roasted garlic oil to each one. Seal on full, then cook in the water bath for 30 minutes before plunging into iced water. Store the clams in an airtight container and use within 3 days.

To finish
Pour 60 g of the gazpacho into a chilled bottle and keep in a very cold fridge or blast-chiller until you're ready to serve. Slice 60 g of the clams on the bias and divide equally between 4 chilled bowls. Shake the soup well and pour over the clams, then slash over some green oil.

Put 100 g of the ube purée into a piping bag and take out 4 crackers. Pipe the purée into the centre of each cracker and gently spread it across to flatten. Cover the crackers with the flowers, then spray them with house pickle and season with smoked salt. Serve on a plate alongside the soup.

cassava terrine, calf brain & morel

During our travels to Lagos, Iré introduced me to cassava in the form of *eba*. Native to South America, the starchy tuber grows perennially and annually in tropical and subtropical regions, and is a fundamental source of carbohydrates after rice and maize. Eba is a common form of *fufu*, a soft ball of dough with a slightly sour taste eaten with soups and used to mop up stews. The version I tried was composed of dried, fermented cassava flour, rehydrated and pounded into a glutinous ball. We pulled off pieces of the starch to spoon up a spinach and cow-offal stew thick with the smell of iru, African fermented locust bean. The dish was deeply delicious, but so filling we both passed out for more than three hours once we were done. I was captivated by cassava, recognizing it as an ingredient with diverse culinary applications. Its potato-like texture was far starchier than any other vegetable I had tried, and the idea of fermenting and then drying it was fascinating.

Serving a dish like eba would most likely put an end to a tasting menu if served at the start, as it would fill the belly and induce a coma. But the idea of serving cow offal and starch as a snack was an opportunity not to be missed. We just needed to find a lighter way to introduce these flavours and this combination of ingredients. We first baked thin slices of the tuber in half brown butter, half aged beef fat, with light sprinklings of *garri* (dried fermented cassava) between each layer. We flattened the slices into a terrine with heavy weights, and the starches, cooling fats and garri fused together to form a bond that shaped the cassava into a neat block.

The offal took the form of a light emulsion of veal brains, seasoned almost like *vitello tonnato*, with slightly acidic components. I wanted to play with the image of the brain in the dish, and liked how much the interconnected web of morel mushrooms look like cerebral lobes. We seared the mushrooms over an exceptionally hot plancha before resting them in smoky butter, and finally seasoned the dish with salted dried cep mushrooms and iru, a nod to the stew I'd eaten in Lagos. While the combination of these ingredients may seem unusual, the result is something totally familiar: crispy, buttery starch, creamy offal and the meatiness of mushroom.

For the brain emulsion
1.2 kg calves' brains
3 kg filtered water, plus iced water for cooling
25 g salt
60 g garlic, sliced
200 g whole milk
10 g Malabar peppercorns
5 g white Penja peppercorns
25 g anchovies in oil
grated zest of 2 lemons
2 Scotch bonnet chillies
30 g chardonnay vinegar
20 g smoked rapeseed (canola) oil
50 g whipping cream
200 g Simple Mayonnaise (page 230)

For the cassava terrine
3 kg cassava, peeled and sliced with a mandoline (be sure to remove any stalk or bark)
25 g fine salt
200 g garri
250 g Rendered Aged Beef Fat (page 230)
250 g Brown Butter (see Suya Butter, page 230)

To make the brain emulsion
Soak the brains in cold running water for 1 hour to clean and remove any residual blood. Bring the measured water to the boil in a pan and add the salt. Drop the brains into the water and simmer over a low heat. After 8 minutes, check the temperature of the brains and remove when they reach 88°C (190°F). Plunge them into the iced water, then carefully remove the membranes and veins from the brains using a paring knife and small tweezers.

Simmer the garlic in the milk in a saucepan for 10 minutes, then allow to cool to room temperature. Strain and reserve the milk for another use.

Toast the peppercorns in a large frying pan, then grind to a fine powder in a spice grinder.

In a blender, blend the brains with the garlic, ground peppercorns, anchovies, lemon zest, chillies, vinegar and smoked rapeseed (canola) oil for 2 minutes. Pass the resulting emulsion through a chinois.

Whip the cream to medium peaks, then fold into the brain emulsion. Stir a third of the brain emulsion into the mayonnaise, then gently fold in the rest. Season to taste, then leave in the fridge to set overnight.

Store the emulsion in an airtight container in the fridge and use within 3 days.

To make the cassava terrine
Preheat the oven to 160°C/Gas Mark 3 and line a large, flat gastronorm with baking parchment.

Arrange a layer of cassava over the parchment, with as few gaps as possible, then sprinkle lightly with salt and garri, followed by a few brushes of beef fat and brown butter. Keep adding layers of cassava until you are 1 cm (½ in) from the top of the gastronorm, repeating the seasoning process at each step. Pour the remaining fat and butter over the top.

Bake for 1½ hours. Check the terrine is done by pushing a knife through it. If it yields easily, remove from the oven, otherwise continue to cook until done. Allow the tray to rest on the worktop for several minutes before placing a heavy weight on top. Leave to set overnight in the fridge, or at least 6 hours.

Once set, slice the terrine into pieces measuring 2.5 × 6 cm (1 × 2¼ in). Store in an airtight container in the fridge and use within 1 week.

For the iru cep salt
20 g iru
400 g dried porcini mushrooms (ceps)
25 g smoked salt

To finish
grapeseed oil, for deep-frying and
  brushing
4 large morel mushrooms
Suya Butter (page 230), for basting

To make the iru cep salt
Preheat the oven to 55°C/130°C.

Place the iru and dried ceps on a silicone baking mat or
parchment-lined baking sheet. Bake for 12 hours, then blitz to
a fine powder with the smoked salt. The iru cep salt will keep in
an airtight container at room temperature for several months.

To finish
Fry 4 of the terrines in the grapeseed oil at 170°C (338°F) for
3 minutes or until golden brown. Leave to rest for 10 minutes
in a warm place.

Brush the morel mushrooms on one side with grapeseed
oil and place on a hot plancha. Leave undisturbed until the
edges look caramelized and crispy. Flip over once and cook
for another 20 seconds, then place the mushrooms over the
bars on a grill, basting with the suya butter, allowing the fats
to spit and release smoky flavours.

Remove from the heat and let the mushrooms rest until
tender but with a slight bite, draining any excess fat.

Place a small quenelle of the brain emulsion (about 20 g) on
to each terrine, followed by a mushroom, pressing gently
down so it sits firmly. Finish with a dusting of the iru cep salt
and serve.

fermented rice, pink peppercorn & raw squid

Iré introduced me to a kind of rice pancake, *sinasir*, based on a northern Nigerian recipe that uses varieties of soft rice. I found it to be simple and delicious, but I wanted to serve something with a more tender consistency and a lighter structure. Our fermented rice pancake is full of air pockets, just like a crumpet but thinner, chewier and crispier, something reminiscent of a blini, but sourer and more varied in terms of its textures. I love how its aerated caverns absorb pools of spiced butter, while the base tastes like caramelized sourdough crust.

We finish the batter with buttermilk and bicarbonate of soda (baking soda), which creates an incredibly beautiful crumb of tiny, circular holes. The batter is cooked on a flat frying pan, starting over a high heat to create more bubbles in the pancake, then finishing over a low heat to just cook it through.

While this pancake is tasty enough to be eaten on its own, I see it as a versatile, canapé-style base for the season's most inspiring ingredients. My favourite topping is our salad of sliced raw squid marinated in pink peppercorn and rose oil, with smoked Scotch bonnet and lightly poached broccoli.

For the fermented rice pancake
465 g jasmine rice
280 g filtered water
65 g yogurt
8 g fine salt
25 g caster (superfine) sugar
3.2 g bicarbonate of soda (baking soda)
25 g butter

For the raw squid
500g whole squid

For the pink peppercorn oil
200 g dried rose buds
50 g pink peppercorns
500 g grapeseed oil

To finish
4 fermented rice pancakes
Suya Butter (page 230), warmed, for greasing
60 g prepared raw squid
10 g smoked salt
pink peppercorn oil
2 heads of gai lan
iced water
20 g extra virgin olive oil
50 g Smoked Scotch Bonnet Emulsion (page 207)

To make the fermented rice pancakes
Soak the rice in the filtered water for 3 hours.

Transfer to a high-powered blender and blitz for 2 minutes. Leave in a warm place at between 22 and 24°C to ferment for at least 12 hours.

When the batter smells sour, with small bubbles forming on the surface, stir in the yogurt, salt, sugar and bicarbonate of soda (baking soda). Store the batter in an airtight container in the fridge and use within 3 days.

When you are ready to cook the pancakes, bring the batter to room temperature for 30 minutes and whisk well. Lightly grease the surface of a non-stick frying pan with the butter and bring to a high heat. Place 7 cm (2¾ in) moulds in the frying pan and pour in the batter 5 mm (¼ in) thick, then immediately reduce the heat to the lowest setting. Cook the pancakes until all the bubbles on the uncooked side appear dry. Remove and leave to cool on a wire rack then store in a sealed container at room temperature until ready to grill. The pancakes will keep for up to 1 day.

To prepare the raw squid
Wash the squid well and remove the tentacles from the body, squeezing the head to remove the beak and entrails. Slice the purple membrane from the body and cut off the fins. Rinse the squid again, then dry well with kitchen towels. Use the tentacles for another recipe and store the squid in an airtight container in the freezer for up to 1 month.

To make the pink peppercorn oil
Blitz the rose buds and pink peppercorns in a high-powered blender for 1 minute until a fine powder forms. Add the oil and blend for a further 8 minutes. Store the oil mixture in the fridge for 48 hours, then strain through a muslin cloth-lined chinois. Store the oil in an airtight container in the freezer and use within 6 months.

To finish
Brush the pancakes with a few smears of warm suya butter and place caramelized-side down on a hot grill until the pancakes are charred and smoky (cook only on the caramelized side). Keep in a warm place until ready to dress.

Using a very sharp knife slice the squid 1 mm thick. Season well with smoked salt and pink peppercorn oil.

Bring a large pan of water to the boil and blanch the gai lan for 30 seconds–1 minute depending on its thickness, then shock in the iced water. Drain the gai lan and slice 2 mm (¹⁄₁₆ in) thick. Season the slices of gai lan with smoked salt and extra virgin olive oil.

Spread the Scotch bonnet emulsion over the 4 pancakes and then evenly distribute the sliced squid on top. Cover the squid with the slices of gai lan all arranged in the same direction.

continued overleaf

langoustine moin moin

Moin moin is a traditional steamed bean dumpling from western Nigeria, comprised of peeled black-eyed peas, onions and peppers. While we call our version of this dish moin moin, it's really something quite different. I'd first come across the texture of ground pulses (legumes) in the form of a broad (fava) bean cake in Turkey, and this was the first thing that came to mind when I tried moin moin. The Nigerian delicacy has a lighter, crumblier texture, and the pulverized beans act like an aerated web that can suspend other ingredients, such as ground beef or shellfish. Although there were no reference points in my own food experience to relate to this technique, it somehow called to my mind *lo bak go*, a Cantonese turnip cake set with rice flour and filled with shrimp, sausage and condiments.

The Ikoyi moin moin is my way of articulating the wonderfully sweet flavours of lo bak go through a different cultural lens. In our version, the turnip and langoustine take centre stage. We decided to use gram flour instead of beans, as this created an even lighter texture that would crisp up better in oil once combined with the grated turnip. The cake batter is comprised of intensely spiced seasonings, smoked dried tuna and a simple seaweed broth. Our langoustines arrive at the restaurant still alive, having been creel-caught (caught in a basket-like cage) from the west coast of Scotland and flown down to London that same day. The meat of the Scottish langoustine is so plump and sweet when it's in season that it only requires gentle warming to firm up its proteins. There is very little cooking involved; we simply baste them gently with brown butter until slightly bouncy.

This is one of the dishes I am most excited about from our menu, because there is something overindulgent about serving each guest a whole, giant langoustine as one of their first bites in the meal. The shimmering langoustine, dripping in suya butter and seasoned with lemon thyme, sits on the caramelized and fluffy moin moin, brushed with a glaze of fermented plums.

For the lacto-fermented plum honey
1 kg plums, gently washed and halved
20 g fine salt
100 g honey
15 g black Urfa biber chilli

For the turnip moin moin
360 g gram flour
500 g Cold-Brew Dashi (page 231)
neutral oil, for greasing
30 g katsuobushi
20 g smoked paprika
20 g black peppercorns
10 g garlic powder
30 g smoke powder
28 g smoked salt
1.2 kg Tokyo turnips, peeled
150 g shallots, sliced
40 g Scotch bonnet chillies
215 g egg whites

To make the lacto-fermented plum honey
Place the halved plums into a large vacuum-seal bag. Add the salt to the bag and toss well. Spread the plums into an even layer in the bag and seal on full. Leave to ferment for 7 days at 24–28°C (75–82°F). If the bag expands too much, 'burp' out the air by making a small incision and then reseal.

Taste the plums after 1 week. If they are sour, with complex, tart flavours, remove the plum stones and drain out most of the liquid, reserving it for another use. Ferment the plums for several more days if required.

Blend the plum flesh with the honey until smooth, then season with the Urfa biber chilli. Store the fermented plum honey in an airtight container in the fridge and use within 1 month.

To make the turnip moin moin
Start by whisking the gram flour into the dashi. Leave to hydrate for 1 hour.

Preheat the oven to 100°C/210°F/Gas Mark ¼ and lightly grease 2 × 10 cm (4 in) rectangular moulds with a neutral oil.

Toast the katsuobushi in a large frying pan until browned and very smoky. Toast the spices with the garlic powder, smoke powder and smoked salt in a wide frying pan until fragrant. Blitz the katsuobushi with the spices and salt roughly in a spice grinder.

In a blender, blend the turnips and shallots with the chillies and ground spice mix for 3 minutes. Fold in the gram flour mixture.

Whisk the egg whites to soft peaks, then gently fold into the turnip batter. Leave the final mixture to sit for 20 minutes to allow the batter to settle.

Pour 50 g of the batter into each mould, filling them to the top. Place the moulds on a tray and tap gently to flatten, then bake for 18 minutes. Cool to room temperature, then blast-chill. Slice each moin moin in half and then store carefully between sheets of baking parchment in an airtight container in the fridge and use within 2 days.

langoustine moin moin

To finish
50 g benne seeds
4 × 80 g langoustines
Suya Butter (page 230), melted, for
    brushing
grapeseed oil, for frying
20 g lemon thyme, picked
10 g smoked salt

To finish
Preheat the oven to 160°C/325°F/Gas Mark 3 and toast
the benne seeds for 15 minutes.

Meanwhile, remove the heads, claws and shells of the
langoustines. Make gentle incisions into the underside of
each langoustine, then place on a tray and brush with suya
butter. Temper the langoustines over the middle rack of a
hot grill, turning frequently. Remove the tails from the grill
when the flesh begins to turn a translucent, pinkish white
and feels bouncy to the touch.

Place a square of baking parchment on a plancha or a hot
frying pan. Fry the moin moin in some grapeseed oil on top
of the parchment for 2 minutes until each side is golden
brown and crispy.

Brush the top of each moin moin with some plum honey,
then place a cooked langoustine on top. Garnish with the
toasted benne seeds and arrange picked lemon thyme on
either side of the langoustine, facing in the same direction.
Finish with smoked salt and serve.

blue poppyseed waffle, smoked honey butter & daikon ganache

We created this fermented plantain waffle to use the trimmings left over from our other plantain servings. As a lover of chocolate hazelnut spread on waffles, I wanted to find a way to use the bountiful daikon grown by Robin and Ikuko at NamaYasai Farm in East Sussex and transform it into a savoury, nut-based ganache. When peeled, mashed and roasted, daikon begins to take on a biscuity (cookie-like) sweetness. We whip the caramelized daikon with some bitter dark (semisweet) chocolate and hazelnut butter to create a rich, vegetal kind of Nutella. After grilling the waffles, we pour lashings of smoked honey butter and chopped salted chicken skin into the crevices. It's important for the waffle to have charred, buttery edges, with a surface similar to that of a perfect grilled cheese, which, when squeezed, oozes fat.

blue poppyseed waffle, smoked honey butter & daikon ganache serves 4 pictured on p. 56

For the fermented plantain
trimmings from 6 plantains
salt

For the blue poppyseed and fermented plantain waffle
350 g Brown Butter (see Suya Butter, page 230)
450 g plain (all-purpose) flour
50 g sorghum flour
120 g cornflour (cornstarch)
70 g blue poppyseeds
50 g bicarbonate of soda (baking soda)
16 g salt
5 eggs, separated
500 g buttermilk
100 g caster (superfine) sugar
400 g whole milk

For the smoked honey butter
500 g butter, softened
220 g honey
7 g turmeric
7 g smoked paprika
5 g smoked salt

To make the fermented plantain
Weigh your plantain trimmings, then calculate 2 per cent of the total weight: this is how much salt you will need. Mix the plantain with the salt in a large vacuum-seal bag. Toss well, then seal on full. Leave to ferment for 7 days. 'Burp' the bags if necessary, by making a small incision, then resealing. Once the plantains have developed a sour, complex flavour, store in an airtight container in the fridge for 1 month.

To make the blue poppyseed and fermented plantain waffle
Preheat the oven to 120°C/250°F/Gas Mark ½.

Heat the butter to 170°C (338°F), then cool to room temperature.

In a large bowl, whisk together all the dry ingredients except the sugar.

Blend the egg yolks with the buttermilk and 400 g of the fermented plantain in a blender for 2 minutes.

Whisk the egg whites to soft peaks, then gradually add the sugar and continue to whip until you achieve a glossy meringue.

In a large bowl, combine the brown butter with the egg yolk and plantain mixture, then slowly whisk in the dry ingredients. Fold in the egg white gently until just combined; do not over-whip. If the dough is too thick, adjust with some of the whole milk to gain an almost pourable consistency.

In batches, roast the batter in a 5 × 5 cm (2 × 2 in) waffle maker for 4–5 minutes, then bake the cooked waffles in the oven for a further 10 minutes to crisp further. Store the waffles in an airtight container and use within 2 days.

To make the smoked honey butter
Prepare a handheld smoker filled with oak chips. Whip the butter in a stand mixer until light and smooth, then fold in the other ingredients. Spread the butter into a thin layer in a large gastronorm and wrap in cling film. Make a small incision in the cling film and insert the tip of the smoker. Smoke the butter for 30 seconds, then seal the hole with another piece of cling film. Leave to infuse for 1 hour, then repeat the smoking process 4 times. Store the butter in an airtight container in the fridge and use within 2 weeks.

For the daikon ganache
5 kg daikon, peeled
150 g rapeseed (canola) oil
300 g Cold-Brew Dashi (page 231)
112.5 g double (heavy) cream
225 g Hazelnut Butter (made using
    peanut butter method on page 81)
75 g black garlic
30 g dark (semisweet) chocolate
30 g black truffle
300 g butter
12 g smoked salt

For the salted chicken skin
500 g chicken skin
20 g smoked salt

To finish
black truffle, sliced

To make the daikon ganache
Blitz the daikon in a food processor until it forms a fine mash. Pour the rapeseed (canola) oil into a wide-based frying pan over a medium heat, add the daikon mash and cook out for roughly 15 minutes until all the moisture has been released and the daikon develops a deep brown colour. Add the cold-brew dashi, then remove the daikon from the heat.

Transfer to a blender and blitz with the double (heavy) cream, hazelnut butter, black garlic, chocolate and black truffle for 3 minutes. Emulsify in the butter until very smooth and season well with smoked salt. Store the ganache in an airtight container and use within 5 days.

To make the salted chicken skin
Preheat the oven to 150°C/300°F/Gas Mark 2 and line 2 baking trays with baking parchment.

Spread the chicken skin out flat and scrape the fat from the underside. Arrange the skins on the prepared trays and bake for 1½ hours. Check the skins and continue to bake until golden and crisp. Drain the fat and cool to room temperature. Chop the skins roughly and toss well with the salt. Store in an airtight container at room temperature and use within 3 days.

To finish
Place the waffles in the centre of a hot grill for 1–2 minutes until caramelized on either side. Transfer to the middle rack of the grill and generously baste the waffles with some of the smoked honey butter. Once golden and caramelized, season the waffles with the salted chicken skin, then pipe on the daikon ganache to cover the top of one. Serve the waffles with slices of black truffle.

lobster, red currants & strawberry vinegar jelly

One of our first bites on the menu in the summertime is this sweet lobster tart with currants from our friend Olly's farm in Cornwall. We quickly steam the meat from the knuckles and claws, then fold it into a simple mayonnaise seasoned with shiso, fresh peppers and preserved kohlrabi. There is something humorously regal-looking about the miniature tart, which protrudes from the plate like a small, jewelled crown, the jelly shimmering as if it were some kind of rare stone. The flavours are classically rich and full of fruity sweetness.

For the lobster salad
800 g lobster claws and knuckles
iced water
120 g Simple Mayonnaise (page 230)
120 g Ikoyi Kimchi (page 234–6), finely
　　diced
20 g shishito peppers, finely diced
5 g shiso, julienned
smoked salt
lemon juice

For the strawberry vinegar jelly
25 g gelatine sheets
iced water
250 g Strawberry Vinegar (see Fruit
　　Vinegar, page 231)
250 g House Pickle (page 230)
25 g hibiscus
5 g agar agar

For the black garlic croustades
8 black garlic cloves
120 g filtered water
3 g smoked salt
75 g plain (all-purpose) flour
25 g cornflour (cornstarch)
50 g eggs
500 g grapeseed oil

To finish
12 mixed currants
8 sorrel flowers (optional)

To make the lobster salad
Blanch the claws and knuckles for 2–4 minutes, depending on their size, then shock in iced water. Pick the meat, slice thinly and fold into the mayonnaise. Add the kimchi, peppers and shiso and fold everything together. Season with smoked salt and a touch of lemon juice. Store the lobster salad in an airtight container in the fridge and use within 1 day.

To make the strawberry vinegar jelly
Bloom the gelatine in iced water.

In a saucepan, bring the strawberry vinegar and house pickle to the boil, then add the hibiscus. Take off the heat and infuse for 1 hour, then strain. Hand-blend the agar agar into the liquid and bring it back to the boil. Remove from the heat and allow to cool to 70°C (158°F). Remove the bloomed gelatine from the iced water and hand-blend it into the mixture, then pour into a 1-litre gastronorm and leave to set for at least 2 hours before slicing into very small brunoise.

Store the jelly cubes in an airtight container in the fridge and use within 1 week.

To make the black garlic croustades
In a blender, blend the black garlic cloves, water and salt to form a paste. Add the flours and blitz on full speed for 10 seconds.

Beat the eggs with a spoon, being careful not to aerate them too much, as this will cause bubbles to form in the base and leave holes in the croustade. Add the eggs to the mixture in the blender and blend for 5 seconds until just combined. Rest the mixture for 2 hours to allow any air bubbles to evaporate.

Heat the grapeseed oil in a medium pot with a timbale mould submerged in the oil until the temperature reaches 170°C (338°F). Carefully dip the base of the timbale in the batter at an angle, holding it for a few seconds to allow the batter to adhere. Now dip the batter-coated timbale 3.75 cm (1½ in) into the oil and leave submerged for up to 10 seconds to cook through. Use small tweezers or an offset spatula to gently remove the croustade shell from the mould and repeat with the remaining batter. Cool the shells on a wire rack, then store in an airtight container and use within 3 days.

To finish
Mix 48 g of the lobster salad with the currants, then divide the salad equally between 4 croustades. Top with a few small cubes of the jelly (5 g for each croustade), followed by the sorrel flowers, if using. Serve immediately.

crab & roasted malted barley bread

When living in Copenhagen for a short period, I consumed a fair amount of *smørrebrød*, open sandwiches consisting of Danish rye bread with toppings of preserved herrings, cold cuts and a variety of cheeses. The taste of deeply caramelized dark bread clashing with fresh, sour accompaniments is a quintessentially Danish culinary tradition that's slowly finding its way into food cultures and communities outside the Nordic region. Although I only spent a few months in Denmark, I knew that one day these flavours would manifest themselves in my cooking in some shape or form.

I became especially fascinated with bitter flavours in dark breads, particularly when there was a sweeter, molasses-like note of unrefined sugars. Bitterness coupled with umami isn't the first combination that comes to mind when creating recipes, since we tend to think of meatiness going well with fat and acidity. For me, the palatable link between bitterness and umami is sweetness, a sensation that rounds out stringent compounds, leading to an intricate and almost indescribable marriage of flavour.

We first explored this idea by using roasted malted barley flour in our breadmaking. As a non-diastatic flour, roasted malted barley flour does not contain the enzymes that promote the conversion of starches into sugars, which yields a better rise. Its concentrated earthiness is used purely for flavour. The bread reminded me a lot of the outer layer of an Oreo cookie: slightly malty, slightly chocolatey; a bit like tasty soil. Since they work so well with a sweet filling, we would do the same. Instead of fructose syrup, rapeseed (canola) oil and artificial flavourings, our filling would be a little more natural: a ragout of confit shallots, caramelized mushrooms, roasted peanut butter and thyme.

Our bread was not flat like its Nordic counterpart, but crispy on the outside, and soft and sugary in the middle. We steamed the dough after proving, then quickly deep-fried it before resting it over the grill to create a beautiful crust, cooking the bread as if it were a piece of meat basting in roasted crab-infused butter. To amplify the presence of crab, and to use the remainder of its parts, we reduced the brains and coral (the brown crab meat) to a concentrate, which we used to season the picked white meat. This recipe is a good example of the way opening your mind to the simplest associations of deliciousness can lead to an unboundaried, flavour-driven approach to cooking.

For the peanut butter
170 g peanuts

For the mushroom ragout
1 kg chestnut (cremini) mushrooms
350 g butter
1 kg shallots, thinly sliced
10 g lemon thyme, picked
35 g Suya Powder (page 233)
90 g Pumpkin Seed Miso (page 237)
5 g smoked salt

For the roasted malted barley bread
25 g filtered water
10 g dried fast-action yeast
365 g strong white bread flour
35 g roasted malted barley flour
100 g Nigerian Guinness
8 g smoked salt
13 g honey
rapeseed (canola) oil, for greasing

To make the peanut butter
Preheat the oven to 160°C/325°F/Gas Mark 3.

Place the peanuts on a roasting tray and roast for 15 minutes. Transfer the roasted nuts to a blender and blend on low until you have a smooth butter. The peanuts will look brittle at first, but eventually the oils will release to form a slick consistency.

To make the mushroom ragout
Blitz the mushrooms to a fine paste in a food processor.

Heat 100 g of the butter in a hot pan until frothing. Add the mushroom paste, leaving undisturbed for 5 minutes. Turn very gently to make sure the mushrooms are browning well and not releasing their juices into the pan. Take off the heat and set aside.

In a separate pan, melt the remaining 250 g butter and add the shallots. Confit over a low heat for 2 hours until very sweet.

Mix 700 g of the warm, reserved mushrooms with 250 g of the confit shallots, reserving the rest for another recipe. Pick the thyme into the mixture and fold in the peanut butter, suya powder, pumpkin seed miso and salt. Leave to cool, then weigh into 25 g balls. Store in an airtight container in the fridge and use within 1 week.

To make the roasted malted barley bread
Heat the filtered water to 42°C (108°F), then mix in the yeast, proving for 10 minutes until activated and bubbling.

In a stand mixer, mix together the flours, beer, salt and honey until just combined without any lumps or dry patches. Leave to sit for 45 minutes, then add the yeast mixture, mixing it well into the dough base. Prove in a warm place for 2 hours, folding the dough over itself twice every 20 minutes.

After 2 hours, punch the air out of the dough, then cover and leave in the fridge to bulk-ferment overnight.

The next day, roll the dough into 50 g balls, then flatten each one with the back of your hand. Place a mushroom ragout ball in the middle of each dough circle, then fold the edges of the dough around the ragout ball to seal. Flatten and roll out gently to a thickness of 1 cm (½ in). Rub the breads with some rapeseed (canola) oil and place on a tray, then wrap in cling film. Prove in a warm place for 30 minutes until well risen. They should look a bit like burger buns.

Preheat the oven to 100°C/210°F/Gas Mark ¼. Flatten the breads slightly with the palm of your hand, then steam in the oven for 10 minutes. Cool the breads to room temperature and use within 1 day.

                    continued overleaf

For the brown crab concentrate
150 g butter
900 g brown crab meat
70 g garlic, chopped to a fine paste
40 g fresh root ginger, chopped to a
    fine paste
100 g shallots, chopped to a fine paste
100 g tomato purée (paste)
1 Scotch bonnet chilli, finely chopped
30 g Suya Powder (page 233)

For the pickled crosnes
600 g crosnes
100 g honey
200 g chardonnay vinegar

For the crab and crosnes salad
900 g king crab meat
ice
50 g Ikoyi Kimchi (page 234–6)
400 g Simple Mayonnaise (page 230)
10 g Aleppo chilli flakes
grated zest of 2 lemons
15 g lemon juice
7 g smoked salt

For the roasted crab butter
20 g black peppercorns
10 g Sichuan peppercorns
10 star anise
10 cloves
15 g ground cinnamon
3 kg butter
2 kg crab shells
100 g tomato purée
50 g fresh root ginger, sliced
100 g garlic, sliced
2 Scotch bonnet chillies, sliced

To finish
grapeseed oil, for deep-frying
Mexican marigold leaves

To make the brown crab concentrate
Melt the butter in a wide pan, then add the brown crab. Caramelize and reduce the crab in the butter until most of the liquid has evaporated. Add the garlic, ginger and shallots and continue to cook for several hours over a low heat.

Stir in the tomato purée (paste) and Scotch bonnet and continue cooking until the paste becomes deeply caramelized with roasted crab flavours. Remove from the heat and stir in the suya powder. Store the brown crab concentrate in an airtight container in the fridge and use within 5 days.

To make the pickled crosnes
Wash the crosnes well in a few changes of water to remove any soil or debris. Combine the honey and vinegar in a pan with 150 g water and bring to a simmer. Cool to room temperature, place the crosnes and the pickling liquid in a vacuum-seal bag and seal. Leave to infuse for 1 week at room temperature, then store the pickles in an airtight container in the fridge and use within 1 month.

To make the crab and crosnes salad
Pick the crab meat carefully over ice to ensure there are no shells or cartilage left. In a bowl, whisk together 100 g of the brown crab concentrate with the kimchi, mayonnaise and Aleppo chilli. Mix the resulting emulsion with the picked crab, 600 g of the pickled crosnes and the grated lemon zest. Season with the lemon juice and salt to taste. Store the salad in an airtight container in the fridge and use within 1 day.

To make the roasted crab butter
Preheat the oven to 130°C/265°F/Gas Mark ½.

Toast all the spices in a wide frying pan until fragrant, then blitz roughly in a spice grinder.

Melt the butter in a large gastronorm and stir in the spices, tomato purée, ginger, garlic and Scotch bonnet chillies. Place the broken crab shells on top and roast in the oven for 1½ hours, stirring every 20 minutes, until the shells are nicely browned.

Blend the contents of the gastronorm in a food processor and then hang in a muslin cloth-lined chinois for 2 hours. Store the butter in an airtight container in the freezer and use within 3 months.

To finish
Heat the oil to 180°C (350°F) in a large pot and deep-fry 2 of the breads for 2 minutes. Continue to cook on the middle rack of the grill on medium heat until the surface of the bread bubbles and blisters, basting generously with the crab butter. Cut the breads in half lengthways so you have 2 semicircles, and garnish alongside each half with a large spoonful of the salad, then scatter over the marigold leaves and serve.

octopus fried in wild rice & yeasted béarnaise

My parents used to take me and my sister for pizza as a special treat when we were still at school. I always found that the most exciting part of the meal was ordering the calamari. Those crispy, greasy rings of semi-tender rubber, doused in lemon juice and then dunked into garlic aioli, helped overcome my anticipation for the pizza. For this reason, I always associate calamari with eating at the family table, squabbling with siblings over the last piece, and asking my father to order that extra portion. I think of calamari as the ultimate starter or side dish: a perpetual crowd pleaser.

At Ikoyi, I prefer to serve squid or cuttlefish raw, or so briefly cooked it hasn't had a chance to firm up. For my reconstruction of fried calamari, I wanted to cook with octopus, which can be meaty, tender and controlled in a way that yields a consistent texture and mouthfeel. We serve our octopus as a single but substantial bite to avoid the troubles of sharing. Instead of a traditional mayonnaise-style sauce, we serve it over a yeasted mushroom béarnaise, a sauce so light yet deep in umami and acidity that it's the ideal accompaniment to the crispy, rice-coated mollusc.

For the roasted yeast powder
1 kg hen-of-the-woods mushrooms, halved
20 g fine salt
100 g fresh yeast
15 g filtered water

For the yeasted mushroom béarnaise
300 g filtered water
12 g dried porcini
6 g dried shiitake
6 g black garlic
5 g baobab powder
12 g kombu
200 g chardonnay vinegar
14 g cubeb peppercorns
7 g red chilli powder
2 star anise
420 g butter
236 g egg yolk
28 g Roasted Mushroom Oil (page 232)
28 g Benne Miso (page 236)
10 g smoked salt

To make the roasted yeast powder
Place the mushrooms into a large vacuum-seal bag. Add the salt and toss well, then spread the mushrooms into an even layer in the bag and seal on full. Leave to ferment for 7 days at 24–28°C (75–85°F). If the bag expands too much, 'burp' out the air by making a small incision and then reseal.

Taste the mushrooms after 1 week: they should be sour with complex, tart flavours. Drain the liquid, reserving for another use. You can ferment the mushrooms for several more days if required to achieve the desired flavour profile.

Preheat the oven to 55°C/130°C, and line baking trays with silicone mats. Place the fermented mushrooms on the prepared trays and dehydrate in the oven overnight.

The next day, remove the mushrooms from the oven and increase the temperature to 160°C/325°F/Gas Mark 3. Mix the fresh yeast with the water to form a paste. Brush the paste on to a silicone baking mat in a flat, even layer and roast for 30–40 minutes, or until totally dried.

Blitz the yeast and dried fermented mushrooms in a spice grinder to form a very fine powder. Store the powder in an airtight container and use within 6 months.

To make the yeasted mushroom béarnaise
Preheat a water bath to 60°C (140°F). In a vacuum-seal bag, combine the water with the dried porcini, shiitake, black garlic, baobab and kombu. Cook in the water bath for 1 hour, then cool to room temperature.

Strain and weigh out 235 g of the resulting mushroom stock.

In a saucepan, reduce the vinegar with the peppercorns, chilli and star anise for 15 minutes to a strained weight of 70 g.

Preheat the water bath to 75°C (167°F). Place the mushroom stock and reduced vinegar into a vacuum-seal bag with all the remaining ingredients (except the smoked salt) and cook in the water bath for 25 minutes.

Blend in a blender with the smoked salt for 2 minutes until very smooth, then pass through a chinois. Chill well. Store in an airtight container in the fridge and use within 3 days.

For the octopus
1 × 2.5 kg octopus, frozen overnight
300 g olive oil
20 g black garlic
25 g uda pods

For the puffed wild rice
300 g grapeseed oil
50 g wild rice

To finish
40 g egg whites
30 g cornflour (cornstarch)
2 kg grapeseed oil
20 g Anchovy Butter (page 230), for
  brushing
5 g smoked salt

To prepare the octopus
Thaw the octopus under cold running water. Remove the head and reserve for use in a stock (see page 232). Place the octopus into a vacuum-seal bag with the oil, black garlic and uda pods. Straighten the legs and steam in a steam oven for 3 hours 20 minutes at 82°C (180°F). Cool in an ice bath, straightening the legs once again. Remove the octopus stock from the bag and reserve.

Slice each tentacle off the body, gently scraping some of the excess gelatine off the octopus so that the surface is smooth, then portion into 15 g pieces. Reserve the gelatine for another use. Store the octopus in an airtight container in the fridge and use within 2 days.

To make the puffed wild rice
In a saucepan, heat the grapeseed oil to 240°C (460°F). Place the rice in a metal strainer and dip into the hot oil for 2 seconds, or until the rice puffs. If there is no reaction, the temperature of the oil is probably too low. Drain the puffed rice on paper towels, then store in an airtight container and use within 2 days.

To finish
Warm 100 g of the béarnaise to 55°C (131°F), then use it to fill a siphon, charging twice.

Take 4 × 15 g portions of octopus and 20 g of the puffed wild rice. Whisk the egg whites to soft peaks, then fold in the cornflour (cornstarch). Brush the resulting paste over the undersides of the octopus pieces, and then dip each one into the wild rice, compacting the grains with your other hand so they stick to the octopus.

Heat the oil to 180°C (350°F) in a large pot and deep-fry the octopus pieces for 30 seconds and then rest for 2 minutes. Fry once more for 10 seconds, then immediately brush with anchovy butter and season with the smoked salt.

Pipe the béarnaise on to 4 pre-warmed plates, placing the octopus on top. Finish by dusting 10 g of the roasted yeast powder over the hot octopus with a tea strainer and serve.

seafood

One of the reasons I've wanted to remain in Great Britain as a chef is the incredible seafood that surrounds the island. We are in a very lucky position to be able to communicate directly with fishermen and boats, accessing fish caught on the line in the early hours of the morning with it arriving at Ikoyi some hours later. What excites me about fish is its purity and energy. When hyper-fresh, there is nearly no taste. The fish almost acts as a vehicle for other flavours, while its texture – which can be melting, dense or bouncy – heightens mouthfeel.

While our meat ages for long periods of time, I prefer to serve fish fresh rather than ageing it for too long. We often dry our fresh fish with a very light cure, applied only for minutes and then brushed off with a dry towel. From the moment fish or shellfish enters our kitchen, it will never come into contact with water again. We use a blast-chiller set to 1°C (34°F) to further desiccate the skin or membrane of the flesh, which makes it easier to grill. Sometimes, we will age larger fish for up to 3–5 days to relax the meat and intensify flavour, especially if the *ike jime* method (see page 100) has been used.

When cooking fish, our job is to make the produce shine, and so there are very few movements involved once we have broken the fish down into fillets. Our preferred methods of cooking use gentle heat – poaching, confiting and baking – followed by a few kisses of flame. Cooking fish beautifully is best achieved by careful observation, watching the colour transform to a fragile pearlescence and noticing the flesh expand in reaction to heat. I like to think of the perfect level of fish 'doneness' as hot-raw: the delicate moment when fish boasts the sheen of bursting juices while having the consistency of flaky tenderness.

line-and-hook-caught
ike jime **mackerel**

see p. 100

89

**line-caught mackerel &
red pepper kelp**

see p. 100

90   **baked turbot with
saffron tomato velouté** **see p. 102**

suya of aged turbot head

see p. 102

skate wing & iru xo see p. 109

93   **monkfish mbongo, sea beets &
seaweed**   **see p. 115**

steamed fonio brioche see p. 105

orkney island scallop with vanilla scallop
roe butter

see p. 105

octopus ndolé & collard greens see p. 111

ike jime trout & gola pepper **see p. 113**

grilled native lobster,
komatsuna & mussel emulsion see p. 118

smoked jollof rice & crab custard   **see p. 121**

line-caught mackerel & red pepper kelp

Although I took over cooking our family meals in my mid-teens, there were still certain maternal plates I craved. One particular dish was smoked peppered mackerel and crushed buttered potatoes. I remember pulling apart the threads of the meat and mashing their oils into the soft, warm potatoes. Because the mackerel came from a packet, it was the kind of nutritious after-school comfort food that could be thrown together in minutes. My childhood memories of mackerel are of a strong-flavoured, stringy-textured fish that really made your mouth water. I also recall the little grains of pepper getting stuck in my teeth, the tiny, tedious bones, and thinking that smokiness was an innate characteristic of mackerel.

My perception of mackerel totally changed when I began working with *ike jime*-prepared line-and-hook-caught mackerel from the southwest coast. Ike jime is a technique originating from Japan, but it is now widely used by fishermen as a humane means of killing fish and a way to optimize the quality of its flesh. After spiking the brain, which causes instant death and prevents the development of unwanted lactic acid and ammonia build-up in the flesh, the gills and the tail are sliced to drain the blood, while the spinal cord ruptures to destroy the nervous system. The process prolongs rigor mortis, allowing for the development of amino acids that contribute to the sensation of umami. At this point, the fish can be aged and stored at a very low temperature for a significant amount of time.

While not all the fish we serve at Ikoyi is prepared in this way, during the slightly warmer months, when the weather is in our favour, some of the day boats practising ike jime can catch exceptional mackerels, up to 800 g (1¾ lb) in size. We tend to only work with this fish when we can get our hands on large specimens, as this allows for a more complex range of textures, from the skin down to the base of the fillet. Unlike the mackerel of my youth, the meat is a delicate and matte pink, the skin shimmering and firm. There is almost no smell, just a faint whiff of the sea. As soon as the fish arrives, we fillet and lightly cure the skin, brushing off the cure without water, as we do with all our fish at Ikoyi. The skin then lies flat on sheets of kelp seaweed for up to 24 hours, depending on its size and thickness. The outcome is skin so crispy it could shatter like glass, and gently flavoured but well-seasoned meat that flakes into soft pillows of fat. For one of the most reasonably priced types of fish, properly handled mackerel delivers some of the most flavoursome meat and luxurious mouthfeels.

Many of our guests, particularly chefs, wonder how we cook this fish, as it's one of those dishes that transforms perceptions of produce. Mackerel can go from its buttery, raw state to stringy white very quickly. I wanted to capture mackerel at medium-rare, when the flesh is gradually warming and therefore breaks down more fluidly in the mouth.

Our approach is to prepare extremely dry skin, brushing it lightly with oil. We cook the mackerel from the fridge to ensure that the intense heat applied to the skin doesn't transfer too far beyond the upper point of the meat. It's only a matter of seconds before the mackerel leaves the plancha. We brush it with a smoked vinaigrette and some anchovy butter, then turn it over from side to side until its grey-pink meat begins to hint at white. At this point, it must be served. We make sure to remove every single bone, slicing the mackerel into hefty mouthfuls so the guest can experience the richness of this fish in all its glory.

For the red pepper kelp sauce
1.4 kg red bell peppers, deseeded and
    roughly chopped
600 g tomatoes, diced
100 g Scotch bonnet chillies, roughly
    chopped
300 g red chillies, roughly chopped
200 g olive oil
60 g honey
120 g Roasted Kelp Paste (from
    Roasted Kelp Oil, page 233)
100 g Cold-Brew Dashi (page 231)
10 g Katsuobushi Salt (page 233)
smoked salt

For the mackerel
1 × 800 g whole mackerel
Fish Cure (page 233), for sprinkling
2 kombu sheets

To finish
30 g rapeseed (canola) oil, for brushing
15 g Anchovy Butter (page 230), for
    basting
25 g Smoked Vinaigrette (page 231), for
    basting and dressing
smoked salt

To make the red pepper kelp sauce
In a blender, blend together the peppers, tomatoes and
chillies. Add this blended mixture to a deep pot, along with
the olive oil, and fry the juice in the oil until it has reduced
by half, becoming caramelized and split with the oil. Return
to the blender, along with the honey, roasted kelp paste,
cold-brew dashi and katsuobushi salt. Blend for 5 minutes
until aerated and totally smooth. Pass through a chinois
and season with smoked salt. Store the sauce in an airtight
container in the fridge and use within 5 days.

To prepare the mackerel
Gut the mackerel by slicing open the belly. Carefully remove
the guts and clean out the insides with paper towels. Dry the
fish well, and then remove the fillets from the spine. Pin-
bone the mackerel, then sprinkle a fine layer of fish cure over
the skin and leave for 30 minutes.

Brush the cure and juices released off the fillets until the fish
is totally dry. Place the fish skin-side down on the kombu and
blast-chill, uncovered, for 10 minutes, to dry out and ensure
that there is no more residual moisture.

Leave the fillets to cure for 24 hours in the fridge, then
remove from the kombu. Place the mackerel skin-side up on
wire racks over a moisture-resistant cloth. Cover the top of
the mackerel with a perforated gastronorm and keep in a 1°C
(34°F) fridge for up to 7 days.

To finish
Remove the mackerel fillets from the fridge and pat the skin
dry. Brush the skin lightly with oil, then cook the fish, skin-
side down on a hot plancha for 10–15 seconds. Let the fish
rest flesh-side down, then give it a few more short blasts of
heat until the skin feels crispy and dried.

Baste the fish with anchovy butter and smoked vinaigrette,
then rest it on the top rack of the grill at a point barely hot
enough to burn your hand. Turn the fish over and around
every few seconds for 2 minutes to allow the heat to slowly
penetrate the meat without overcooking either side.

Leave the fish to rest in a warm place, under the heat lamps
or beside the stove, until it feels delicately warm, turning
a glistening white. Flip it over on to the skin side and carve
each fillet into 6 × 2 cm (¾ in)-wide slices. Be sure to use an
extremely sharp knife to make a clean, straight edge on the
skin, which can be brittle and fall apart easily. Use the length
of your slicer to lift the fish from under the skin and gently
turn the fish back around. Baste the insides of the exposed
flesh with more anchovy butter, then divide each sliced fillet
into two. Warm four spoonfuls of red pepper kelp sauce and
spoon them into the centre of your plates, followed by the
mackerel. Dress with the smoked vinaigrette and season with
smoked salt before serving.

baked turbot &
suya of aged turbot head

Receiving a 7 kg (15½ lb) turbot in our small kitchen always sends a ripple of anticipation through the team. The majestic turbot yields pearlescent, succulent fillets, and gives different textures of skin, tissues, fat and gelatine. The experience of consuming the multifaceted parts of a whole turbot is so varied that some recommend the fish requires no accompaniments or side dishes at all. I'd taken Iré to the Basque Country to celebrate his thirtieth birthday, and we were eager to learn the art of turbot-grilling. Chef Aitor Arregi, of the world famous Elkano restaurant in Getaria, discouraged us from ordering anything else on his menu, insisting that a whole turbot would substantiate a balanced meal and quell our hunger. The locally caught fish was beautifully blistered and silken, with a vinaigrette of its own fat. As I lifted the large spoon to break into the fish, Aitor quickly grabbed it from my hand and proceeded to pull apart the meat in front of us, pointing out his favourite parts, and spooning morsels of cheek and skin into our mouths. We couldn't help but fall for his passion and the connection he had to his home and native produce. I left Getaria in bittersweet contemplation of the turbot we'd just eaten. Iré and I were from such disparate cultures that our articulation of turbot-cooking could never express the kind of connectedness and sense of place we had experienced at Elkano.

I decided I wanted our version of turbot to retain elements of Basque fish cookery – the gelatinous skin, springy flesh and fatty, sour glaze – but also to incorporate influences of our own. For me, there is a lightness to the flavour of the flesh of ultra-fresh fish, making it a clean medium for absorbing rich but smooth sauces of herbs, spices and butter. The plump fillets of turbot would be served with seasonal veloutés of summer tomatoes or caramelized winter artichokes, depending on the time of year. We wanted to relate that cosy feeling of a chowder and its comforting sweetness, spiking it with sour herbs and bright, smoky peppercorns. While the fillet would be served as an immaculate slice, we wanted the guests to eat the head in a more carnal way. After curing it in a miso of heirloom peas and suya spices, we slowly cook the head high up over the grill until almost falling apart, blasting it over flames just at the end. We brush it with copious brown butter and smoked vinaigrette during the cooking process, and stuff it with preserved wild garlic and grated citrus. The guests are encouraged to eat with their hands and suck the sticky meat off the softened, jelly-like bones.

Our turbots come from Devon and Hastings on the south coast of England. We prepare the fish by separating the head and collar, then slicing it into large tranches kept on the bone. Each piece, which is big enough to serve between four and six people, rests in a salt/sugar cure to dry out both sides of the fish. We leave the fish to rest in the fridge overnight, which makes the skin crispy and easier to cook with, as excess moisture is drawn out. Our favourite way to cook the fish is by starting it off in a pan with butter, dried chillies, garlic and thyme. The smell of caramelizing milk solids, fish proteins and aromatics is close to the joyous aroma of butter-basting dry-aged beef. The fillets bake at a very low temperature, and we serve them slightly warmer than other kinds of fish, as the amount of collagen in turbot requires a little more energy for it to liquify. At close to 46°C (115°F), the turbot slips off the bone like a block of soap. We mix some of the baking juices with lobster garlic butter to form a sauce, using the off-cuts and skin in the velouté, so nothing goes to waste.

For the lobster garlic butter
1 kg lobster heads
20 g ground cumin
20 g black peppercorns
15 g smoked paprika
3 kg butter
300 g garlic
25 g smoked salt
2 Scotch bonnet chillies
20 g lemon thyme

For the saffron tomato velouté
4 kg Roasted Fish Bone Stock (page 232)
40 g kombu
25 g katsuobushi
600 g whipping cream
4.5 g saffron strands
300 g butter
300 g fennel, brunoised
150 g garlic, brunoised
80 g fresh root ginger, brunoised
300 g celery, brunoised
15 g coriander seeds
25 g white Penja peppercorns
10 g green Penja peppercorns
30 g smoked paprika
500 g white wine
1.4 kg seasonal tomatoes, sliced
3 Scotch bonnet chillies
500 g smoked haddock, flaked
lemon juice
smoked salt

For the turbot head
1 × 600 g turbot head
50 g Suya Butter (page 230), melted
25 g Suya Pea Miso (page 236)

To make the lobster garlic butter
Preheat the oven to 130°C/265°F/Gas Mark ½.

Place the lobster heads in a food processor and blitz for 1 minute to break apart.

Toast all the spices in a wide frying pan until fragrant, then blitz roughly in a spice grinder.

Melt the butter in a large gastronorm. Add the blitzed lobster heads, along with the ground spices, garlic, salt and chillies. Bake for 1½ hours, stirring every 20 minutes, until the butter is aromatic and deep red from the roasting lobster shells.

Remove from the oven and stir in the thyme, then allow the butter to cool before passing it through a muslin cloth-lined chinois. Store the butter in an airtight container in the freezer and use within 3 months.

To make the saffron tomato velouté
In a large pot, heat the fish stock to 70°C (158°F). Take off the heat and add the sheets of kombu. Wrap the top of the pot well in cling film and then leave to infuse for 1 hour.

Remove the kombu and bring the stock to the boil. Add the katsuobushi, infuse for 15 minutes, then strain and set aside.

In a separate pan, bring the cream to a simmer, then take off the heat and add the saffron. Leave to infuse while you begin the next stage.

Melt the butter in a deep, heavy-based pot. Add the fennel, garlic, ginger, and celery, and sweat down in the butter until soft and sweet but almost colourless. Toast the dried spices in a wide frying pan until fragrant, then blitz roughly in a spice grinder. Add the spices to the sweating vegetables, then deglaze the pan with the white wine and reduce until fully absorbed. Add the tomatoes and Scotch bonnet chillies, then bring to the boil and reduce the liquid by half.

Pour over the fish stock, followed by the smoked haddock and the saffron cream, and simmer for 1 hour over a low heat.

Blend the velouté in a blender for 5 minutes, then pass through a chinois and season with salt and lemon juice. Store the velouté in an airtight container in the freezer and use within 3 months.

To prepare the turbot head
Brush the turbot head with the melted suya butter, then rub in the suya pea miso. Leave to cure overnight in the fridge.

baked turbot &
suya of aged turbot head

To finish

1 × 500 g tranche of turbot
rapeseed (canola) oil, for frying
butter, for basting
2 cloves garlic, peeled and left whole
2 whole dried red chillies
1 thyme sprig
100 g Negi onions
50 g mixed herbs: shiso, cinnamon basil,
　black mint, fat hen spinach
20 g grated yuzu zest
20 Pickled Wild Garlic Capers (page
　231)
30 g Smoked Vinaigrette (page 231)
30 g mizuna
lemon juice
smoked salt

To finish

Remove the turbot head and the tranche of turbot from the fridge to temper for at least 1 hour before cooking. Preheat the oven to 115°C/240°F/Gas Mark ½ and preheat the grill to a temperature barely hot enough to roast.

Place the turbot head in a roasting tray over the top rack of the grill and roast for 30 minutes, turning it over every 10 minutes. Once the skin and cartilage have softened, baste the head and lower it on to the flames to crisp up the skin, allowing the fat to atomize and infuse with flavour.

Meanwhile, heat a little rapeseed (canola) oil in a large frying pan over a high heat until smoking. Carefully drop the turbot into the pan, white-skin-side down. Press gently, letting the underside crisp up, adjusting the heat so the skin doesn't burn. You will feel the small air bubbles in the skin dissipating when the side is fully in contact with the base of the pan. Flip and continue to caramelize the dark side of the skin. Reduce the heat and add a generous spoonful of butter, along with the garlic and dried chillies. Baste the fish, moving it around the pan in a circular motion to evenly distribute the heat, and flipping again to ensure both sides are in contact with the browning butter. Remove the fish and place on a wire rack over a roasting tray. Top with the thyme, then pour the buttery juices all over. Bake for 5 minutes until the internal temperature reads 40°C (104°F). The fish will continue to cook once out of the oven, but should be served not long after cooking, resting for a maximum of 5 minutes and reaching up to 48°C (118°F).

Place a fork under the skin and curl it backwards around the fork, as if you're rolling up a carpet. Push the fillets off either side of the bone, keeping the engawa – small, gill-like pieces – attached to the fillet. Slice the turbot into 4 pieces. Brush with the pan juices and some lobster butter and keep warm.

Toss the Negi onions in some rapeseed (canola) oil, then place them in an even layer on a hot plancha for 30 seconds, leaving them untouched to char and develop a smoky aroma. Season with smoked salt and keep aside.

In a saucepan, warm through 250 g of the velouté; it should thicken slightly and coat the back of your spoon. Remove from the heat and add the mixed herbs, allowing them to break down slightly while still keeping their crunch and freshness. Quickly distribute the velouté between 4 pre-warmed plates. Place a nest of Negi onions in the middle, followed by the turbot. Finish with some of the fresh yuzu zest, spoonfuls of lobster butter and smoked salt.

When the turbot head is ready, garnish it with capers, yuzu zest and the smoked vinaigrette. Dip the mizuna in some of the turbot roasting-fat and season with smoked salt and lemon juice. Serve the mizuna leaves alongside the head and the bowls of velouté.

orkney island scallops, vanilla scallop roe butter & steamed fonio brioche

Not long before Swedish chef Mikael Jonsson's London restaurant Hedone closed its doors for good in 2019, I ate a dish at that changed the way I thought about scallops – and cooking in general. Sitting at the restaurant's kitchen counter, I lifted the flat ceramic bowl containing a giant scallop. Picking it up, I felt as though I was holding a burger in a slider bun, or a compact hockey puck cast from white marble. I'll never forget the moment I cut into it and the knife resisted. The scallop's texture was firm, as if it was in rigor mortis, and it defied my blade. Then it gave way, the knife slipping through the meat as though gliding through cold, just-tempered butter. The cut was totally smooth, the turgid flesh breaking apart into distinct cubes. Inside, there was a glow, like an opaque stone illuminated by a lantern. The scallop itself was so fresh that it had almost no aroma or detectable flavour other than a subtle, underlying sweetness. It served as the perfect vehicle for the 'jamón extraction', a warm, clear broth of cured ham with shavings of white truffle. The scallop had been popped out of the shell right before cooking, passing through the steamer for an instant, before kissing the bars of a red-hot grill. The flavours of the soup revealed nuanced hints of the Jinhua ham broth and dried scallops I'd eaten as a child in Hong Kong, while the musky woodiness of the white truffle unlocked instances of decadence I'd parcelled deep in my memory.

Mikael used a simple technique, gently coaxing the scallop from raw to warm with short bursts of steam and fire. It was as if, along the spectrum of doneness, he knew at exactly which point to stop. The meat was so rigid and alive. I'd only ever eaten scallops with a similar density to this at Magnus Nilsson's Fäviken in Sweden. As well as the texture, I was also captivated by Mikael's inventiveness of the flavour combinations, and that impacted the way I wanted to cook. As I picked up the scallop, I felt as though it was the sort of food experience that changes the way you think about produce, calling into question your previous standards of deliciousness and technique. I vowed never to cook with scallops until I could find and cook them at this quality.

I began working with the Scottish supplier Keltic Seafare in 2020, after we discovered that their fishers were hand-diving for scallops off the northern coast of Scotland and the Orkney Islands. Weighing up to 300 g, the scallops were colossal, and so fresh it took some might to open them. We cleared out an undercounter fridge to make a dedicated, temperature-controlled environment in which they could rest, maintaining a consistently cold atmosphere to keep their density alive. At first, we tried shucking and freezing them, as well as storing them out of their shells in the fridge, but though they still had a clean flavour, they no longer held their form in that exceptional way. They had to be healthily alive and in their shells right up to the point of being cooked.

Cooking the scallops seemed easy in comparison to sourcing and storing them. We simply poached them in gently warmed, smoked oil, touching and observing them until they arrived at our idea of 'perfection', that firm-but-melting texture I'd dreamed about ever since my meal at Hedone. We made an intense broth using the roe and skirt, emulsifying it into a vanilla and butter sauce. On the side, we added a small dollop of caramelized Koginut squash, mimicking the image of the roe, with aged citrus and chillies hidden beneath the scallop to give the dish that essential kick.

For the scallop roe and skirt stock
1.5 kg scallop roe and skirt
200 g filtered water

For the scallop roe butter emulsion base
7 g gola peppercorns
10 g garlic, sliced
⅓ Madagascan vanilla bean
300 g white wine
10 g Pumpkin Seed Miso (page 237)
400 g butter, diced
0.9 g xanthan gum
maple verjus
smoked salt

For the Koginut purée
1.2 kg Koginut squash
200 g dashi
130 g chardonnay vinegar
130 g honey
20 g fine salt
120 g smoked rapeseed (canola) oil

To make the scallop roe and skirt stock
Preheat a water bath to 95°C (203°F). Rinse the roe and skirts very well and remove the black stomach sacs. Vacuum-seal with the water and cook in the water bath for 1 hour. Allow the bag to cool, then pass the stock through a muslin cloth-lined chinois into a pan.

Reduce the liquid to 350 g and keep warm until needed, or store in an airtight container in the fridge and use within 2 days.

To make the scallop roe butter emulsion base
Gently toast the gola peppercorns until fragrant, then grind in a spice grinder. Place into a saucepan with the garlic and the seeds from the vanilla bean. Add the wine and reduce to 150 g.

Strain the reduced wine into 350 g of the warm scallop stock and add the pumpkin seed miso. Transfer this mixture to a blender, along with the butter, vanilla bean and xanthan gum. Blitz on full speed for 3 minutes, then season with maple verjus and smoked salt.

Store the emulsion in an airtight container in the fridge and use within 1 week.

To make the Koginut purée
Preheat a water bath to 85°C (185°F).

Peel the squash of all its hard and inedible skin. Slice in half and scoop out the seeds. Reserve the skins and seeds for another recipe. Blend the squash flesh to a paste in a blender and weigh out 1 kg.

Place this in a large vacuum-seal bag, along with all the remaining ingredients except the smoked rapeseed (canola) oil. Cook in the water bath for 16 hours.

Transfer the content of the bag to the blender and blend with the smoked rapeseed (canola) oil for 10 minutes until completely smooth and glossy. The resulting purée should be very light, sour and well-seasoned. If there is still a slight graininess to the texture, add a touch of water and keep blending until it's completely clean and smooth. Store the purée in an airtight container in the fridge and use within 5 days.

**For the caramelized steamed fonio
  brioche**
20 g filtered water
9 g dried fast-action yeast
500 g strong white bread flour
10 g salt
355 g eggs
50 g caster (superfine) sugar
270 g fridge-cold butter, cubed
baking spray, for greasing
50 g whole milk
50 g honey
60 g fonio seeds

To make the caramelized steamed fonio brioche
Heat the filtered water to 42°C (108°F) then mix in the yeast, proving until activated and bubbling.

In a stand mixer, mix together the flour, salt, eggs and sugar until just combined, ensuring there are no lumps or dry patches. Leave to sit for 45 minutes, then add the yeast mixture, mixing it well into the dough base. Knead for 13 minutes.

Slowly add the fridge-cold butter, piece by piece, until the dough is smooth and elastic and detaches from the sides of the bowl.

Prove the dough at 32°C (90°F) for 2 hours until doubled in size. Knock back the dough, then reshape into a clean ball and carefully place into a storage container to continue proving overnight in the fridge.

The next day, roll the dough into 52 g balls and reserve in the fridge.

Grease 4 × 10 cm (2.5 in) moulds with baking spray and remove four dough balls from the fridge. Flatten and fold each dough ball 4 times over, then tuck and push in the seams. Seal the seams, then very gently roll each piece of dough into a round log. Place the logs into the greased moulds and prove again until tripled in size.

Preheat the oven to 190°C/375°F/Gas Mark 5.

In a bowl, combine the milk with the honey, then brush over the dough, sprinkling well with fonio seeds. Bake the bread for 13 minutes with 50 per cent steam. Make sure the sides of the brioche are golden before removing from oven. Leave the breads to cool on a wire rack and use within 1 day.

orkney island scallops, vanilla scallop roe butter & steamed fonio brioche

To finish

4 × 100 g Orkney scallops
100 g smoked rapeseed (canola) oil
300 g rapeseed (canola) oil
2 × brioche
1 g soy lecithin
Honey Butter (page 230), for brushing
2 teaspoons Citrus Kosho (page 236)
Roasted Garlic Oil (page 232)

To finish

To shuck the scallops, gently push open the scallop shells from the flat side, then take a quick swipe to release the flesh. Using a thin-rimmed spoon, scoop the scallop out of its skirt and roe in one motion. Once all the scallops have been shucked, dry them with more paper towels to make sure there is no surface moisture remaining. Line the scallops on a clean kitchen cloth and leave in the blast-chiller for 10 minutes to dry and set the flesh further. The scallops must be used shortly after shucking.

Preheat the oven to 180°C (356°F).

Heat the smoked and regular rapeseed oils in a deep pan to 50°C (122°F). Drop the scallops into the oil and make sure the oil maintains its temperature by tempering next to a hot stove. They should take about 10 minutes to heat, but remove them once they reach 42°C (108°F).

In a saucepan, bring the scallop roe butter base to a simmer, then shear in the lecithin with a hand-blender for 1 minute to aerate bubbles into the sauce. Leave to stand in a warm place and allow the bubbles to firm up.

Roast the brioche in the oven for 2 minutes. Brush with a tablespoon of the honey butter and roast for a further 1 minute.

To plate, place ½ teaspoon citrus kosho on each plate, positioning it off-centre and to the right. Glaze the scallops with some of the roasted garlic oil and place on top of the citrus kosho. Place a precise, teaspoon-sized quenelle of the Koginut purée next to each scallop, pushing them close together as if connected. Spoon the roe butter emulsion over and around the dish, and then serve the scallops alongside the brioche.

skate wing & iru xo

Although skate refers to a number of different types of fish, when we talk of skate at Ikoyi, we're referring to the blonde, cuckoo, spotted, thornback and small-eyed rays of Cornwall. Skates tend to be slow-growing fish, producing only a small number of eggs each year, and they are vulnerable to overfishing. Their spiked backs make them susceptible to being caught in nets, so it's nearly impossible to avoid catching larger rays in trawls. At Ikoyi, we tend to avoid seeking out this species of fish because of the difficulty in rebuilding populations of rays. However, on the off-chance that a boat brings in rays as by-catch, we jump at the chance to work with this fish for its unique physiology, high collagen content and filament-like texture.

Though skate tends to be relatively inexpensive, we believe it should be treated with great respect and care, as it's something of a rarity. Once you've managed to strip the slimy, thorned outer skin from its wings, you're left with the fairly straightforward task of removing the giant fillets off the webbed fan of bones, which look like something between a shark's fin and a boomerang. We tend to receive mainly blonde rays, which are the largest of the Cornish rays and can reaching more than 1 metre (40 in) in length. The thickness of their fillets allows the blade to slice under the tube-like fibres of meat, which remain held together by a film of collagen. The beauty of this thin web is that it not only holds the strands of the skate together, but it also like a buffer to high-temperature cooking. We cure our skates to draw out some of their moisture, then cook them skin-side down on a searingly hot grill. The rich collagen melts away at such a high temperature, basting the fish as it gives way, releasing the delicate but thick and meaty fibres.

We brush our skate with iru XO, a condiment of fermented locust beans, chillies, dried mushrooms, cured ham and aged beef fat, slowly baked to a dark, jammy consistency. Aromas of roast beef, smoked chillies and earthy umami transform the prehistoric-looking fish into something that tastes almost like a great burger. A few crisp bites of French sorrel brighten up the interaction of collagens, making this one of the most comforting ways to eat this magnificent fish.

For the iru XO sauce

600 g boiling water, for soaking, plus 400 g for the crayfish
400 g dried porcini mushrooms (ceps)
400 g dried shiitake mushrooms
300 g dried crayfish
1.6 kg vegetable oil
250 g jamón Iberico, finely diced
450 g Rendered Aged Beef Fat (page 230)
6 Scotch bonnet chillies, minced
300 g garlic, minced
150 g fresh root ginger, minced
500 g shallots, minced
100 g rum
75 g tamari
50 g maple verjus
75 g light brown sugar
3 star anise
20 g chipotle powder
20 g hot red chilli powder
50 g iru
smoked salt

For the skate wing

1 kg skate wing
Fish Cure (page 233), for sprinkling

To finish

Suya Butter (page 230), melted, for brushing and drizzling
8 sorrel leaves, halved

To make the iru XO sauce

Pour 600 g of boiling water over the mushrooms and leave to soak overnight.

The next day, pour the remaining 400 g boiling water over the crayfish and leave to infuse for 1 hour. Strain the mushrooms and crayfish, and squeeze out any excess liquid. Reserve 500 g of the mushroom soaking water.

Preheat the oven to 145°C/295°F/Gas Mark 1½.

Heat the vegetable oil in a deep, heavy-based pan over a low heat. Add the ham and beef fat and cook until crisp and golden. Add the crayfish and continue to cook until the mixture is a rich golden colour. Add the chillies, garlic, ginger and shallots and cook, stirring continuously, until the mixture begins to bubble around the edges and the vegetables start to caramelize. Pour everything into a deep gastronorm, then deglaze the pan with the rum and the reserved mushroom stock, scraping it well before adding the liquid and anything left in the pan to the gastronorm.

Cook in the oven on full dehydration for 1 hour, turning the mixture after 30 minutes. After 1 hour, add the tamari, maple verjus, brown sugar, star anise, dry chilli powders and iru. Reduce the oven temperature to 120°C/250°F/Gas Mark ½ and bake for a further 3–4 hours until the mixture is really dark and caramelized. Blend the iru XO in batches in a blender to a coarse paste, then season well with smoked salt. Store in an airtight container in the freezer and use within 3 months.

To prepare the skate wing

Make an incision in the inner part of the wing to lift up the skin. Dry the fish well. Use a towel to grip the skin, pulling away and rolling the skin back. Use your other hand to hold the fish down and prevent the flesh from tearing. Remove the thick cartilage at the inner part where the fillet meets the bone. Make a cut into the thickest part of the fillet and draw the knife through in long, sweeping motions, peeling the fillet away from the bone. Once the skin has been removed, lightly sprinkle the fish cure on either side of the skate and leave for 10 minutes, or slightly longer if it's a very thick fillet. Brush the cure off well, then leave the skate uncovered in the blast-chiller for 30 minutes to further dry out the fillet. Portion into four equal pieces.

To finish

Brush the skate fillets with some suya butter, then place them, collagen-side down, on to a hot plancha, gently pressing down on the fish to make sure it comes into full contact with the cooking surface. Leave for up to 45 seconds, depending on thickness, lifting it gently to check the skin is caramelizing and breaking down. Flip the fish on to a warm tray and leave somewhere warm above your grill until the fish has an internal temperature of 46°C (115°F).

Brush with the iru XO sauce, then lightly blowtorch the fish. Drizzle some more suya butter over the fillets, then season with some smoked salt. Serve each piece of skate with some sorrel leaves.

octopus ndolé & collard greens

My first taste of white Penja peppercorn reminded me of American-style pepperoni pizza. There was an animal-like musk of bacon, roasted chicken stock and oregano, followed by wild aromas of burned herbs and dried wood. Grown in a volcanic valley in Penja, Cameroon, this rare peppercorn is the gastronomic equivalent of a fine wine. Harvested in very low yields and grown in balanced, mineral-rich soil with natural spring water, the flavour of the Penja truly speaks of its complex terroir. The berries are hand-picked in bunches just before full ripeness, and the spicier outer core is removed to leave the uniform milk-white centre.

Until I came across French explorer and gastronome Erwann de Kerros' *Pepper: From Around the World: Stories and Recipes*, I had never given the same level of thought to the cultivation and history of my dry ingredients and spices as I did to my locally sourced produce. Reading about the volcanic terrain of Cameroon and its humid equatorial climate, I was inspired by the growing potential of the region, which produced pineapples, bananas, papaya, coffee and many other bounties. The Penja peppercorn made me realize how much character and potency can be imparted to a meal with the addition of carefully grown spices.

I wanted to create a dish that alluded to the pepper's place of origin while also portraying some of the ideas we'd developed in the kitchen. I saw a recipe for *ndolé*, a kind of soup of bitter greens, shellfish, nuts and garlic. I immediately thought of our growers, who were producing vibrant spinach, mustard leaves and earthy cress. For my ndolé, I blend the raw greens into a roasted nut milk so they retain their bitter flavour. Roasted garlic, black garlic, crayfish and the all-important peppercorns are infused into brown butter to form a paste, which serves the same sort of purpose as a Thai shrimp paste. All the components are brought together in a cold state to prevent the leaves from cooking until the final moment, when the warming of the sauce releases the chlorophyl, transforming its colour to a deep green.

Although the Ikoyi ndolé sauce works well with any meaty fish, we like to serve it with octopus, which seems to pair extremely well with the barbecue flavours of the Penja peppercorn. We confit our octopus in black garlic and uda pod oil, cooling it in its own cooking juices before slicing it into clean, graphic portions. The extended cooking time, coupled with the way we smooth out the octopus, creates an even surface for caramelization, with tiny fissures that absorb the buttery glazes and sauce. It's important that the octopus offers al dente resistance at first, but ultimately melts in your mouth.

The first time Doug, one of my chefs, tasted our octopus ndolé, he told me that it reminded him of takeaway pizza. I was happy to hear that my free-thinking and random associations were coming out through our cooking.

For the ndolé sauce
100 g cashew nuts
100 g peanuts
800 g Cold-Brew Dashi (page 231)
300 g watercress, sliced
100 g mustard leaves, sliced
200 g spinach, sliced
1 garlic bulb
250 g Brown Butter (see Suya Butter,
    page 230)
50 g black garlic
25 g fresh, shelled crayfish
15 g white Penja peppercorns
15 g black Penja peppercorns
30 g shallot
2 Scotch bonnet chillies
15 g smoked salt
10 g chipotle powder
10 g smoked paprika

For the octopus
1 × 2.5 kg octopus, frozen overnight
300 g olive oil
20 g black garlic
25 g uda pods

To finish
rapeseed (canola) oil, for roasting
25 g Anchovy Butter (page 230),
    melted, for basting
4 collard green leaves, finely julienned

To make the ndolé sauce
Preheat the oven to 160°C/325°F/Gas Mark 3.

Put the cashews and peanuts into a roasting tin and roast for 15 minutes, then transfer to a saucepan with the dashi. Bring to a simmer for 15 minutes, then immediately transfer to a blender. Blend for 4 minutes. The result should be a slightly thick, pourable cream. Blast-chill until very cold.

Once cold, add the watercress, mustard leaves and spinach to the blender with the cold roasted nut dashi cream and blend for 4 minutes.

Increase the oven temperature to 170°C/340°F/Gas Mark 3½. Wrap the garlic bulb in foil and bake for 30 minutes. Leave to cool, then squeeze out the cloves and discard the skin.

In a blender, combine the brown butter with the roasted garlic, black garlic, crayfish, peppercorns, shallot and chillies and blend to form a smooth paste. Whisk the paste and the green sauce together and season with smoked salt. Store in an airtight container in the fridge until needed, and use within 1 week.

To prepare the octopus
Thaw the octopus under cold running water. Remove the head and reserve for use in a stock (see page 232). Vacuum-seal the octopus with the oil, black garlic and uda pods.

Straighten out the legs and steam the octopus in a steam oven for 3 hours 20 minutes at 82°C (180°F). Cool in an ice bath, straightening the legs once again. Once cool, remove the octopus stock from the bag and reserve. Slice each tentacle off the body, then gently scrape some of the excess gelatine off the octopus so its surface is smooth. Slice the octopus into 40 g portions. Store the octopus in an airtight container in the fridge until needed, and use within 2 days.

To finish
Roast the octopus on a hot plancha with rapeseed (canola) oil to caramelize the surface. Then place directly on your grill for several seconds to pick up some of the smoky flavours and baste with the anchovy butter. Leave to rest on the middle rack of your grill, turning and basting the octopus until it reaches 70°C (158°F) and feels soft and crispy to the touch.

In a saucepan, warm the ndolé sauce until it starts to thicken and darken, making sure to just make it hot rather than cooking out.

At the very last minute, cook the collard greens on the plancha with some rapeseed (canola) oil until the edges begin to crisp. Add a splash of water to briefly steam the greens, but make sure they don't deflate too much; you want them to keep their nest-like form.

Serve the octopus and collard greens with a large spoonful of ndolé sauce.

ike jime trout & gola pepper

This serving is inspired by some of the best raw fish dishes I've had in my life, most while travelling in Japan. While the end product is very different, I wanted to create something very pure, focused on the quality of the trout and an understanding of how to age it. I practised, tasted and observed, breaking down each section of the fish to determine the most tender parts for a raw serving. I was excited by the idea of creating our own perspective on raw fish that was as delicious and umami-driven as sushi, but also distinct.

Our friend Albert Tucker supplies us with gola peppercorns directly from ethical farms in Sierra Leone, and the peachy aromas of this peppercorn add a dimension of sweet spice to the lean, firm trout. After ageing and lightly salting the fish with a citrus peppercorn cure, we slice the thickest part of the top loin and quickly marinate the fillet in a fermented Scotch bonnet ponzu sauce before glazing it in fragrant gola oil. Ageing the fish brings out some of the rich oils in the trout, creating an even greater depth of flavour. We work with the wonderful citrus farmers Perinne and Étienne from Agrumes Bachés in southern France, who supply us with ultra-fragrant yuzu, sudachi and Buddha's hand lemons to infuse our dressing.

For the trout
1 × 4 kg ike jime trout
Citrus Fish Cure (page 233), for
  sprinkling

**For the fermented Scotch bonnet and
  citrus dressing**
120 g red bell pepper
60 g Lacto-Fermented Scotch Bonnet
  Chillies (page 234)
30 g lemon juice
440 g aged mirin
40 g honey
80 g palm wine
400 g white soy sauce
300 g Cold-Brew Dashi (page 231)
40 g kombu
40 g dried porcini mushrooms (ceps)
20 g sudachi juice
80 g grated Buddha's hand lemon zest
40 g orange juice
40 g grated yuzu zest
12 g katsuobushi

To finish
Gola Peppercorn Oil (page 232)

To age the trout
Gut the trout and remove the gills and head. Clean the fish extremely well with paper towels to ensure no blood or residual slime is left on the fish. Leave the fish to age for 5 days at 2°C (36°F).

To make the fermented Scotch bonnet and citrus dressing
Put the red pepper into a blender with the fermented Scotch bonnet and lemon juice and blend to combine, then set aside.

Place the mirin, honey and palm wine in a saucepan and reduce by 15 per cent.

Preheat a water bath to 60°C (140°F). Vacuum-seal the reduction with the white soy, cold-brew dashi, kombu and mushrooms, and cook for 1 hour in the water bath. Cool to room temperature, then transfer to a bowl and add all the remaining ingredients. Leave to age for 48 hours, then strain through a muslin cloth. Store the dressing in an airtight container in the fridge until needed, and use within 1 month.

To cure the trout
Once the trout has been ageing for 5 days, fillet both sides of the trout and remove the belly, keeping it for another use. Skin the fillets and delicately apply the citrus cure to both sides of the fish. Leave for 10 minutes, then brush off the cure until the surface of the trout is very dry. Slice out the pin bones on either side of the spine. Repeat with a second cut to remove the bloodline of the trout. Reserve the thickest part of the loin for this dish (about 80 g), and use the rest of the fish for another recipe. Store the trout on a wire rack in the fridge and use within 3 days.

To finish
Slice the trout loin horizontally into eight pieces (two per person). Brush the trout pieces with the dressing and leave for 5 minutes before arranging on chilled plates. Glaze each piece with a few drops of gola oil and some of the dressing just before serving.

monkfish mbongo, sea beets & seaweed

Mbongo tchobi, also known as *mbongo*, is a black stew eaten by the Bassa people of Cameroon. The stew has a rich, velvety texture, and its dark colour comes from the burning of mbongo tree bark ground with *ehuru* – a type of nutmeg – dried onions, peppercorns and grains of paradise. The flavour is intoxicating, tropical and elusive, with the aromas floating between sour, sharp and strawberry-like. I ate this dish for the first time when I cooked it while researching sauce inspirations for our menu. I used a recipe I found online, and while I can't say that my version was totally accurate, the familiar ingredients of ginger, spring onions, chillies and fish made creating the base of the sauce easy to follow. The mysteriousness of the white fish submerged in the split black coating enhanced the freshness of the spices and kept my palate continually guessing. I really focused in on this particular kind of black, which gleamed with red-tinted oil, formed by caramelizing tomatoes and chillies.

The burning tartness of the grains of paradise was like a new addition to my vocabulary. Little did I know that this spice, once called 'African Pepper' by Roman poet Pliny, was actually a replacement for black pepper in Europe during the 14th and 15th centuries, and was extensively traded by the Portuguese in the Gulf of Guinea. Even the British imported thousands of kilos per year during the late 19th century, as a means of adding aroma to their gins, liquors and cordials. In West African cultures, the medicinal properties of this pepper were thought to aid digestion, even possessing folkloric powers of divination and a magical ability to determine whether an accused person was guilty or innocent. I was surprised to learn that this tiny seed's history spanned hundreds of years over countless cultures around the globe. Its exceptional flavour and story fit well within the narrative of my menu.

I fell for the alliteration of 'Monkfish Mbongo', the title of my interpretation of this enigmatic dish. At the restaurant, we make sure to blend the sauce for an extended period of time to achieve an uninterrupted, matte texture, which later gains a murky sheen from the caramelized tomato oil. The sea-beet leaves become enveloped in mbongo, their emerald green colour disappearing into obscurity, like folds of an oil-slicked blanket.

For the mbongo sauce
250 g rapeseed (canola) oil
2.6 kg canned plum tomatoes, diced
100 g Scotch bonnet chillies, roughly
   chopped
150 g olive oil
300 g shallot, sliced
80 g lemongrass, sliced
50 g fresh root ginger, sliced
70 g grains of paradise
10 g ehuru
200 g Cold-Brew Dashi (page 231)
70 g squid ink

For the monkfish
1 × 2 kg monkfish tail
300 g fresh dulse
iced water

For the citrus kosho emulsion
130 g egg yolks
20 g fine salt
30 g Dijon mustard
20 g honey
300 g smoked rapeseed (canola) oil
1 kg rapeseed (canola) oil
200 g chardonnay vinegar
110 g pickled onion juice
40 g Lacto-Fermented Scotch Bonnet
   Chillies (page 234), finely chopped
100 g Roasted Kelp Paste (from
   Roasted Kelp Oil, page 233)
40 g Citrus Kosho (page 236)

To make the mbongo sauce
Pour the rapeseed (canola) oil into a deep, heavy-based pan. Add the tomatoes and chillies and fry until the oil is split and the tomato is well reduced. There should be a pool of oil on top as it bubbles away and the tomatoes and chillies turn a dark red.

Pour the olive oil into a separate pan over a low heat, and gently confit the shallots, lemongrass and ginger for 1 hour, stirring every 10 minutes and checking to make sure they're not catching or developing any colour. They should be translucent, sweet and aromatic. Leave to cool in the pan.

In a wide frying pan, toast the grains of paradise and ehuru until fragrant, then blitz to a fine powder in a spice grinder.

Strain most of the oil out of the tomatoes and pass the strained oil through a chinois. Set aside. Transfer the tomatoes to a blender, along with the shallot mixture and the ground spices. Add the cold-brew dashi and squid ink and blend for 8 minutes, then pass through a chinois. Add a quarter of the strained red oil back to the mbongo to give it has a black and red split consistency. Store the sauce in an airtight container in the fridge and use within 1 week.

To prepare the monkfish
Remove the cheeks from the monkfish and reserve for another recipe. Cut through the skin with scissors up to the end of the tailbone. Remove the skin by holding it with a towel, then pull it by holding on to the fish's jaw. Wipe the fish clean, then remove the 2 fillets from the bone. Trim any greyish bands of collagen, and trim the sides of flabby meat and skin so that you have 2 neat, round fillets. Reserve any trim and bones for stock or other recipes.

Rinse and soak the dulse until it's totally clear of excess salt and sand. Roll out a piece of cling film on a flat surface and then line it with the dulse. Place the monkfish fillets on top and season with fine salt – lightly, as the seaweed will also act as a seasoning for the fish. Roll the monkfish tightly in the dulse-lined cling film and leave to cure overnight.

The next day, preheat the oven to 70°C/160°F. Steam the monkfish on a wire rack in the oven until it reaches an internal temperature of 40°C (104°F). Plunge it into iced water to stop the cooking process. Once cool, slice the fish into 50 g rounds, carefully removing the cling film but keeping the dulse intact. Store the fish on wire racks in the fridge and use within 3 days.

To make the citrus kosho emulsion
In a bowl, mix together the egg yolk, fine salt, mustard and honey, then slowly begin to add the oils. Balance the consistency of the mixture with the chardonnay vinegar and pickled onion juice, whisking constantly until it has fully emulsified into a mayonnaise. Add the fermented Scotch bonnet chillies, kelp paste and citrus kosho and fold in. Store the emulsion in an airtight container in the fridge and use within 1 week.

For the pickled Citron (Cedro) lemon
250 g Citron (Cedro) lemons, halved,
    deseeded and very thinly sliced
8 g fine salt
80 g chardonnay vinegar
80 g filtered water
60 g honey
5 g long peppercorns

To finish
rapeseed (canola) oil, for brushing
Roasted Chicken Wing Jus (page 231–2)

To prepare the pickled Citron (Cedro) lemon
Toss the lemon slices in the salt and leave for 1 hour.

In a saucepan, bring the vinegar, water and honey to the boil
and add the long peppercorns, then cool to room temperature.
Transfer the lemon slices and pickling liquid to a vacuum-seal
bag, then seal and leave to marinate for 1 week before using.
Store the pickles in an airtight container in the fridge and use
within 1 month.

To finish
Preheat the oven to 60°C/140°F. Brush four monkfish portions
with some rapeseed (canola) oil and place on a flat metal tray
lined with baking parchment. Wrap the tray in cling film and
steam in the oven for 7–9 minutes until the fish reaches 42°C
(108°F). Remove the fish from the tray and pat dry, then place
the fish on a hot grill very briefly to char the seaweed coating.
Rest the fish in a warm place above your grill, serving the
monkfish at 45°C (113°F).

To serve, place a circle of the citrus kosho emulsion on a plate,
then top with a spoonful of the mbongo sauce. Baste the fish
with chicken wing jus and top with a few pieces of the pickled
Citron (Cedro) lemon.

grilled native lobster, komatsuna & mussel emulsion

We like to work with the older, native lobsters from Devon during the late summer and early autumn. Their deep blue carapace encases crimson-edged flesh that is so naturally sweet that the crustacean needs little seasoning. The tail is rich, with a slightly crunchy and bouncy texture, while the claws are salty and sweet, perfect for a salad. The meat from the knuckles, legs and head lends itself perfectly to be folded into a rich mash.

After quickly spiking the brain, we remove the head from the tail, separating the coral and the tomalley. The tails are frozen, then thawed briefly to release the flesh from the shell, before being laid on kelp to marinate overnight. We roast the shells, then infuse them in suya butter, which becomes the cooking bath for the cured tails the next day.

There is almost nothing better than a perfectly grilled lobster tail. I like to baste the tail in a rich butter infused with its roasted shells, revealing smoky flavours as we slowly turn the tail over the grill. As soon as there is a delicate firmness in texture, we stop applying heat and serve the lobster immediately. I like to pair it with other peppery, bitter and sweet ingredients, seasoned with a deeply oceanic umami sauce. But the only way the dish can be exceptional is if you start with a near-perfect lobster.

For the pickled kelp
50 g honey
60 g apple cider vinegar
200 g fresh kelp, rinsed well

For the Tokyo turnip velouté
8 g Penja peppercorns
900 g peeled and finely diced Tokyo
    turnip (prepped weight)
100 g extra virgin olive oil
60 g buttermilk
80 g butter
170 g whipping cream
12 g smoked salt

For the mussel emulsion
2 kg mussels
500 g filtered water
20 g gola peppercorns
20 g garlic, sliced
600 g white wine
25 g Pumpkin Seed Miso (page 237)
800 g butter
1.8 g xanthan gum
lemon juice
smoked salt

To make the pickled kelp
In a saucepan, combine the honey and vinegar with 80 g water and bring to the boil to make the pickling liquid. Put the kelp in a large bowl, then pour the pickling liquid over the top. Leave to marinate overnight.

The next day, slice the kelp into 1-mm-thick strips and return to the pickling liquid. Store the pickles in an airtight container in the fridge and use within 1 month.

To make the Tokyo turnip velouté
Toast the peppercorns in a wide frying pan until fragrant, then blitz in a spice grinder to a fine powder.

Preheat the oven to 95°C/200°F. Mix the turnip with the olive oil and place on a flat gastronorm wrapped in cling film. Steam in the oven for 1 hour. Strain, then place the strained turnips in a blender with the buttermilk and blend for 3 minutes. Add the butter, cream and salt and peppercorns, then blitz for 30 seconds more. Store the velouté in an airtight container in the fridge and use within 5 days.

To make the mussel emulsion
Preheat the oven to 95°C/200°F. Place the mussels into a vacuum-seal bag with the filtered water. Seal and steam in the oven for 2 hours.

Strain the liquid through a muslin cloth-lined chinois into a pan and reduce to 700 g.

In a wide frying pan, gently toast the gola peppercorns until fragrant, then blitz in a spice grinder. Add the ground peppercorns to a saucepan with the garlic and wine and reduce to 300 g.

Strain the reduced wine into the still-warm mussel stock and add the pumpkin seed miso. Transfer the mixture to a high-powered blender, along with the butter and xanthan gum. Blitz on full speed for 3 minutes, then season with lemon juice and smoked salt. Store the emulsion in an airtight container in the fridge and use within 5 days.

continued overleaf

grilled native lobster, komatsuna & mussel emulsion

For the lobster
4 × 600 g native lobsters
2 kombu sheets
300 g Suya Butter (page 230)

For the malt XO sauce
140 g pork fat
260 g Iru XO (page 110)
6 g smoked salt
50 g malted barley extract
30 g white soy sauce
5 g Cabernet Sauvignon vinegar

To finish
1 g soy lecithin
8 komatsuna leaves
1 sudachi, cut into segments
smoked salt

To prepare the lobster and lobster suya butter
Spike the lobster heads down the centre with a strong, sharp knife. Pull the heads away from the tails and remove the claws. Freeze the tails for at least 5 hours.

Thaw for 15 minutes, then peel the shells from the tails with scissors, cutting down the belly side and along the frills. Make small incisions along the underside of each tail to flatten it out. Crack the claw shell on the narrow side with the back of a knife to remove the bottom half of the shell. Carefully break the thumb-like piece and remove the claw through the open end of the shell. Pat the claw and tail dry and rest on the kombu sheets to cure overnight. Reserve the shells. Store the lobster on wire racks in the fridge and use within 1 day.

Preheat the oven to 160°C/325°F/Gas Mark 3.

Roast the shells in a roasting tray for 1 hour. Transfer to a food processor and grind to a paste.

In a pan, heat the suya butter to 80°C (175°F), then add the shell paste. Infuse for 1 hour, then strain. Store the strained butter in an airtight container in the freezer and use within 3 months.

To make the malt XO sauce
Render the pork fat slowly in a wide-based pan for 30 minutes. Take off the heat and add all the remaining ingredients, then emulsify using a hand-blender. Store the resulting mixture in an airtight container in the freezer and use within 3 months.

To finish
Bring 100 g of the mussel emulsion base to a simmer and shear in the lecithin with a hand-blender for 1 minute to aerate bubbles into the sauce. Leave to stand in a warm place and allow the bubbles to firm up.

In a pan, heat the lobster suya butter to 55°C (131°F). Drop in the lobster tails and the claws and place above your grill to warm through. Turn and baste the lobster until it reaches an internal temperature of 38°C (100°F). Briefly place the tails and claws on the grill, with their undersides touching it directly, then take off the heat and leave to rest until they reach a serving temperature of 45°C (113°F), continually basting the lobster in its juices and the infused butter.

Very gently warm through 80 g of the Tokyo turnip velouté, taking care not to boil the cream.

Brush the komatsuna leaves with some of the lobster butter and place on a very hot plancha, making sure they're well spread out. Add a few drops of water to steam and caramelize the leaves at the same time. Brush the undersides of the leaves with 40 g of the malt XO sauce and keep warm.

Place a generous spoonful of the velouté in the centre of each plate. Wrap the tails in pickled kombu leaves and season with smoked salt, placing the lobster on the velouté. Wrap and fold the komatsuna leaves around the lobster tails, dropping a few spoonfuls of the mussel emulsion around the vegetables. Hide the sudachi segments under the tails.

smoked jollof rice & crab custard

My friendship with Iré has always been centred around the celebration of rice. I suppose we both come from strong rice-eating cultures, so it's no wonder that we have always reverted to cooking rice with prawns (shrimp) and roast chicken on the occasions that we hang out together. Of all the dishes we have created for Ikoyi, our jollof rice is probably one of the most complex technique-wise, but also one of the most personal in terms of storytelling. Though most Ikoyi dishes are born out of subjective and abstract inspirations, jollof rice is an existing culinary tradition – and a fiercely debated one, at that. During our research trip to Lagos, we listened to many conversations on the topic among our Ghanaian, Senegalese and Gambian friends, and it became clear that the origins and supposed 'best versions' of jollof rice were polemical topics.

My intention was never to attempt to elevate any pre-existing concept, but instead to elaborate on an original recipe centred around the core ingredients of the dish: tomatoes, onions, peppers, chillies, spices and a variety of meat, fish or vegetables. I was scared to call the dish jollof, however, and asked Iré whether he thought 'smoked rice' might be more appropriate, or at least less incendiary. He insisted we stick with jollof, espousing the open-minded belief that there was no one true authority on the dish. But if I was to create a half-Chinese, half-Canadian jollof, I knew it would have to stand up in terms of flavour. I went on to create the greatest defence mechanism I could think of: a powerful jollof broth, a vehicle of umami-laden depth, followed by layers of aroma, smokiness and an all-out assault on the palate. If our guests were going to argue over the dish's authenticity, at least they would be doing it over inarguably delicious spoonfuls of rice.

After witnessing the smoking firewood under pots of jollof cooked in Lagos, I knew that the concept of burning must lie at the heart of our dish, too. In our recipe, we burn and smoke the vegetables over the grill until blackened and blistered, before blending them into a broth of roasted chicken, dried mushrooms, spices, condiments, seaweed and caramelized tomatoes. We gently toast the rice grains before steaming them in the broth to a very al dente, almost undercooked, consistency. The rice is then dried, rubbed by hand with oil and cooled before we finish it off by roasting it in hot, aromatic beef fat and our *wok hei* paste. My father introduced me to wok hei on the very rare occasion that he cooked Hainanese chicken rice. After finely chopping ginger, spring onions and garlic, he poured boiling hot oil over the vegetables, which bubbled and fizzled in the inferno of wok-breath heat. I've been mesmerized with the sounds, aromas and process of this dipping sauce ever since, and knew its fragrance would add its own dimension of smokiness to our jollof.

When we roast the rice, we are aiming for crisp, separated grains with bouncy centres. I know if the jollof has been cooked correctly by listening to the frequency of the sizzle as the pan draws near the pass for plating. If the pan is silent, or has been sitting just 30 seconds too long, I know the grains will have an oily, bland consistency and will require re-cooking. For some reason, most of the cooks at Ikoyi think the rice section is the easiest, but it actually requires a surprising amount of attention to detail to execute an exceptional bowl of rice. Timing and temperature are everything. As the rice cooks, we simultaneously warm the crab custard, which acts as a glaze, added at the last moment, before we smoke the entire dish. Crispy, chewy, creamy, crunchy, smoky, spicy, sweet, salty, it's the kind of food you want to eat when you're hungover or sitting in front of the TV with a beer.

For the jollof broth

2.5 kg Roasted Chicken Wing Stock (page 231)
80 g kombu
80 g dried porcini mushrooms (ceps)
90 g chipotle powder
90 g hot paprika
60 g black peppercorns
30 g red Kampot peppercorns
15 g black Penja peppercorns
90 g madras curry powder
45 g ground cinnamon
30 g ground cumin
200 g grapeseed oil
4 kg tomatoes, quartered
1.5 kg red bell peppers, deseeded and sliced into large segments
1.5 kg red onions, sliced into large segments
150 g fresh root ginger, diced
150 g garlic, diced
30 g Scotch bonnet chillies, deseeded and sliced
90 g crayfish powder
30 g Tabasco sauce
60 g tamari
30 g fish sauce
30 g Worcestershire sauce
100 g black garlic, diced
200 g light brown sugar
60 g smoked salt

For the crab custard

300 g whipping cream
300 g whole milk
900 g brown crab meat
200 g egg yolks
60 g fresh root ginger, sliced
40 g garlic, sliced
20 g Scotch bonnet chillies, roughly chopped
12 g smoked salt

For the wok hei paste

125 g garlic, sliced
250 g fresh root ginger, sliced
300 g spring onions, sliced
125 g grapeseed oil
30 g Scotch bonnet chillies, deseeded and finely diced

To make the jollof broth

In a large pot, bring the chicken stock to 70°C (158°F), then add the kombu and dried mushrooms. Take off the heat and leave to infuse for 1 hour, then strain.

Toast all the spices in a wide frying pan until fragrant, then blitz to a fine powder in a spice grinder.

Heat 150 g the grapeseed oil in a deep pot until smoking hot, then add the tomatoes. Leave the tomatoes to fry in the oil until they begin to split and catch on the bottom of the pan. Stir, then continue to fry over a high heat until most of the liquid has been reduced.

Preheat the plancha to high. Toss the peppers, onions, ginger, garlic and chillies lightly in the remaining grapeseed oil and place in an even layer on the hot grill. Allow them to smoke and burn, but make sure they don't overcook on the inside, and turn them to ensure they are all evenly blistered. Add them to the pot with the reduced tomatoes, along with all the spices and the crayfish powder, Tabasco, tamari, fish sauce, Worcestershire sauce, black garlic, sugar and smoked salt. Add the infused chicken stock and simmer the broth, covered, until all the vegetables are cooked through.

Blitz the broth in a blender for 5 minutes until very smooth, adding some filtered water if necessary, then pass through a chinois. Store the broth in an airtight container in the fridge and use within 1 week.

To make the crab custard

In a blender, blitz together the whipping cream, milk, crab, egg yolks, ginger, garlic and Scotch bonnet for 2 minutes.

Pour the resulting custard into a wide pan and cook gently, whisking and scraping the edges with a spatula, until the mixture coats the back of a spoon. Pass the custard through a chinois and season well with smoked salt. Store the custard in an airtight container in the fridge and use within 2 days.

To make the wok hei paste

Place the garlic, ginger and spring onions in a food processor and blitz to form a smooth paste. Place the paste into a deep pot. In a separate pan, heat the oil to 280°C (536°F) and then carefully pour it over the paste, stirring quickly.

Let the paste cool, then fold in the diced Scotch bonnets. Store in an airtight container in the fridge and use within 1 week.

For the rice
1 kg fragrant Thai jasmine rice
1 kg jollof broth (see opposite)
grapeseed oil
filtered water (optional)

To finish
40 g Rendered Aged Beef Fat (page
   230)
60 g wok hei paste (see opposite)
100 g crab custard (see opposite)
50 g turnip tops
Roasted Garlic Oil (page 232), for
   brushing
smoked salt

To prepare the rice
Rinse the rice gently, changing the water until it runs clear, then drain and allow the grains to dry.

Preheat the oven to 100°C/210°F/Gas Mark ¼.

Bring 1 kg of the jollof broth to a simmer.

Toast the rice grains in grapeseed oil, then place into large, flat gastronorms. Pour over the broth; it should equal the weight of the rice. Loosen each tray of rice with some filtered water if necessary, then steam in the oven for 20 minutes.

Remove from the oven and steam for a further 2–3 minutes until the rice is spongy but al dente. Leave to cool at room temperature, breaking it up with your hands and adding some cold butter and oil to further break apart the grains. Once cool, the rice can be stored in an airtight container in the fridge for up to 3 days.

To finish
Heat a non-stick frying pan over a high heat, then add the beef fat, along with 70 g of rice per person and the wok hei. It should take only 30–45 seconds to cook the rice if the pan is hot enough. The grains should be shiny (but not oily) and extremely fragrant.

At the same time, warm 100 g of the crab custard in a small pot until barely warm. The residual heat of the rice will continue to heat the custard.

Prepare a handheld smoker filled with oak chips. Quickly grill the turnip tops and brush with roasted garlic oil and smoked salt. Divide the rice between two sharing bowls and glaze with the custard so it evenly coats the top layer of rice. Finish with the turnip tops and firmly place a lid on top. Insert the nozzle of the smoker under the lid, smoke the rice and leave to infuse for 1 minute before serving.

vegetables

Vegetables are the foundation of the menu at Ikoyi. Every day we speak to our small network of local farms and producers to select the produce for the week. Instead of building the vegetable menu based on particular recipe ideas, we leave it to the farmers to dictate what's in peak season and ready for picking. We would much rather cook with the crispest, sourest sorrel coming to the end of its season than tuck into another growth of cinnamon basil.

We are obsessed with harnessing the life force of our beautiful produce. The farmers harvest our vegetables in the early hours of the morning and deliver them to Ikoyi in full vigour before midday: succulent leaves dripping with dew, crumbs of earth still clinging to young roots. Everything is washed in ice-cold water, wrapped in damp towels and packed away with furious haste. Ultra-sharp blades slice through root ends to reveal clean edges and score the flesh of halved marrows. Our theory is to prep each vegetable with extreme care and minimal waste, treating it with utmost respect from the very moment it arrives at Ikoyi. Our fast, almost clinical approach ensures that all of the vegetables are ready to be cooked with, and that they retain their integral form and have the longest possible shelf life.

kohlrabi & pumpkin seed egusi see p. 132

127 **gratin of cabbages &
bread sauce**

see p. 134

robin's koginut, cuttlefish &
meyer lemon see p. 137

confit cep, girolles groundnut &
smoked quince

see p. 139

grilled squash glazed with
roasted pumpkin seed oil

see p. 142

varieties of summer squash   **see p. 142**

kohlrabi & pumpkin seed egusi

I fell for peeling and slicing vegetables when I started working with kohlrabi. I'd eaten the innocuous brassica of the cabbage family during my time in Denmark. Used to it as a pickled, fermented or shredded condiment, I had never experienced kohlrabi as the main component in a dish. Served in a raw state, its mild taste often went unnoticed, providing more of a textural benefit to remoulade or sour cream. When cooked just enough to tenderize the consistency, however, the flavour becomes incredibly mellow, nutty and sweet.

The process of carving the kohlrabi is an act of beauty. I spent many sleepless nights with the vision of my peeler gliding over its smooth, apple-like surface, effortlessly fashioning perfectly round edges along the lunar shapes. I loved the idea of its starkness, that there was nowhere to hide uneven lines. Armed with a razor-sharp knife, I could execute my vision. I thought it was incredible that chefs got the chance to re-enact sculpture, applying considered craftsmanship to raw materials in order to produce defined forms from vegetables.

At Ikoyi, we serve the kohlrabi with our pumpkin seed *egusi*, one of the first sauces we developed for the menu. Unlike traditional egusi, a Nigerian soup that is cooked with meat, fish, palm oil and bitter leaves, our version focuses mainly on the practice of using the seeds as a stock thickener and emulsifying agent. We make the sauce creamy and aerated with hints of bitterness from the pumpkin seed. Its pure colour and rounded flavour serve as a subtle backdrop to the sculpted and sweet kohlrabi.

For the pumpkin seed egusi
600 g whipping cream
20 saffron strands
200 g pumpkin skin
800 g pumpkin seeds
2 kg Cold-Brew Dashi (page 231)
50 g extra virgin olive oil
100 g butter
80 g sage leaves
100 g bird's eye chillies, sliced
50 g chipotle powder

For the kohlrabi
1 × 300 g kohlrabi
60 g Roasted Mushroom Oil (page 232)

To finish
1 tablespoon Pumpkin Seed Miso Butter
   (page 237)
smoked salt

To make the pumpkin seed egusi
In a saucepan, bring the whipping cream to a simmer, then add the saffron. Turn off the heat, then wrap the top of the pan in cling film and leave to infuse for 1 hour.

Meanwhile, preheat the oven to 160°C/325°F/Gas Mark 3.

Arrange the pumpkin skins in a roasting tray and roast for 30 minutes until lightly browned. Remove from the oven, then increase the oven temperature to 180°C/350°F/Gas Mark 4 and roast the pumpkin seeds for 15 minutes. Blitz the roasted seeds in the food processor to form a powdery crumble, then set aside.

In a large saucepan, bring the cold-brew dashi to a simmer. Add the roasted skins, then take off the heat and leave to infuse for 1 hour, then strain.

Fry the blitzed seeds in the olive oil and butter in a pan for 4 minutes, then slowly add the pumpkin skin-infused cold-brew dashi, a ladleful at a time, as if cooking a risotto. Keep adding all the stock until the mixture has a thickened consistency.

Transfer the thickened stock to a blender and blend with the sage leaves, saffron-infused cream, bird's eye chillies and chipotle for 4 minutes until the sauce is totally emulsified. When small air bubbles begin to form on the top and the colour is a uniform light brown, the sauce is ready. Store in an airtight container in the fridge and use within 5 days.

To prepare the kohlrabi
Preheat the oven to 90°C (194°F).

Remove the kohlrabi leaves, then slice the top and bottom off the kohlrabi. Peel the sides, rotating the vegetable as you do so. Place the flat side of the kohlrabi on a chopping board, then slice in half. Turn each half cut-side down, then slice each half into 2 thick wedges. Carefully peel the round side of the kohlrabi again until the outer edge is completely smooth, ideally in a single motion to minimize waste.

Place the kohlrabi slices into a vacuum-seal bag with the roasted mushroom oil. Seal and steam in the oven for 15–20 minutes until the kohlrabi pieces become slightly translucent and give ever so slightly when pressed. Cool to room temperature, then store in an airtight container in the fridge and use within 1 week.

To finish
Warm 4 large spoonfuls of the egusi until barely hot. If you boil the sauce, it will thicken and ruin the smooth texture. Stir in the pumpkin seed miso butter, then pour the sauce into the centre of each plate. Place 4 kohlrabi portions into a steamer at 60°C (140°F) for 8 minutes, then slice the kohlrabi into narrow strips, with the straight side pointing away from you. Season with smoked salt and glaze with a little of the roasted mushroom oil and plate directly on to the pumpkin seed egusi sauce.

gratin of cabbages &
bread sauce

My mother has always insisted that the more bitter the greens, the better their flavour will be. I only really witnessed this idea in culinary action when, staging at Noma in London, I stood grilling ramson leaves and winter cress over coals, brushing their fuming surfaces with a scallop paste. Cooking transforms the acrid raw leaves into something soulfully comforting and meaty. In line with my mother's thinking, greens at the bitterest end of the scale tend to exhibit this taste conversion most intensely.

My obsession with these flavours stems from eating stir-fried greens during my childhood in Hong Kong: crunchy gai lan with oyster sauce, pea shoots with garlic and fermented yellow beans, choi sum with rice wine and soy sauce, all with that characteristic wok hei, the smoky flavour released from oil in an extraordinarily hot wok. One thing that has stayed with me is the centrality of texture in Chinese cooking, particularly with respect to green vegetables.

Rather than only serving the softest, tenderest parts of the vegetable, I like there to be variations in texture, and elements that require more chewing. As soon as our vegetables arrive from the farm, we wash them in very cold water and trim them as little as possible, removing only the thready roots that have dried out and become inedible. We store the vegetables under damp towels and make sure to cook them within one day of their harvest. The idea behind grilling the greens is to blister and char the exterior, but not so much that the leaves turn brown. This means the process must be executed very quickly. The edges have to be smouldering and crispy, with a gradient towards the centre where the leaves are still crunchy. I like to leave everything that is edible as close to intact as possible, even if this means a slightly uneven cooking surface by the root and stem.

The cabbages are thinly sliced, then steamed à la minute to tenderize them slightly before we caramelize their sides like a mille-feuille with honey-sweetened roasted walnut butter. The kale becomes an extra-terrestrial translucent green as it emerges from a buttery emulsion of roasted ceps. The gai lan stems are steamed, partly submerged in boiling water, to ensure that their thicker ends cook through. Then we finish the whole vegetable over the grill while basting it with a reduction of benne hoisin. Our guests experience a spectrum of cooking techniques and tastes, and may even begin to question whether meat really needs to be present in order for the flavour and sensation of meatiness to be achieved.

For the benne hoisin
15 g kombu
20 g crayfish powder
10 g dried shiitake mushrooms
700 g filtered water
100 g Benne Miso (page 236)
15 g malted barley extract
5 g black Urfa biber chilli

For the roasted walnut butter miso
370 g Roasted Walnut Butter (made
    using peanut butter method on page
    81)
150 g Pumpkin Seed Miso (page 237)
175 g honey
35 g apple cider vinegar
100 g filtered water

For the bread sauce
50 g filtered water
10 g dried fast-action yeast
365 g strong white bread flour
60 g roasted malted barley flour
200 g Guinness
8 g smoked salt
13 g caster (superfine) sugar
600 g black smoked porter beer
200 g red onions, sliced
50 g garlic, sliced
50 g Scotch bonnet chillies, sliced
2 cloves
2 star anise
2 bay leaves
10 g white Penja peppercorns
10 g gola peppercorns
5 g uda pods
1 kg whole milk
600 g Aged Beef Stock (page 231)
160 g whipping cream
50 g Pumpkin Seed Miso (page 237)
110 g white miso
40 g malted barley extract
100 g honey
80 g maple verjus

To make the benne hoisin
Preheat a water bath to 55°C (131°F). Place the kombu, crayfish and dried shiitake mushrooms in a vacuum bag, along with the water, and cook in the water bath for 1 hour. Strain and measure out 600 g of the liquid. Blend the liquid with the miso and freeze overnight.

The next day, hang the frozen miso water in a muslin cloth, allowing the melting liquid to strain through into a bowl as it thaws. Reduce the strained liquid until it is thick enough to coat the back of a spoon, then whisk in the malted barley extract and Urfa biber chilli. Store the hoisin in an airtight container in the fridge and use within 1 month.

To make the roasted walnut butter miso
Add the miso, honey, vinegar and water to the roasted walnut butter in a blender and blend for a further 2 minutes to form a smooth paste. Store in an airtight container in the fridge and use within 2 weeks.

To make the bread sauce
Heat the filtered water to 42°C (108°F), then mix in the yeast, proving until activated and bubbling.

In a stand mixer, bring together the flours, Guinness, salt and sugar together until just combined, making sure there are no lumps or dry patches. Leave to sit for 45 minutes, then add the yeast mixture, mixing well to combine. Leave to prove in a warm place for 2 hours, folding the dough over itself twice every 20 minutes.

After 2 hours, punch the air out of the dough, then cover and leave in the fridge to bulk-ferment overnight.

The next day, roll the dough into 2 small loaves, place on a tray and prove again for several hours until doubled in size.

Preheat the oven to 180°C/350°F/Gas Mark 4.

Bake the rolls for 15 minutes, then leave to cool on a wire rack.

Reduce the oven temperature to 150°C/300°F/Gas Mark 2. Shred 500 g (1 lb 2oz) of the bread into breadcrumbs, then toast in the oven for 12 minutes.

In a saucepan, reduce the porter to 200 g, then set aside.

In a separate pan, sweat the onions, garlic and chillies until soft without any colour.

In a wide frying pan, toast the spices, then add to the onions, garlic and chillies. Pour over the milk and beef stock and heat until the liquid reaches 80°C (176°F). Remove from the heat and wrap the pan in cling film, then leave to infuse for 2 hours.

Once it's been infusing for 2 hours, strain the milk and add the toasted breadcrumbs. Transfer the mixture to a blender and blitz for 2 minutes. Place the mixture in a pan and heat

     continued overleaf

**For the roasted mushroom benne
emulsion**
40 g benne seeds
1 kg boiling filtered water
400 g butter, diced into small cubes
7 g xanthan gum
50 g Roasted Mushroom Oil (page 232)
smoked salt

To finish
1 Kalibos cabbage, quartered
rapeseed (canola) oil, for brushing
Anchovy Butter (page 230), melted, for
    brushing
40 g Ren's Iru Vadouvan (page 233)
4 elephant ear kale leaves
2 heads of gai lan, sliced in half
iced water
smoked salt

to 80°C (176°F), holding at this temperature while stirring
until a thickened consistency is achieved.

Stir in the cream, misos, malt extract, honey, beer reduction
and verjus, and season with smoked salt. Store the bread
sauce in an airtight container in the fridge and use within
5 days.

To make the roasted mushroom benne emulsion
Preheat the oven to 160°C/325°F/Gas Mark 3.

Roast the benne seeds in the oven for 15 minutes.

Place the boiling water in a blender, along with the butter,
xanthan gum and roasted mushroom oil, and blend for
2 minutes. Season well with smoked salt and fold in the
toasted benne seeds. Use immediately.

To finish
Place the cabbage quarters on a perforated tray and steam
for 5–7 minutes in an oven until slightly tender. Brush the
sides with rapeseed (canola) oil and cook on a searing hot
plancha until the edges are heavily darkened. Baste the sides
in roasted walnut butter miso, followed by anchovy butter,
and move to the middle rack of the grill to gratin the surface
and caramelize the sugars. Cover the cabbage with the iru
vadouvan.

In a pot, bring the roasted mushroom benne emulsion to a
simmer and poach the elephant ear kale in the emulsion until
it begins to turn a clear, bright green. Remove and drain on
paper towels, then season with smoked salt.

Submerge the thicker ends of the gai lan in boiling water
for 1–2 minutes, then shock in iced water. Brush with some
rapeseed (canola) oil and cook over the grill. As the edges
begin to darken and blister, remove from the heat and baste
with the benne hoisin. Return to the grill and keep turning
to ensure each portion is evenly charred and glazed.

Arrange the different cabbages on the plates with enough
space between each piece so that the residual juices
don't overlap. Spoon the bread sauce evenly between the
cabbages and serve.

robin's koginut, cuttlefish & meyer lemon

We are lucky enough to work with farmers who source seeds grounded in flavour. The 110-day matured Koginut squash hails from Row 7, the cutting-edge seed company based in Hudson Valley, New York, that breeds plants for flavour and soil health. The result is an exceptionally sweet squash with smooth, supple flesh and undertones of citrus and vanilla.

I've always loved a traditional butternut squash soup, with a base of chicken stock, lots of butter, cream and some chives. But in this case, I wanted to concentrate on the raw, herbaceous aroma of the squash and not mask it too much with rich dairy. Here, we steam the flesh of the squash until tender, retaining the moisture, which helps to create a creamy consistency when blending the soup. We slowly bake the skins, seeds and flesh scrapings to a sugary dark brown, and then infuse our cold-brew dashi with these different elements. The trimmings steep like tea leaves and perfume the soup with roasted notes once blended with the steamed flesh. Hints of molasses and cane sugar intermingle with the lemony squash.

This dish explores the sensations of hot and cold. In the base of the bowl, we place a spoonful of lightly whipped, very good cream over slices of grilled confit cuttlefish and Meyer lemon. The bowl is so hot to the touch it can barely be handled, while the cream is served ice cold. We warm the soup to a gentle simmer and pour it over the cold cream. The chilled fattiness of the cream doesn't allow the soup to intersperse; instead, the viscous liquids merge away from each other like moving tides. We dust the soup with cinnamon pumpkin seed miso sugar, which makes the experience of eating this dish at once comforting and complex.

For the Koginut soup
1 kg Koginut squash flesh, chopped
250 g Koginut skin, seeds and residual
   flesh
2.5 kg Cold-Brew Dashi (page 231)
65 g light brown sugar
10 g smoked salt

For the candied Meyer lemons
1 kg Meyer lemons
iced water
100 g chardonnay vinegar
70 g caster (superfine) sugar
salt

For the cuttlefish
1 × 1 kg cuttlefish
100 g extra virgin olive oil
iced water

For the cinnamon miso sugar
200 g Pumpkin Seed Miso (page 237)
25 g ground cinnamon
50 g caster (superfine) sugar

For the salted whipped cream
0.375 g xanthan gum
2 g salt
250 g whipping cream

To finish
smoked salt

To make the Koginut soup
Preheat the oven to 80°C/175°F.

Place the squash flesh in a large gastronorm. Cover with cling film
and steam in the oven for 1 hour until tender and falling apart.

Increase the oven temperature to 160°C/325°F/Gas Mark 3.

Arrange the squash skin and seeds in a roasting tray and roast for
25 minutes.

Bring the cold-brew dashi to the boil, then add the roasted skins and
seeds. Take off the heat and infuse for 1 hour, then strain.

Transfer the strained dashi to a blender, along with the steamed
squash flesh and all the sugar and salt. Blend for 4 minutes until you
have an ultra-smooth soup. Store in an airtight container in the fridge
and use within 1 week.

To make the candied Meyer lemons
Preheat a water bath to 80°C (176°F). Slice the lemons into quarters,
then remove the flesh and slice the pith from the skins. Squeeze the
juice from the flesh and set aside. Blanch the skins in a pan of salted
water for 20 seconds, then refresh in iced water. Place the lemon skins
into a vacuum-seal bag with the vinegar, sugar and 50 g water. Seal
and cook in the water bath for 30 minutes, then shock in iced water.

Strain the liquid from the bag and mix with the reserved lemon juice.
Brunoise the lemon-peel petals. Store in the liquid in an airtight
container in the fridge, and use within 6 months.

To prepare the cuttlefish
Preheat a water bath to 58°C (136°F). Rinse the cuttlefish and
carefully remove the ink and guts from the inside. Dry well, then
remove the membrane from the inside by scraping it away with your
knife. Cut the cuttlefish in half lengthways. Place the cuttlefish in
a vacuum-seal bag with the olive oil and cook in the water bath for
3 hours, then shock in iced water.

Dice the cuttlefish and divide into 25 g portions. Store in an airtight
container in the fridge and use within 3 days.

To make the cinnamon miso sugar
Place the pumpkin seed miso in a blender with the cinnamon and
sugar and blend to a fine powder. Store in an airtight container at
room temperature and use within 6 months.

To make the salted whipped cream
Stir the salt and xanthan into the cream, then whip the cream to very
soft peaks. Use immediately.

To finish
Quickly sear 4 portions of the cuttlefish in a hot pan to crisp it up,
then season with smoked salt. Mix with 40 g of the pickled Meyer
lemon, then portion into 4 hot bowls. Divide the salted whipped
cream between the bowls.

Warm 160 g of the Koginut soup to a simmer, then pour it directly
over the cream. Dust the cinnamon miso sugar over the top and serve
immediately.

confit cep, girolles groundnut & smoked quince

I think of our groundnut sauce as one of the Ikoyi 'mother sauces'. The concept of this sauce relates to the Nigerian peanut-based soup known as groundnut stew, which is also found in other West African countries. While recipes vary slightly, most I have come across contain chicken, tomatoes, broth, Scotch bonnets and spices. Throughout my restaurant experience, I have seen many sauce techniques but nothing quite like this, which uses pulverized nuts to flavour and bind the cooking liquids. We use a combination of peanuts and Piedmont hazelnuts for our nut butter, which creates a rounded, toasted flavour. The Ikoyi version is the distillation of our desire for the stimulating sensations of peppery spice, rich fats and sweet caramelized vegetables.

Mushrooms burn in a single layer over a smoking hot pan, with just enough oil to make them sizzle brightly. I always know whether the cooks have heated the pan adequately on hearing the pitch of the crackling girolles. If the flame is too low, there is a slow gurgle as the mushrooms begin to steam in their own juices. We aim to brown their outsides without causing them to release any liquid. They are essentially scorched, raw mushrooms, which retain a fresher, earthier taste compared to mushrooms that have gone soggy and limp. The onions caramelize with smoked chillies until fudgy and deeply sweet, and we then blend the sauce with a stock for an extremely long period of time to break down the particles until the texture becomes that of a glossy cream. The aesthetics of the sauce are the first indication we give the diner of our attention to detail: the first hint of intensity, or, as American Author Harold McGee puts it in *On Food and Cooking,* 'an anticipation of pleasures to come'. An uncompromising approach to sauce consistency has become a fundamental tenet of the Ikoyi kitchen.

I wanted our cep to be cartoonishly plump and graphic. Like the humanoid mushroom head of the well-known video game character, the cep would pop out of the lustrous patina of the groundnut sauce with a strong, three-dimensional presence, making it seem even more mushroom-like than before it was cooked. When submerged in smoked oil, the mushroom retains all of its water content and remains firm in texture. Brief blasts of the fire crisp up its outermost layer, leaving its insides exploding with juice. We serve the cep and groundnut with a smoked quince relish, which conjures up memories of peanut butter and jelly and reflects my childish fascination with playful flavours and cartoon imagery.

For the girolles groundnut
600 g red onions, sliced
70 g butter
36 g garlic, sliced
36 g Scotch bonnet chillies, sliced
15 g Malabar peppercorns
25 g sweet paprika
3 cloves
500 g girolles mushrooms
200 g hen-of-the-woods mushrooms
rapeseed (canola) oil, for frying
1.6 kg Cold-Brew Dashi (page 231)
450 g whipping cream
100 g Hazelnut Butter (made using
    peanut butter method on page 81)
75 g Peanut Butter (see page 81)
20 g smoked salt

For the smoked quince relish
45 g gola peppercorns
37.5 g smoked paprika
30 g ancho chillies
30 g pasilla chillies
6 kg quinces, quartered and deseeded
600 g caster (superfine) sugar
82.5 g smoked salt
900 g shallots, finely brunoised
360 g maple verjus

To make the girolles groundnut
In a large saucepan, slowly caramelize the onions in the butter until they are very sweet and dark. Add the garlic and Scotch bonnets towards the end.

Toast all the spices in a wide frying pan until fragrant, then blitz in a spice grinder to a fine powder. Add to the onion mix.

Wash the mushrooms to remove dirt and debris, then lay out on a kitchen cloth to dry in a warm place. Heat a frying pan until searing hot and toss handfuls of the mushrooms in a light coating of rapeseed (canola) oil. Roast the mushrooms in the pan, working in small batches so to avoid overcrowding. Leave the mushrooms to char on their sides, moving them as little as possible, as any movement will cool down the pan and cause the mushrooms to release moisture.

Transfer the cooked mushrooms to a blender with the onion mixture and all the remaining ingredients. Blend for 5 minutes. The final consistency should be an aerated, nutty cream that is totally smooth. Pass through a chinois, then store the sauce in an airtight container in the fridge and use within 5 days.

To make the smoked quince relish
Preheat the oven to 125°C/260°F/Gas Mark ½.

Toast the spices and chillies in a wide frying pan until fragrant, then blitz in a spice grinder to a fine powder. Mix with all the other ingredients and divide the mixture between 2 large gastronorms. Bake for 3 hours, stirring every 30 minutes. The resulting relish should be deep red, sweet and smoky, with good acidity and a slightly chunky consistency.

Prepare a cold smoker with oak chips. Blend the relish in a blender for 2 minutes until smooth, then pour into a large gastronorm. Cold-smoke the relish and infuse for 1 hour. Store in an airtight container in the fridge and use within 1 month.

For the ceps
2 × 150 g ceps
100 g smoked rapeseed (canola) oil

To finish
Coffee Buckwheat Shoyu (page 237–8),
    for basting
smoked salt

To prepare the ceps
Preheat the oven to 100°C/210°F/Gas Mark ¼.

Use a damp brush to clean the ceps of dirt and debris. Carve off any broken or mouldy edges and reserve any off-cuts for other recipes. Slice each cep in half and carefully trim the cup at the head of the cep so that it has a uniform shape. Place the ceps in a shallow container, cut-side down. Pour over the smoked rapeseed (canola) oil and wrap the container tightly in cling film.

Steam for 25 minutes in the oven, then leave the ceps to cool in the oil. Store the ceps, still in their oil, in an airtight container in the fridge and use within 2 weeks.

To finish
Remove the ceps from the cooking oil, reserving it for another recipe. Brush the cut side of the ceps with coffee buckwheat shoyu and cook directly over the grill, cut-side down, to roast the mushroom. Flip the mushroom over and baste once more with the shoyu, then continue to cook for 30 seconds. Move to the middle rack of your grill and leave to rest and warm through.

Warm 4 large spoonfuls of the groundnut sauce until barely hot. If you allow it to boil, it will thicken and the smooth texture will be ruined. Pour the groundnut sauce into the centre of 4 pre-warmed plates and tap the undersides to flatten the sauce. On each plate, place 1 teaspoon of the smoked quince relish to the left of the sauce, then place a cep in the centre. Season it with smoked salt before serving.

varieties of summer squash

I started working with Calixta Killander after visiting her Cambridgeshire farm, Flourish Produce, in 2019. After walking through the rows of brassicas, rare-breed tomatoes and mustard greens, I was particularly inspired by the varieties of courgettes (zucchini) and squash she had cultivated. The little crookneck squash were like tiny still-life objects: pristinely yellow and waxy, they seemed almost synthetic. Most impressive were the avocado squash, which were dark green and oval, with an intensely creamy flesh that tasted slightly bitter, with a vegetal and earthy aroma. When I cut through the giant Trombetta, beads of sap emerged from its pores.

I wanted to preserve this image of fecundity when cooking with courgettes of such profound beauty. I conceived of serving them as warmed to just above the state of being raw, almost as one would cook fish, delicately coaxed to the point of doneness without applying too much direct heat. Our hot, raw courgettes would feel like they'd just been pulled from the ground, firm enough to resist on biting and retaining the tannic freshness of their sap.

There is something repetitive and unnatural about plating perfectly consistent produce. Serving each guest a unique set of geometrically distinct courgettes makes our work as cooks a lot more exciting and challenging. Each plate ends up having its own personality, and while based on a similar theme, the oddities and disfigurements of each piece of squash speak of the unpredictable beauty of nature.

The different varieties of squash sit atop a velvety sauce of vibrant summer greens, spinaches and wild cress emulsified into a base of roasted nuts, caramelized onions, Scotch bonnet chillies and fermented locust beans. The idea behind the sauce comes from *efo riro*, the one-pot stew from Nigeria comprised of layers of deep flavours and complementary ingredients. Efo riro literally means 'stirred greens' in the Yoruba language. In my recipe, our greens are blended in a near-raw state with the chilled condiments to preserve the greenness of the leaves and alleviate the pungent aromas of the iru. The fats glisten through the bright green glaze, which shines like paint as we splash it on to our white plates.

For the efo sauce
2 kg Roasted Chicken Wing Stock (page 231)
20 g madras curry powder
25 g ehuru, plus extra for grating
10 g Cameroon chilli flakes
20 g green peppercorns
800 g red onions, sliced
250 g butter
50 g fresh root ginger, sliced
100 g garlic, sliced
80 g tomato purée
170 g cashew nuts
60 g Scotch bonnet chillies, sliced
30 g iru
1 kg spinach
300 g watercress
200 g turnip tops
iced water
lemon juice
smoked salt

For the preserved Buddha's hand lemons
7 g long peppercorns
100 g honey
5 g fine salt
130 g chardonnay vinegar
400 g Buddha's hand lemons, very thinly sliced on a mandoline
iced water

To finish
2 avocado squash
4 crookneck squash
Pumpkin Seed Miso Butter (page 237), melted, for brushing
Roasted Pumpkin Seed Oil (see Nut & Seed Oils, page 232)
smoked salt

To make the efo sauce
Freeze half of the chicken stock.

Toast the curry powder, ehuru, chilli flakes and peppercorns in a wide frying pan until fragrant, then blitz to a fine powder in a spice grinder.

In a pan, caramelize the red onions in the butter until dark and sweet. Towards the end of the onion cooking process, add the ginger, garlic, tomato purée, cashews and Scotch bonnet chillies.

Blanch the iru in boiling water and drain well, then add the iru to the pan with the onions, along with the toasted spices. Add the non-frozen chicken stock and reduce by half until thickened to a rich sauce. Remove the frozen chicken stock from the freezer and break it into small frozen cubes.

Blanch all the greens in boiling water for 30 seconds, then shock in iced water. Remove the leaves from the iced water once they are cold and squeeze through a muslin cloth to get all the water out. Cool the thickened sauce to near frozen, then transfer to a blender, along with the frozen chicken stock and blanched greens. Blend for 3 minutes until extremely smooth and glossy.

Season the sauce with lemon juice, smoked salt and grated ehuru, then store in an airtight container in the fridge and use within 3 days.

To make the preserved Buddha's hand lemons
Preheat a water bath to 70°C (158°F). Toast the long peppercorns until fragrant, then add to a saucepan with 90 g water, along with the honey, salt and vinegar. Bring to the boil, then pour this liquid over the sliced lemons. Place the sliced lemons into a vacuum-seal bag with the liquid and cook in the water bath for 30 minutes. Chill in an ice bath and leave to infuse overnight. Store the lemons in an airtight container in the fridge and use within 1 month.

To finish
Slice the avocado squash in half and score the cut side diagonally at 1-mm intervals. Make fine incisions, 1–2 mm (1/16 in) apart, in the crookneck squash. Season both well with smoked salt and leave for 15 minutes.

Preheat the oven to 80°C/175°F. Place the vegetables on a gastronorm and wrap in cling film. Steam in the oven for 10–15 minutes until slightly tender. Brush the squash pieces with pumpkin seed miso butter, then brûlée with a blowtorch. Glaze with the roasted pumpkin seed oil. Finely chop 60 g of the preserved Buddha's hand lemon and scatter along each of the squash pieces.

Warm 80 g of the efo sauce and swirl it around each of the plates so that there are different places where the vegetables can be dipped. Season the squash pieces generously with smoked salt and arrange in a circle around the plate. Serve.

meat

The meat servings at Ikoyi are an expression of terroir, much like the distinct aromas and flavour profiles in great wine, which are shaped by numerous environmental factors. While our main focus is beef from Cornwall and Devon, we also work with aged mutton, game and rare-breed pork. As with our vegetable farmers, we let our beef farmers select the meat that will be aged for the restaurant. The result is beef that is as seasonal and varied as our bounty of greens.

Our cattle and sheep graze rotationally on pasture grass, moorland areas and between coppiced forestry. Every time I taste meat from one of the many native breeds we serve, I'm surprised by its distinct textural and aromatic characteristics, which vary depending on the time of year. Beef killed towards the end of summer finishes on richer grass, and so the meat is sweeter with a greater covering of fat, while winter beef tends to be slightly leaner.

Because we age our beef for up to five months, at any given moment in the year we may have up to 40 ribs of beef and sheep hanging in the ageing facility in Cornwall. Although the animal's kill date normally determines the order in which we cook our meat, selecting from the menu of ribs sometimes feels like perusing a fine wine list. However, the inspiring people behind the produce and the exceptional care with which they handle their animals makes it a difficult but exciting choice.

native breed beef, peppercorn blend &
goat horn pepper

see p. 152

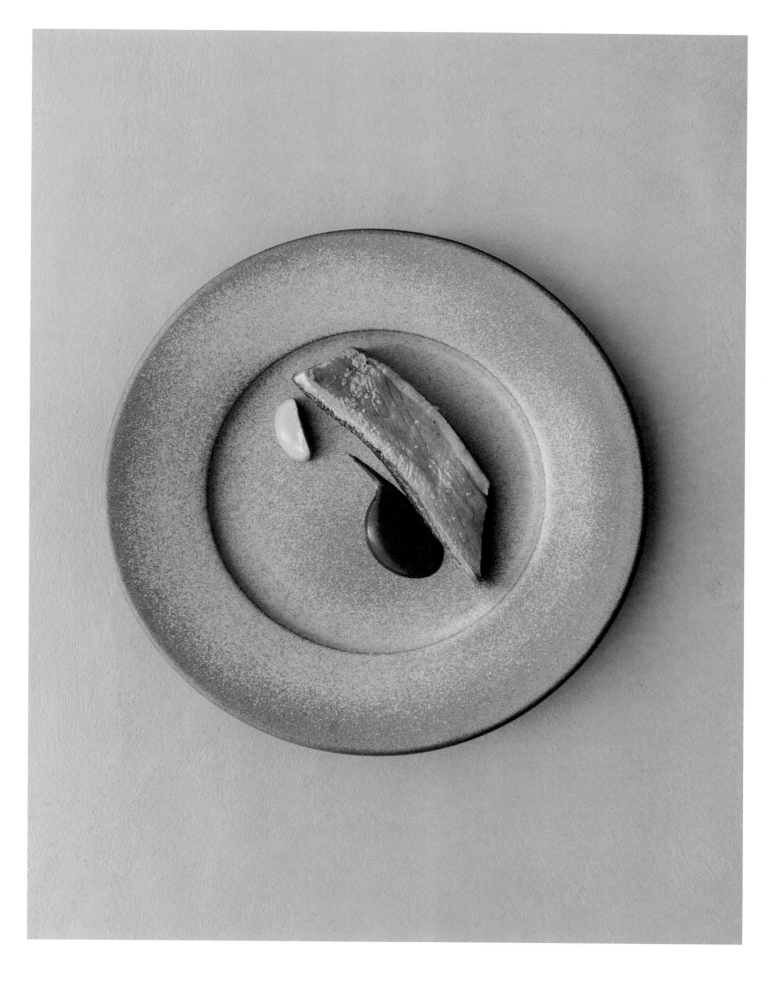

wild duck & preserved beetroot **see p. 155**

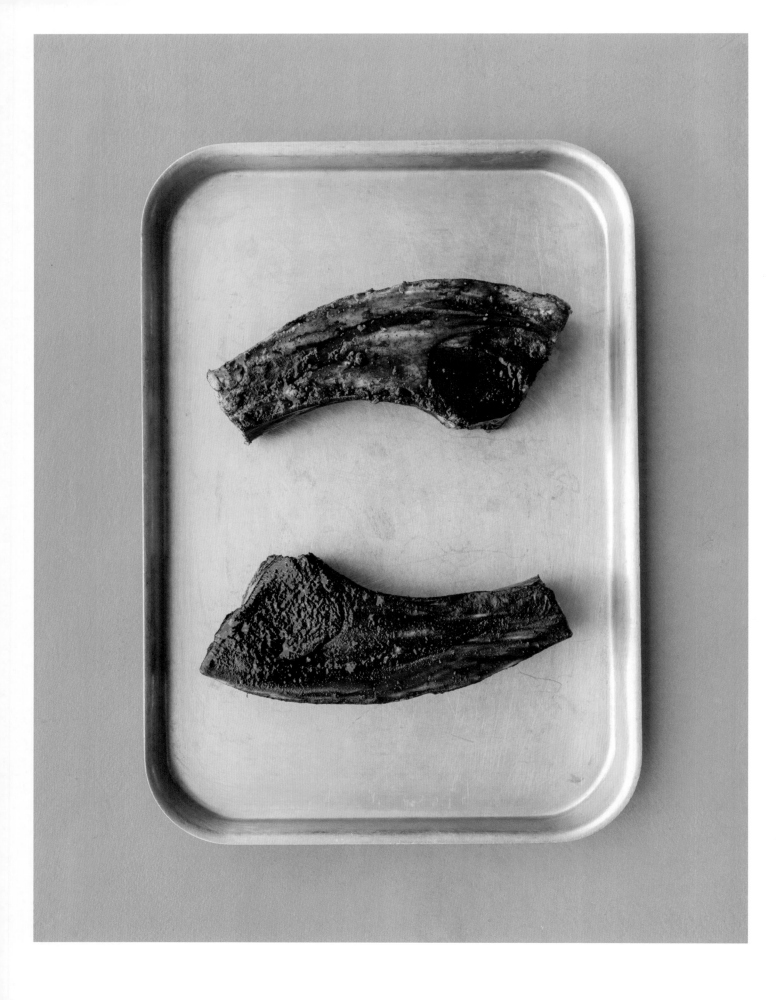

cured cull yaw before plating see p. 158

149   cull yaw cured in burned
       seaweed & asun relish   see p. 158

**sheep from crocadon farm,
coffee & shiso**

see p. 160

151 **noire de bigorre pork suya,**
hibiscus miso & onion caramel

see p. 163

native breed beef, peppercorn blend & goat horn pepper

Our beef arrives at Ikoyi late at night, so most mornings I set my alarm early to ensure that I'll get to the kitchen before any of the other chefs. Perhaps out of selfish excitement, or maybe out of a fear that it will be mishandled, I want to be the one to unwrap the pink butcher's paper to reveal today's forerib: it's an Angus. The aroma is intoxicating, like honey, chestnuts and roasted cheese, a profound odour that is both sweet and rich. It's perfectly aged. I admire the forerib like a work of art or a prized carving from a Greco-Roman temple. It has such a cohesive structure: densely aged, it is an antique covered in light grey fur, the mark of controlled decay.

I sharpen my boning knife and slicer and begin to remove the central bone and ribs. As I peel back the rib cap, the parting of aged flesh and tissue fills my ears like the ripe sound of branches crunching on a forest floor. I make use of every single part: the ribeye and its deckle muscle; the trim for a serving of raw beef; the bones for a rich jus; and the fat, which becomes the lifeforce of our kitchen and finds its way into nearly every one of our recipes. The ritual of breaking down the animal is an act of respect and adoration for the entire process of life and death. My devotion to this ritual is almost monastic, except in this case, the apotheosis centres on flavour.

A truly deep love and passion for British beef is entwined with an appreciation of the very system that produces that beef. It's taken about two years for me to fully comprehend the work of our butcher and farmer Ian Warren. Aside from the journeys down to Launceston in Cornwall, I've also spent many months learning from the Warrens: having conversations, receiving late-night texts and examining intricate photos of the perfect, glistening cut-through, then discussing with them a particularly impressive piece of beef from that night's service. I am obsessed.

Our focus is on native breeds: Aberdeen Angus, South Devon, Hereford and Dexter, to name a few. The calves are raised by suckling method for up to a year, wandering the weathering terrains of the Cornish moors before grazing over rich, Jurassic soil, rotating from pasture to pasture and consuming a plethora of nutrients from the organic grass, herbs and plants covering the downs. The beef is rich in character. Its 'beefiness' comes from the muscles, which are bursting with haemoglobin having used the cardiovascular system well during life outdoors. The fat storage is remarkable, with thin layers like cracks of marble between the dense, dark meat, a sign of health and vitality. Our ribs are carefully aged for at least two months. During the first two weeks, they are placed in high humidity, which encourages microbial growth and helps the desired flavour compounds develop. The following four weeks serve to harness and deepen the effects of ageing. The meat tenderizes while becoming imbued with character.

The only way I could imagine honouring this meat would be to serve it with an interpretation of au poivre sauce with a blend of our carefully sourced peppercorns. While the flavour profile is quite classical, we lay the foundations with caramelized Jerusalem artichokes, and finish the dish with fermented mushroom juices and a pickled peppercorn relish.

For the peppercorn relish
1 kg red carrots, halved lengthways
20 g fine salt
200 g caster (superfine) sugar
250 g apple cider vinegar
20 g Aleppo chilli flakes
150 g green peppercorns
150 g pink peppercorns
50 g Pickled Wild Garlic capers (page 231)

For the fermented mushroom juice
500 g hen-of-the-woods mushrooms
250 g cep mushrooms
250 g morel mushrooms
20 g fine salt

For the beef preparation
1 × rib of beef, aged for 8 weeks

To make the peppercorn relish
Place the carrots into a large vacuum-seal bag with the salt and toss well. Spread the carrots out into an even layer and seal on full. Leave to ferment for 7 days at 24–28°C (75–82°F). If the bag expands too much, 'burp' out the air by making a small incision and then reseal. Taste the carrots after 1 week: they should be sour, with complex, tart flavours. You can ferment the carrots for several more days if required, to achieve the desired flavour profile. Once they're ready, remove from the bag and brunoise finely, reserving their juices.

In a saucepan, combine 150 g water with the sugar and vinegar and bring to a simmer. Once the sugar has dissolved, add the Aleppo chilli and the peppercorns. Cool to room temperature, then transfer to a vacuum-seal bag. Seal and infuse overnight.

The next day, fold 1 part pickled peppercorn mixture into 2 parts fermented carrots, then fold in the wild garlic capers. Store the resulting relish in an airtight container in the fridge and use within 1 month.

To make the fermented mushroom juice
Freeze the mushrooms for 24 hours, then slice in half and place into a large vacuum-seal bag. Add the salt to the bag and toss well. Spread the mushrooms out into to an even layer and seal on full. Leave to ferment for 7 days at 24–28°C (75–82°F). If the bag expands too much, 'burp' out the air by making a small incision and then reseal. Taste the mushroom juice after 1 week: it should be sour, with complex, tart flavours. You can ferment the mushrooms for several more days if required, to achieve the desired flavour profile. Once they're ready, remove the mushrooms from the bag and strain the juice, reserving the mushrooms to use in a different recipe. Freeze the fermented mushroom juice, and thaw in a muslin cloth-lined chinois. Store the clarified juice in an airtight container in the fridge and use within 1 month.

To prepare the beef
Remove the rib bones and chine from the meat. Slice off the top fat cap and outer rib muscles, fibres and tendons until you reach the deckle muscle, the thinner piece enveloping the ribeye. Carefully remove the deckle and trim any excess tough tissue. Reserve the beef fat for rendering, the aged bark of the meat for stock and the rib-cap trimmings for tartare.

Slice the ribeye in half lengthways so that you have 2 long, rectangular pieces. Portion the beef into 150 g servings: this is the serving size for 2 people. Weigh the deckle muscle and divide the weight by the total number of ribeye portions, allocating a piece of deckle to each ribeye, so that the guests can try both parts of the rib. Store the beef on wire racks in the fridge and use within 3 days.

continued overleaf

**native breed beef, peppercorn blend &
goat horn pepper**

For the sauce au poivre

2.5 kg Jerusalem artichokes, peeled
100 g butter
100 g Rendered Aged Beef Fat (page
    230)
120 g garlic, sliced
25 g black peppercorns
20 g Madagascan peppercorns
15 g white Penja peppercorns
10 g gola peppercorns
10 g grains of paradise
10 g Sichuan peppercorns
15 g uziza peppercorns
40 g smoked paprika
700 g brandy
25 g uda pods
4.5 kg Aged Beef Stock (page 231)
1 kg whipping cream
60 g Worcestershire sauce
200 g maple verjus
smoked salt

To finish

500 g Rendered Aged Beef Fat (page
    230)
Suya Pea Reduction (page 237), for
    basting
Suya Butter (page 230), melted, for
    basting
4 goat horn peppers
smoked salt

To make the sauce au poivre

Process the artichokes in a food processor to a fine paste, then transfer to a pan with the butter and beef fat and caramelize over a medium heat until very golden brown. Add the garlic and continue to cook until caramelized and fragrant.

In a wide frying pan, toast all the peppercorns until fragrant, then blitz all the spices (except the uda pods) in a spice grinder to form a fine powder. Add these ground spices to the pan with the artichokes and stir well. Deglaze the pan with the brandy and reduce until most of the liquid has been absorbed. Wrap the uda pods in a muslin cloth and add this to the pan, along with the beef stock. Reduce until the sauce is thick enough to coat the back of a spoon, then stir in the cream and Worcestershire sauce. Lift out the muslin cloth containing the uda pods, then transfer the sauce to a blender and blend for 7 minutes until very emulsified. Season with the verjus and smoked salt. Store in an airtight container in the fridge and use within 1 week.

To finish

Heat the beef fat to 52°C (126°F). Sear 2 × 150 g beef ribeye portions on a very hot plancha to colour each side, then drop the ribeye portions into the fat. Make sure the fat maintains temperature by tempering it next to a hot stove. The ribeye portions should take about 30 minutes to cook, but remove them from the fat once they reach 42°C (108°F).

Brush the ribeye portions with the suya pea reduction, then roll them on the grill to brown the sides further and add smoky flavours. Leave the ribeye portions on the highest level of the grill to slowly come up to temperature.

Brush the smaller deckle pieces with the suya pea reduction and sear directly on the hot grill. Temper the ribeye and deckle until a temperature of 48°C (118°F) is reached. Brush the beef once more with the suya pea reduction and grill a final time. The meat should be gradually brought to a serving temperature of 52°C (126°F) without any long resting periods. Carve each portion into 2 and baste with suya butter, seasoning with smoked salt.

Grill each pepper until blistered and crispy but still green. Heat 4 spoonfuls of the au poivre sauce with a spoonful of the peppercorn relish. Season the sauce to a sharp flavour using a few drops of the fermented mushroom juice, then pour into the centre of each plate. Place the ribeye portions directly on top of the sauce, with the deckle muscles to the right, then add the grilled peppers. Serve.

wild duck & preserved beetroot

When Iré and I had more time to go out and eat as friends rather than business part-ners, one of the spots we frequented was Four Seasons on Gerrard Street in London's Chinatown. There we would share a whole Cantonese-style barbecued duck on the bone. Our first few experiences there were hit-and-miss. At times, the meat was dry and mangy-looking, seemingly pulled off leftovers and then reattached to the carcass, then swathed in a lacquer to hide its imperfections. But when we went to eat there with my old flatmate, Zhen, the duck we were served was considerably better: plump fillets cushioned by layers of quivering duck fat, intricately arranged on the plate. My favourite part was the skin, which had been roasted to a dark, crispy con-sistency, then partially hydrated in a sweet-and-salty duck soy sauce infused with subtle aromatics and spice.

Four Seasons seemed to be a very successful venture. There was always a queue outside, and while lining up we felt great anticipation. Would we score a delicious duck, or one of the old fowls that had been left on display for the past few days? Would we be seated in the overcrowded, windowless basement, the eerie converted flat on the upper level, or the esteemed ground-floor dining room? While it probably didn't hurt that Zhen was Chinese and would order in Cantonese, he told us the secret to getting a 'good duck' was to insist on a fresh one. The first time I witnessed this exchange between Zhen and our waiter, the dialogue was comprised of a curt back and forth, accompanied by furrowed brows, as the staff member insisted all the ducks were the same. But from our many experiences at Four Seasons, we knew this wasn't the case. Despite the slightly painful interaction, we received a gleaming bird fit for a VIP. Since taking Zhen's advice, our ducks have become much more consistent – and the disgruntled reactions from the servers on hearing our adamant requests have stayed the same, too.

I realized from eating at Four Seasons that this is the ultimate way to eat duck. Unlike Beijing duck, which requires more tableside ceremony and pancake-building, I love the way Cantonese-style duck drips fat into your steamed rice, creating the perfect meat marinade with its hints of cassia bark, anise and ginger. Having soaked up the sauce, the duck skin goes from crispy to slightly chewy, offering a textural contrast to the fat and rice.

The duck at Ikoyi takes inspiration from this ideal skin texture and barbecue-spiced seasoning. Served as a main course, the duck is accompanied by a complex, mole-like sauce of beetroot (beet) and roasted duck juices, and guests spoon morsels of the meat on to their plates alongside our smoked rice. The recipe for our Ikoyi-style duck is composed of almost 40 ingredients, all of which are completely essential to achieving the orgiastic mingling of flavours. While its Chinatown counterpart hangs in windows alongside slabs of pork belly and soy chicken, our wild duck hangs on the bone for two weeks before cooking, its rich meat flavour intensifying as the skin dries out.

For the hibiscus dashi
2.5 kg filtered water
60 g dried porcini mushrooms (ceps)
30 g garlic
25 g black garlic
25 g hibiscus
20 g Roasted Kelp Paste (from Roasted Kelp Oil, page 233)
30 g kombu

For the preserved beetroot (beet) sauce
1.4 kg purple beetroots (beets)
120 g honey
125 g smoked rapeseed (canola) oil
4 Scotch bonnet chillies, deseeded and sliced
300 g garlic, sliced
160 g black garlic, sliced
200 g overripe plantain, peeled and sliced into thin rounds
150 g Rendered Aged Beef Fat (page 230)
25 g red Kampot peppercorns
20 g pink peppercorns
10 g grains of paradise
50 g ancho chillies
5 g allspice berries
8 cloves
125 g maple verjus
150 g apple cider vinegar
150 g dark (semisweet) chocolate
50 g beetroot (beet) powder

For the sour carrot baobab purée
15 g uda pods
10 g uziza peppercorns
1.2 kg red carrots, peeled
120 g filtered water
175 g chardonnay vinegar
30 g baobab powder
150 g caster (superfine) sugar
20 g fine salt
70 g smoked rapeseed (canola) oil

To make the hibiscus dashi
Preheat a water bath to 55°C (131°F). Place all the ingredients into a vacuum-seal bag. Seal and cook in the water bath for 1 hour. Leave to infuse in the fridge for 15 hours, then strain through a muslin cloth-lined chinois. Store the dashi in an airtight container in the fridge and use within 3 days.

To make the preserved beetroot (beet) sauce
Preheat the oven to 100°C/210°F/Gas Mark ¼.

Place the beetroots (beets) in a food processor and blitz to a fine paste. Transfer the puréed beetroot to a vacuum-seal bag with the honey and 2.4 kg of the hibiscus dashi. Seal and steam in the oven for 90 minutes. Cool the cooked beetroot to room temperature and reserve.

Heat a wide frying pan until smoking hot. Add the smoked rapeseed (canola) oil and cook the Scotch bonnet chillies and both types of garlic, leaving them undisturbed until the chillies are golden and blistered. Transfer the garlic and chillies to a gastronorm, along with the beetroots, and wrap tightly with cling film, leaving them to soften further in their own residual heat.

In a separate pan, caramelize the plantain in the beef fat until golden brown.

In a wide frying pan, toast the peppercorns and spices until fragrant, then blitz to a fine powder in a spice grinder.

Transfer the plantain to a blender, along with the beetroot mixture, beetroot powder, maple verjus, apple cider vinegar, dark (semisweet) chocolate and the spices. Blend everything together for 8 minutes to ensure a smooth, emulsified sauce. Store the beetroot sauce in an airtight container in the fridge and use within 1 week.

To make the sour carrot baobab purée
Preheat the oven to 100°C/210°F/Gas Mark ¼.

In a wide frying pan, toast the uda pods and uziza peppercorns, then wrap in a muslin cloth.

Place the carrots in a food processor and blend to a fine paste. Place all the ingredients except the smoked rapeseed (canola) oil into a vacuum-seal bag. Seal and steam in the oven for 2 hours.

Remove the uda pods and uziza in their muslin cloth and transfer the carrot purée and cooking liquid to a blender. Add the smoked rapeseed (canola) oil and blend for 18 minutes until completely smooth. Store the purée in an airtight container in the fridge and use within 1 week.

For the roasted duck jus
1 kg duck legs
3 kg Roasted Chicken Wing Stock (page
   231)
lemon juice

To finish
2 × wild duck crowns, aged for 2 weeks
Roasted Malted Barley Bread Spice
   Glaze (page 234), for basting
Katsuobushi Salt (page 233)

To make the roasted duck jus
Caramelize the duck legs in a wide-based pot until the fat is
well rendered and the legs are browned evenly all over. Strain
out most of the duck fat and place the legs back into the
pot. Keep the strained duck fat for another use.

Pour over the stock and bring to the boil, scraping any bits
of skin or meat stuck to the bottom of the pot. Reduce the
heat to low and simmer for 3 hours. Strain the stock through
a muslin cloth-lined chinois and reduce to a jus. Season the
jus with lemon juice. Store in an airtight container in the
fridge and use within 1 week.

To finish
Remove the duck crowns from the fridge 1 hour before
cooking. Score the skin on both breasts and dry well with
paper towels. Sear the duck crowns on the plancha to
render some of the fat and begin warming the flesh, then
move them to the top of the grill and continue to sear the
duck skin until very crispy. Baste the duck with the roasted
malted barley bread spice glaze and sit the crown directly
over the grill to infuse the meat and skin with smoky flavours
and to thicken the glaze.

Once the duck breasts have reached 45°C (113°F), remove
them from the crown, and then baste on either side with the
glaze once more. Rest the breasts under a salamander or on
top of the grill until they reach an internal temperature of
54°C (129°F).

Warm through 4 spoonfuls of the beetroot (beet) sauce and
divide between 4 plates. Place a medium quenelle of the
carrot purée to the left centre of each plate.

Hold each duck breast down firmly on the plancha for a few
seconds to crisp up the skin one last time, then trim the
breasts and slice in half, seasoning with the katsuobushi salt
and rolling the duck in the residual glaze and juices.

Place the duck portions in the centre of the beetroot sauce
and glaze with the roasted duck jus before serving.

cull yaw cured in burned seaweed & asun relish

Whenever I drive down south to visit our farmers, I'm always happy to visit Matt Chatfield and his sheep on his bucolic pastures. The grass is sturdy and tall in and around the ancient coppice, a small woodland where the podgy ewes bounce around gaily like barrels of cotton. Otherwise known as the Cornwall Project, the ongoing cull yaw programme that Matt started in Devon and Cornwall is a system whereby mothering sheep, usually deemed to be at retirement age, are grazed and fattened in higher welfare conditions on forested pasture. The term 'cull yaw' refers specifically to an older female yaw (ewe) that is too old for breeding. Stereotypes surrounding older sheep or 'mutton' lead many customers and chefs to question the textural challenges of this kind of meat, asking whether the bite would be too tough or 'sheepy'. Mutton often also conjures up an image of a scrawny, withered beast, lacking that supple tenderness of young lamb.

When we received our first eight-year-old ewe, we were amazed at the fat covering, which was so vast we could barely discern the eye of the loin, that tender piece of meat that sits between the leg and the rack. What lay before us seemed more like a perversely plump Iberico pork rack than a side of elderly ewe. The texture was sublime: gentle resistance followed by a pillowy melting in the mouth. The flesh flavour was delicately subtle due to the fact that sheep over the age of five stop producing lanolin, the wax secreted by the sebaceous gland of wool-bearing animals.

I like to serve the cull yaw as a chop, leaving it attached to an untrimmed but polished rib bone so that it can be eaten almost like a lollipop. There is a certain decadence in eating such a refined piece of meat in a caveman-like manner, the clean craftsmanship of the butchering contrasting with the primordial act of gnawing flesh directly off the rib. As you chew the morsel of connective sinew that adheres the meat to the bone, notes of liquorice and toffee seep out of the roasted seaweed marinating the sheep, its salty enzymes tenderizing the proteins and providing a complex depth of seasoning.

For the asun relish

300 g red onions, finely brunoised
400 g red bell peppers, deseeded and
    finely brunoised
100 g rapeseed (canola) oil
10 g uziza peppercorns
15 g gola peppercorns
20 g smoked paprika
50 g tomato purée (paste)
75 g demerara (turbinado) sugar
50 g apple cider vinegar
25 g Suya Pea Reduction (page 237)
10 g Worcestershire sauce
10 g Ikoyi Hot Sauce (page 234)
50 g House Pickle (page 230)
100 g 7082 Pickles (page 214), finely
    chopped
50 g Lacto-Fermented Scotch Bonnet
    Chillies (page 234), finely chopped
20 g lemon juice
15 g smoked salt

For the cull yaw preparation

1 × middle rack of cull yaw, aged for
    6 weeks
100 g Roasted Kelp Paste (from
    Roasted Kelp Oil, page 233)

To finish

rapeseed (canola) oil, for brushing
Roasted Garlic Oil (page 232)

To make the asun relish

Toss the onions and red peppers in some rapeseed (canola) oil to lightly coat, then sear them in batches on a very hot plancha to char the outsides. Quickly remove them from the heat and cool on a large open surface so they don't overcook.

Toast the peppercorns in a wide frying pan until fragrant, then blitz to a fine powder in a spice grinder with the paprika.

In a saucepan, cook the tomato purée (paste) with the sugar, vinegar, suya pea reduction, Worcestershire sauce, hot sauce and house pickle until the mixture reaches a glaze-like consistency, then fold in the spices. Leave to cool completely, then mix into the onions and peppers.

Add the pickles and fermented Scotch bonnets, then season with the lemon juice and smoked salt. Store the relish in an airtight container in the fridge and use within 1 week.

To prepare the cull yaw

Place the middle rack bone-side down and cut along the base of the fillet, trimming the fat around the top of the loin and any inedible tissue. Cut down in between the ribs to remove the intercostal meat, cutting down against the bone. Scrape the membrane off the bones up to the end of the rib. Once the membrane is loosened, it can be peeled off with a towel. Slice each rib portion and rub the meat generously with the roasted kelp paste. Store the sheep on wire racks for 24 hours and use the next day.

To finish

Take the cull yaw chops out of the fridge 30 minutes before cooking. Brush the chops with some rapeseed (canola) oil and grill over a high heat on either side, turning frequently until both sides are well caramelized. Move the chops to the top rack of your grill to rest and continue cooking on a lower heat. Once the chops reach 50°C (122°F), give them another quick blast on a hot plancha to ensure an evenly browned surface. Slice the chops off the bone and carve into bite-sized pieces, then place on plates along with the bones.

Divide 120 g of the asun relish into 4 quenelles and place them to the right of each chop. Brush some roasted garlic oil over the chops and season with smoked salt, then serve.

sheep from crocadon farm, coffee & shiso

Crocadon farm is set against the idyllic backdrop of rolling Cornish fields. Walking among the biodiverse farmland, I felt as though I was standing in a wild botanical garden. Mexican marigolds, rows of artichokes, calendula and squash congregate in between pathways of dense pasture and cover crops. Dan Cox, who began farming on this land in 2017, built the system from scratch, restoring the soil with the help of nutrient-rich seeds and a herd of rare-breed sheep. When I first visited Dan's farm in 2019, I was amazed by the verdant pasture and diverse plant life on which his sheep grazed. Their diet resembled a selection of organic salad greens much like we would serve at the restaurant. And the herd of sheep was diverse itself; in selecting and cross-breeding sheep with specific physical characteristics, Dan had created a flock that was a multicoloured patchwork of shapes and fleeces.

There were two specific cross-breeds that I will never forget: the Jacob × Zwartble and Romney × Vendeen. I noticed a refined geometry to the bone structure of these sheep, and a robust and well-balanced meat-to-fat ratio. The flesh was dark red, while the fat was dry and crumbled, almost like cheese. As I marvelled at these striking specimens, I contemplated the American writer Michael Pollan's idea of 'you are what what you eat eats.' The flavour was unlike anything I had tried before, mild but with a natural salinity and sweetness that spoke to the sheep's terroir.

Our cooking technique for Dan's sheep depends on the cut. After ageing for two months, we normally remove some of the tender leg muscles and use them for steaks or tartare. We mince parts of the shoulder and excess fat for kebabs, and keep some of the tougher muscles for braising. The most exciting part to cook with is the middle loin on the bone. I like to deeply score the fat and cook the loins fat-side down, high up above the grill. As the cap renders, it remains encased in a brittle layer. You know the fat's ready when it becomes translucent and the scoring splits open, at which point we flip over the loin to allow more heat into the meat. We serve Dan's sheep with one of the Ikoyi 'mother sauces', our coffee shito, which is a bittersweet blend of caramelized fish, coffee and blackened aubergines (eggplants).

For the coffee shito sauce
250 g shallots, sliced
225 g butter
800 g aubergines (eggplants)
1 kg cod fillets, chopped into small
  chunks
1 kg seasonal tomatoes, chopped
30 g Scotch bonnet chillies, chopped
200 g red chillies, chopped
75 g rapeseed (canola) oil
125 g Cameroon Boyo coffee grounds
25 g Roasted Kelp Paste (from Roasted
  Kelp Oil, page 233)
200 g black garlic
100 g Octopus Stock (page 232)
2.5 kg filtered boiling water

For the pickled shiso
80 g honey
100 g apple cider vinegar
90 g filtered water
50 purple shiso leaves

For the roasted sheep jus
1 kg sheep rib and shoulder trimmings
100 g butter
3 kg Aged Beef Stock (page 231)

To make the coffee shito sauce
In a pan, confit the shallots in 75 g of the butter until very soft but uncoloured.

Burn the aubergines (eggplants) directly on a hot grill until completely blackened. Once cool enough to handle, scrape out the flesh and discard the skin.

In a frying pan, fry the cod in the remaining 150 g butter until it is broken apart, golden and caramelized.

In a separate pan, fry the tomatoes, Scotch bonnets and red chillies in the rapeseed (canola) oil until thickened and the liquid has reduced by half.

Place the coffee, roasted kelp paste, black garlic and octopus stock in a blender and pour over the boiling water. Add the shallots, aubergine (eggplant) flesh, cod and tomatoes and chillies and blend everything together for 5 minutes. Store the resulting sauce in an airtight container in the fridge and use within 1 week.

To make the pickled shiso
In a saucepan, bring the honey, vinegar and water to the boil, then pour over the shiso leaves in a heatproof bowl. Cool the pickle to room temperature, then transfer to a vacuum-seal bag and seal. Leave to infuse for 1 week until the shiso is tart and fragrant. Store the shiso in an airtight container in the fridge and use within 3 months.

To make the roasted sheep jus
Caramelize the trimmed sheep meat in the butter in a wide-based pot until evenly browned all over. Strain out most of fat and return the meat to the pot. Pour over the stock and bring to the boil, scraping any bits of skin or meat stuck to the bottom of the pot. Reduce the heat to low and simmer for 2–3 hours. Strain the stock through a muslin cloth, then reduce to a jus consistency. Store the jus in an airtight container in the fridge and use within 1 week.

continued overleaf

**sheep from crocadon farm,
coffee & shiso**

To finish

500 g tranche of sheep middle loin on
   the bone
fine salt
4 habanada peppers, stems removed,
   sliced into rings
150 g House Pickle (page 230)
Rendered Aged Sheep Fat (see
   Rendered Aged Beef Fat, page 230),
   for basting
smoked salt

To finish

Remove the sheep middle from the fridge 1 hour before cooking.

Score the sheep fat diagonally, then season well with fine salt and place, fat-side down, on the top rack of your grill. While the sheep is cooking, compress the sliced habanada peppers in the house pickle in a vacuum-pack machine.

As soon as the fat on the sheep begins to split open and become translucent, turn the loin over and grill the underside, basting the sides with the aged sheep fat. It's important not to render too much of the fat cap, but instead to soften it to a bone-marrow consistency. Repeat the process of grilling and slow-roasting the sheep by turning it and briefly touching the loin on the grill until the meat reaches an internal temperature of 48°C (118°F). Carve the loin off the bone and portion into 4 pieces, basting the cut sides with residual juices. Lift each portion and brush the fat cap quickly over a hot plancha to crisp up the outermost layer. Roll the exposed underside of the meat on the grill and season with smoked salt.

Warm 4 spoonfuls of the coffee sauce and divide between the plates. Slice 4 pickled shiso leaves into strips and warm up together with the roasted sheep jus.

Place the meat pieces in the centre of the plates on top of the coffee sauce, and garnish with the pickled peppers and pickled shiso, seasoning them with smoked salt. Glaze the meat and peppers very lightly with the sheep jus and serve.

noire de bigorre pork suya,
hibiscus miso & onion caramel

One of my favourite memories of Lagos is of Iré and I eating roadside suya, mouth-wateringly spiced and savoury meat skewers, similar in taste to bouillon cubes. Lines of customers, many of whom were Chinese and in search of a snack not too dissimilar to the kinds of skewers found in China, awaited the sizzling tripe and beef smoking over the open fires. While many cultures practise the culinary tradition of grilling meat on sticks, it is the Nigerian spice mix known as *yaji* that gives suya its distinctively fiery character. Although the beef suya I ate in Lagos was slightly dry, the seasoning caused such intense salivation that the meat disintegrated instantly in my mouth.

Originally from northern Nigeria, the spice mix varies from region to region and is often tailored to personal taste. Thin slices of beef, goat, chicken, offal and seafood are marinated in peanut powder and a variety of spices, including dried chillies, garlic, ginger and uda pods. Fresh tomato and red onion are typical accompaniments to the dish, which is usually served in sheets of newspaper. For my version, I wanted to apply the peanut-umami spice to a lesser degree, as a way to enhance and cut through the sweet richness of pork.

At Ikoyi, we created our own yaji inspired by the flavours of Nigerian barbecue. The Noire de Bigorre pork we use for our suya comes from a farming cooperative in the Pyrenees, and is one of the oldest breeds in France. The pigs grow so slowly and are so fatty that they almost reached the point of extinction before the breed was revived some 30 years ago, when chefs and farmers realized the exceptional quality of its fat made it perfect for use in ham-making. The pork's sweetness is a result of the pigs' nourishing diet of chestnuts, fruits and mountain pasture, and acts as a sponge for the savoury nut-spiced yaji and suya butter with which we baste the meat.

For the hibiscus miso
1 kg Cox apples, peeled, cored and
 sliced
1.2 kg kohlrabi, peeled and sliced
60 g hibiscus
175 g butter
120 g black garlic
200 g white miso
110 g apple cider vinegar
12 g smoked salt
50 g honey
20 g smoke powder

For the onion caramel
10 kg Roscoff onions, quartered
150 g rapeseed (canola) oil
500 g butter
45 g smoked sherry vinegar

For the tomatoes and onion
300 g Raf tomatoes, sliced horizontally
 into rounds
10 g smoked salt
10 g fresh oregano
50 g Green Oil (page 232)
1 Roscoff onion

For the suya peanut condiment
180 g peanuts
60 g Suya Powder (page 233)

To make the hibiscus miso
Put the apples, kohlrabi and hibiscus into a deep saucepan and pour over enough filtered water to cover the contents by 1 cm (½ in). Bring to the boil, then reduce the heat to very low and simmer for 45 minutes until everything has broken down. Strain into a blender, reserving the liquid. Add the remaining ingredients and blend for 5 minutes, adding some of the strained liquid if necessary, until you have a smooth purée. Pass the purée through a chinois and chill. Store the purée in an airtight container in the fridge and use within 1 week.

To make the onion caramel
Preheat the oven to 160°C/325°F/Gas Mark 3.

In a roasting tin, toss the onions in the rapeseed (canola) oil to coat, then roast for 1 hour 15 minutes.

Preheat a water bath to 85°C (185°F). Vacuum-seal the onions and their roasting juices and cook in the water bath for 16 hours.

Strain the onions and their juices through a chinois, reserving the liquid, then squeeze the onions well through a muslin cloth, discarding the pulp. Reduce the strained liquid in a large saucepan over a low heat until it reaches the consistency of a dark caramel and coats the back of a spoon. Season with the smoked sherry vinegar. Store the caramel in a squeezy bottle in the fridge until needed and use within 2 weeks.

To prepare the tomatoes and onion
Season the tomatoes with smoked salt and a few oregano leaves. Vacuum-seal the tomato slices in the green oil 1 hour before serving and set aside at room temperature.

Peel and very thinly slice the onion 1 hour before serving and set aside under damp paper towels.

To make the suya peanut condiment
Preheat the oven to 160°C/325°F/Gas Mark 3.

Roast the peanuts in a roasting tin for 20 minutes, then blast-chill to −22°C (−7.6°F). Transfer to a blender and blitz to a very fine powder. Fold the suya powder into the powdered peanuts. Store in an airtight container in the freezer until needed; it will keep indefinitely.

For the pork
320 g Noire de Bigorre pork chop
35 g Suya Powder (page 233)
35 g smoked rapeseed (canola) oil
Suya Butter (page 230)

To finish
smoked salt

To prepare the pork
Preheat a water bath to 58°C (136°F).

Whisk together the suya powder and smoked rapeseed
(canola) oil in a small bowl, then rub this mixture all over the
pork chop. Vacuum-seal the pork and cook in the water bath
for 2 hours, then leave to rest at room temperature for
5 minutes. Brush the pork with the suya butter and grill on
all sides for 2 minutes before carving into 4 portions. Baste
the insides of the fillet generously with suya butter and
season with smoked salt.

To finish
Place 1 large quenelle of hibiscus miso on the left side of each
plate, with the tomatoes just to their right. Layer some raw
onion petals across the tomatoes in a single direction. Place
the pork below the tomatoes to the right, then drizzle the
onion caramel around the pork. Add a small teaspoon of the
peanut condiment to the right of the tomatoes and serve.

desserts

Dessert marks an important end to a great meal. Not only is the dessert the last taste impression we leave our guests with, but it can also be the tipping point as to how they feel physically at the end of their experience. Funnily enough, sweet is my least favourite taste, so I've never been particularly fond of desserts and tend to take inspiration from vegetables and other savoury produce when creating this last course for our guests. I have much respect for chefs in Japan who serve a simple, lightly sweetened but perfectly executed egg cube as the ultimate farewell bite. Perhaps, subconsciously, it was my admiration for this tradition that influenced the first dessert I ever put on the menu at Ikoyi, which we teasingly named 'yam and eggs'. My dislike of overly sweet desserts was so strong that I wanted to create something ironic, a tongue-in-cheek interpretation of a classic breakfast food, the fried egg. The white was comprised of an aerated, candied yam mousse, which enveloped a golden orb of duck egg yolk cured in treacle and malt. It turned out to be a divisive dessert, with some of our guests slightly revolted by the suggestion that they were eating an egg at the end of their meal, while others were taken with the concept and its contrast of rich and light sensations. Since then, I have continued to create desserts that are focused on idiosyncratic concepts or embedded with ingredients that have a strong, often savoury or vegetal personality. Our desserts must be fun but precise, clean but comforting, an inside joke that I can share with others.

169   **buttermilk vanilla &**
smoked uda mousse

see p. 178

caramelized cep, cameroonian coffee &
semi-thawed candied blackberries see p. 181

ogbono & sicilian mango **see p. 183**

**brown butter apples, cinnamon berries,
custard & rhubarb**

see p. 186

benne seed miso cookie see p. 189

grains of peace see p. 191

**pistachio, muscat grape &
grains of peace**   **see p. 191**

rice & peas

We put this dish on one of our first tasting menus, and I don't think I'll ever make another dessert quite like it. I love the clean simplicity of the concept, but also how it makes you think of a comforting bowl of rice and buttery red- or black-eyed peas. When I first made this dish, I felt the weight of expectation from a lot of our guests for there to be patent references to the African kitchen in our cooking. Since I'd never claimed to be cooking African food, I playfully both embraced and rejected the pressure, interpreting these ingredients based on my own experience.

The notion of cooked pulses (legumes) in a dessert was something I'd come across during my childhood in Hong Kong. I recalled the cold sensation of red and black bean paste emanating from a frozen membrane of glutinous rice. For our interpretation, we use a black variety toasted until very smoky and reminiscent in smell of popped corn. The peas simmer in a light syrup of burned sugar until tender, before marinating in a caramel of dark sake and brown butter. To enhance the savoury profile of the dessert, we dry our pea miso and bake it into a cookie-textured meringue.

For the black rice ice cream
350 g black rice
1 kg filtered water
3.5 kg soy milk
100 g tapioca starch
30 g smoked salt
200 g dextrose
700 g honey
200 g ice cream stabilizer

For the brown butter sake caramel
200 g caster (superfine) sugar
120 g Brown Butter (see Suya Butter,
    page 230)
180 g whipping cream
5 g smoked salt
15 g lemon juice
10 g dry sake

For the pea miso meringue
315 g egg whites
390 g caster (superfine) sugar
37.5 g Suya Pea Miso (page 236)
30 g baobab powder

For the sugar syrup peas
200 g caster (superfine) sugar
100 g red peas, soaked overnight and
    then drained
600 g filtered water

To make the black rice ice cream
Toast the rice in a wide frying pan until it smells of popped corn. Soak the toasted rice overnight in the filtered water.

The next day, boil the rice in the soaking water in a pot until totally mushy and broken down. Weigh out 800 g of the cooked rice for this recipe and keep the rest for another recipe.

In a saucepan, combine 2 kg of the soy milk with the tapioca starch. Bring to the boil and quickly whisk, then take off the heat and set aside.

Working in batches, blitz the cooked rice in a blender with the tapioca soy milk, the remaining 1.5 kg soy milk and the other ingredients, blending the mixture for 6 minutes. Pass the mixture through a chinois, then freeze overnight. Store in an airtight container in the freezer and use within 6 months.

To make the brown butter sake caramel
In a saucepan, caramelize the sugar until it turns dark amber, then add the brown butter, whisking constantly. Slowly add the cream, taking the pan on and off the heat until the caramel is emulsified. Allow to cool, then whisk in the salt, lemon juice and sake. Store the caramel at room temperature in an airtight container and use within 3 days.

To make the pea miso meringue
Preheat the oven to 90°C/195°F.

Whisk the egg whites to very stiff peaks. Fold in the sugar, 1 spoonful at a time, ensuring each addition is fully incorporated before adding the next. Keep whisking until you have a stiff, glossy meringue. Gently fold in the other ingredients. Using a palette knife, spread out the meringue in a flat, even layer on 4 silicone baking mats. Leave to dry at room temperature for 1 hour, then bake in the oven for 2½ hours. Store the meringue in airtight containers for up to 1 month, breaking it into shards for use in this recipe.

To make the sugar syrup peas
In a saucepan, caramelize the sugar until it turns a dark, mahogany colour, then deglaze with the water, whisking well to ensure the caramel is evenly dissolved. Add the drained peas and cook over a low heat until the liquid has reduced by half and the peas are tender.

Cool to room temperature, then store the peas in the cooking syrup in the fridge for up to 1 week.

To finish
Churn 250 g of the ice cream 2 hours before serving and keep at -9°C (16°F).

Mix the peas into the caramel and divide between 4 pre-chilled bowls. Place a 50 g quenelle of the black rice ice cream in each bowl on top of the caramel peas, followed by a shard of the pea miso meringue. Serve.

buttermilk vanilla & smoked uda mousse

This dessert exemplifies my fascination with complexity and texture, and the attempt to leave long and lingering flavour memories. I wanted to create something with underlying familiarity and comfort but just enough contrast and intensity to force the guest to question their palate and their senses. In search of something more intriguing, I turned to the flavour profile of vegetables and spices to create a dessert bordering on savoury but reminiscent of a classic.

The base of the dessert is a caramel that is dark in colour, light in texture and seasoned with black garlic, which conjures the earthy roasted flavours of molasses and balsamic vinegar. On top we garnish the caramel with a chewy but slightly crunchy cookie of caramelized milk and salted dried baobab fruit powder. This component reminds me of the crunchy part of a crumble, though it's far more seasoned and visceral. In the centre of the dessert is a Madagascan vanilla and buttermilk ice cream enriched with a high ratio of egg yolks. The eggy richness adds more body to the lactic sourness of the buttermilk, which makes this much more layered than a straightforward vanilla ice cream.

We cover a generous spoonful of the ice cream with a marshmallow-like mousse of smoked uda pod and rum cream. Uda pods originate from Nigeria and have a powerful smoked leather and gunpowder aroma. These are some of the best peppercorns I have ever used, and it's always exciting to employ them in our desserts. We finish with a sprinkling of spiced roasted miso sugar to give the dish an extra kick. When I close my eyes and bite into the soft layers of the rum-infused mousse licked with the bitter finish of the caramel, I think of tiramisu.

For the buttermilk vanilla ice cream
1 Madagascan vanilla bean
250 g whole milk
250 g whipping cream
184 g egg yolks
112 g caster (superfine) sugar
112 g dextrose
7.2 g ice cream stabilizer
500 g buttermilk, cold

For the smoked uda mousse
15 g uda pods
5 g long peppercorns
280 g whole milk
110 g whipping cream
20 g rum
3 g agar agar
68 g caster (superfine) sugar

To make the buttermilk vanilla ice cream
Preheat a water bath to 60°C (140°F). Scrape the vanilla pod and place the seeds and pod into a vacuum-seal bag with the milk and cream. Seal and cook in the water bath for 1 hour. Cool to room temperature, then infuse overnight in the fridge. The next day, strain the infusion and heat to 80°C (176°F).

In a large pot, whisk together the egg yolks, sugar, dextrose and ice cream stabilizer until light and frothy. Slowly add a third of the hot milk and cream mixture, still whisking vigorously. Once combined, incorporate the rest of the milk and cream and heat to 82°C (180°F), continuously scraping the sides of the pot.

Remove from the heat and strain through a chinois into a large, flat gastronorm set over ice. Whisk in the cold buttermilk and leave the ice cream mixture to mature in the fridge overnight before freezing. Store in an airtight container in the freezer and use within 6 months.

To make the smoked uda mousse
Toast the spices in a wide frying pan until fragrant, then blitz roughly in a spice grinder.

Preheat the water bath to 60°C (140°F). Place the milk, whipping cream and spices into a vacuum-seal bag. Seal and cook in the water bath for 1 hour. Cool to room temperature then leave to infuse overnight in the fridge.

The next day, prepare a handheld smoker filled with oak chips. Strain the cream mixture and add the rum. Pour the rum and cream mixture into a large, flat gastronorm and wrap the container with cling film. Make a small incision in the cling film and insert the tip of the smoker. Smoke the cream for 30 seconds, then seal the hole with another piece of cling film. Leave to infuse for 1 hour, then repeat the smoking process 4 times.

Measure out 100 g of the cream base and place into a saucepan. Add the agar agar and sugar and whisk to combine, then bring to a simmer. Once thickened, transfer to a blender with the remaining cream base and blitz for 3 minutes until it has a smooth, thickened consistency. Pour the cream base into a shallow metal container over ice and chill for at least 2 hours until completely set. Blend for 1 minute in a blender, then store the uda mousse in an airtight container in the fridge and use within 3 days.

buttermilk vanilla &
smoked uda mousse

For the black garlic caramel
200 g caster (superfine) sugar
120 g butter
180 g whipping cream
75 g black garlic
30 g filtered water
4 g smoked salt
3 g lemon juice

For the roasted milk crumb
280 g butter, softened
320 g milk powder
160 g plain (all-purpose) flour
10 g smoked salt
160 g caster (superfine) sugar
10 g baobab powder

For the spiced miso sugar
5 g black peppercorns
5 g uda pods
2 g cloves
1 kg Benne Miso (page 236)
100 g caster (superfine) sugar

To make the black garlic caramel
In a heavy-based pan, melt the sugar and caramelize until it turns medium brown. Add the butter and cream, whisking constantly until fully incorporated. Continue to cook the caramel until smooth and glossy. Place the caramel with the black garlic and water into a blender, then blitz for 2 minutes. Season with the smoked salt and add the lemon juice. Store the caramel at room temperature in an airtight container for up to 2 weeks.

To make the roasted milk crumb
Preheat the oven to 125°C/260°F/Gas Mark ½.

In a stand mixer, mix the butter with all the remaining ingredients to form small crumbs. Spread out the crumb mixture in an even layer on 2 silicone baking mats and bake for 20 minutes. Stir the crumb and continue to bake for another 15–20 minutes until completely golden.

Freeze the milk crumb overnight until solid, then blitz into a fine powder in a blender. Store in an airtight container in the freezer and use within 1 month.

To make the spiced miso sugar
Toast the spices in a wide frying pan until fragrant, then blitz in a spice grinder, along with the benne miso, to form a fine powder. Mix with the sugar and store in an airtight container. Use within 6 months.

To finish
Churn 250 g of the ice cream 2 hours before serving, then keep at -11°C (12°F) until ready to serve.

Fill a siphon with 200 g of the smoked uda mousse and charge twice. Take out 4 pre-chilled bowls and drop 1 teaspoon of the caramel into each one, followed by 1 teaspoon of the milk crumb. Lay a generous quenelle of ice cream on top of the crumb, then siphon the mousse on top, giving it plenty of height and making sure to cover the surface of the ice cream. Dust the miso sugar over the mousse using a tea strainer. It should have the appearance of burned marshmallow. Serve.

caramelized cep, cameroonian coffee & semi-thawed candied blackberries

While mushrooms were my most feared food as a child, they have become one of the most creatively inspiring and flavour-enhancing ingredients in my career as a chef. Because they have such a high water content, it's often difficult to taste their core flavour without careful cooking and moisture management. There is an uplifting sweetness that bursts out of a well-roasted mushroom, or one cooked at low temperature. At Ikoyi, we tend to either confit mushrooms or grill them on an incredibly high heat, to ensure they don't lose their juices but still develop the deep flavours of caramelization.

When thinking about mushrooms in an ice cream, I knew there would have to be other elements, such as eggs, butter, milk or other liquids, which could potentially dilute the fresh mushroom flavour. So I decided to integrate the aroma of dried mushrooms into the base, and found that the careful roasting of the dried mushrooms revealed other dimensions of flavour buried deep within the ceps. When I asked Iré to try the ice cream for the first time and tell me its flavour, he guessed salted caramel, hazelnut, toffee or butterscotch.

To give the ice cream more body, we added a small percentage of extremely overripe plantain, which we happened to have left over. While introducing a hint of 'banoffee' into the taste profile, it was also a natural way to use up the entire plantain in both savoury and sweet dishes. Given the depth and complexity of the ice cream and the process of creating it, we wanted to serve it with simple but contrasting elements. The coffee, transformed into a murky, tar-like oil, sits inside the ice cream like a viscous pool of dark (semisweet) chocolate. We serve the dish with semi-thawed candied blackberries, which provide a refreshingly tart and sweet crunch that enhances the interaction of the coffee and caramelized ceps.

For the caramelized cep ice cream

100 g dried porcini mushrooms (ceps)
900 g cep mushrooms
220 g egg yolks
250 g whipping cream
740 g whole milk
100 g ice cream stabilizer
260 g overripe plantain
424 g caster (superfine) sugar
62 g dextrose
90 g honey
15 g smoked salt
140 g Brown Butter (see Suya Butter, page 230)

For the Cameroonian coffee oil

220 g Cameroonian coffee
600 g grapeseed oil
15 g Madagascan peppercorns

For the semi-thawed candied blackberries

75 g honey
25 g filtered water
5 g smoked salt
100 g blackberries
50 g caster (superfine) sugar

To make the caramelized cep ice cream
Preheat the oven to 160°C/325°F/Gas Mark 3. Roast the dried mushrooms for 30 minutes, then blitz to a fine powder in a spice grinder.

In a blender, blitz the fresh ceps with the egg yolks, cream and mushroom powder for 1 minute. Transfer the mixture to a saucepan and heat to 85°C (185°F), keeping it at this temperature for 5 minutes.

Transfer back to the blender and add the milk, stabilizer, overripe plantain, sugar, dextrose, honey, salt and brown butter. Blend for 2 minutes until very smooth. Leave the mixture to mature overnight before freezing. Store in an airtight container in the freezer and use within 6 months.

To make the Cameroonian coffee oil
Preheat a water bath to 62°C (144°F).

Place the coffee and oil into a blender and blitz for 8 minutes.

In a wide frying pan, lightly toast the peppercorns, then add to the blender and blend for another minute. Transfer the mixture to a vacuum-seal bag. Seal and cook in the water bath for 1 hour. Allow to cool to room temperature, then leave to infuse overnight.

The next day, strain the oil through a muslin cloth-lined chinois and store the oil in an airtight container in the freezer and use within 6 months.

To make the semi-thawed candied blackberries
In a bowl, whisk together the honey, water and salt. Add the blackberries and leave to marinate in the mixture for 30 minutes.

After 30 minutes, remove the blackberries from the marinade and spread them out in a single layer on a silicone baking mat. Dust with the sugar. Store the blackberries in an airtight container in the freezer and use within 1 month.

To finish
Churn 250 g of the ice cream 2 hours before serving, then keep at -12°C (10°F) until ready to serve. Remove the oil from the freezer and hold in the chiller alongside the ice cream. Thaw 8 blackberries until they give slightly if pressed between thumb and forefinger, then reserve in the same chiller as the other parts.

Take out 4 pre-chilled bowls and place a generous quenelle of the ice cream into each. Make a small indentation in the top of each spoonful of ice cream using a warm teaspoon. Fill the indentations all the way to the top with coffee oil. Place 2 blackberries on either side of the ice cream in each bowl and serve.

ogbono & sicilian mango

Iré introduced me to ogbono seeds when we ate ogbono soup together in Lagos at his aunt's restaurant. Originating in southern Nigeria, these fatty seeds come from the fruit known as bush mango. Apart from the deep flavours of bitter leaves, palm oil, okra, smoked fish and chillies, the soup had a mucilaginous texture, known as 'draw', which bounced from the bottom of my spoon, down into the thick stew and back up again like a bungee rope. While I usually appreciate slimy consistencies, this was not for me.

I came across ogbono seeds again during my ingredient exploration of the market stalls in Peckham. As I recalled the springiness of the soup, I wondered whether I could manipulate this textural property of ogbono in a way that suited Ikoyi's style of cooking. I applied a microscopic dose of the ground seeds to salted caramel, which gave my caramel a beautiful sheen and elasticity at room temperature.

We used the caramel on our Sicilian mango parfait, coupled with flavours of fresh citrus and sour cream. I love the sculptural look to this dish; it seems almost as if it were made of plastic, created from a kind of three-dimensionally printing device.

For the Sicilian mango parfait
600 g mango flesh
1.2 kg whipping cream
225 g egg yolks
200 g caster (superfine) sugar
15 g ground turmeric
270 g glucose
17.5 g gelatine sheets
iced water

For the ogbono caramel
15 g ogbono seeds
400 g caster (superfine) sugar
200 g butter, cubed
1 kg whipping cream
30 g smoked salt

To make the Sicilian mango parfait
In a blender, blend the mango flesh with 200 g of the whipping cream for 1 minute. In a separate bowl, whip the remaining cream to soft peaks.

In a stand mixer, whisk the egg yolks with the sugar, turmeric and glucose for 6 minutes. Transfer to a bain-marie and cook until the mixture reaches 82°C (180°F).

Bloom the gelatine in iced water. Transfer the mango cream to a saucepan over a low heat. Remove the gelatine from the water and add it to the pan, letting it gently melt into the mango cream.

Fold the mango cream base into the egg-yolk mixture. Once combined, pour into a siphon. Charge the siphon once and pipe the parfait mixture into 12 rectangular moulds 7.5 × 10 cm (3 × 4 in). Tap the moulds, then smooth over with a palette knife. Cover the moulds with a tray, then wrap in cling film. Leave to set in the freezer overnight. Store the parfaits in an airtight container in the freezer and use within 1 month.

To make the ogbono caramel
Preheat the oven to 170°C/340°F/Gas Mark 3½.

Place the ogbono seeds into a roasting tray and roast for 25 minutes until very nutty and dark. Blitz to a fine powder.

In a saucepan, combine the sugar with 50 g water and cook until a dark caramel forms. Slowly add the butter in pieces, followed by the cream. Cook the caramel and whisk until smooth and homogenous.

Remove the caramel from the heat, then add the ogbono powder and smoked salt. Whisk well. Store the caramel in squeezy bottles at room temperature and use within 3 days.

For the citrus cream glaze
160 g mandarin juice
800 g buttermilk
600 g crème fraîche
30 g grated yuzu zest
300 g icing (confectioners') sugar

For the sorghum bone marrow crumb
150 g sorghum flour
7 g smoked salt
100 g light brown sugar
250 g plain (all-purpose) flour
5 eggs
1 kg whole milk
200 g bone marrow

To finish
8 slices of fresh Sicilian mango
smoked salt

To make the citrus cream glaze
Pass the mandarin juice through a strainer, then place into
a blender with all the other ingredients. Blend for 1 minute,
then pass through a chinois. Store the cream in an airtight
container in the fridge and use within 1 week.

To make the sorghum bone marrow crumb
Preheat the oven to 140°C/275°F/Gas Mark 1.

In a bowl, whisk all the ingredients together until very
smooth. Lightly grease a non-stick frying pan and fry the
batter in an even layer over a low heat to make thin crêpes.

Place the crêpes on flat baking sheets and roast for
30 minutes.

Once cool enough to handle, chop the crêpes into a crumb.
Store the crumb in an airtight container in the freezer and
use within 1 week.

To finish
Remove 4 parfaits from their moulds and place on a wire
rack positioned over a flat gastronorm. Pour 100 g of the
citrus cream glaze over the parfaits until they are fully
covered, tapping the tray so that the cream falls smoothly
over the edges. Return the parfaits to the freezer for 30
minutes to set.

Remove them from the freezer and repeat the process with
another 100 g of the citrus cream glaze. Hold the parfaits in
a chiller set to -9°C (16°F) for up to 3 hours.

Take out 4 pre-chilled bowls and place a spoonful of the
sorghum crumb into each one. Slash the parfaits horizontally
with the ogbono caramel. Sprinkle the mango slices with
smoked salt and place 2 slices in each bowl on top of the
crumb, followed by the parfaits. Serve.

brown butter apples, cinnamon berries, custard & rhubarb

This serving is a reimagining of the apple and rhubarb crumble I used to eat at school in the north of England. When I think of British pudding – an English word that encompasses all desserts – it's the flavours of custard, tart fruit and buttery crumble that first come to mind. I wanted to make a dish that paid tribute to these memories and that would be somewhat familiar to our local audience in London, and I settled on the idea that it would be compelling to reverse the states of each of the components, concentrating their flavour in different ways. The custard, in the form of a frozen cookie enriched by egg yolks, became the crumble; then the butter was infused into an intense apple ice cream, while the rhubarb, boiled and then blended into a clean gel, became the sauce.

The flavours, when I tasted them, also reminded me of apple pie, and so we decided to add an element of spice to the dessert by using cinnamon berries, the dried fruit of the cinnamon tree, which have a peppery, floral character, and help give the dessert another familiar edge. We burned the apples heavily over the grill and left them wrapped up in foil to soften and take on the smoky aromas of the charred skin. The ice cream was an intense emulsion of the barbecued apples, brown butter and spice, making for a flavour that was rich but clean in a very Ikoyi way.

For the grilled apple ice cream
9 g gelatine sheets
iced water
10 g cinnamon berries
1.7 kg seasonal apples, each cored and
    quartered
9 eggs
12 g smoked salt
450 g caster (superfine) sugar
20 g ice cream stabilizer
150 g milk powder
400 g Brown Butter (see Suya Butter,
    page 230)

For the custard crumb
250 g butter, softened
80 g caster (superfine) sugar
40 g egg yolks
80 g custard powder
40 g milk powder
120 g plain (all-purpose) flour
2 g fine salt

To make the grilled apple ice cream
Toast the cinnamon berries in a wide frying pan until fragrant, then blitz to a fine powder in a spice grinder.

Grill the apples, skin-side down, over a barbecue at a high heat. Leave them to completely burn until the flesh begins to bubble and wilt, then transfer the apples to a deep gastronorm and wrap the container in cling film. Leave to marinate and cool for 1 hour.

Bloom the gelatine in iced water.

Working in batches if necessary, transfer the apples to a blender and blend for 3 minutes to create a purée. Add the eggs, ground cinnamon berries, salt, sugar, ice cream stabilizer and milk powder and blitz for another 2 minutes.

Transfer the mixture to a deep pot and cook until it reaches 82°C (180°F) and is thick enough to coat the back of a spoon. Add the brown butter and gelatine and then hand-blend until smooth. Leave the ice cream mixture to mature in the fridge overnight before freezing. Store in an airtight container in the freezer and use within 6 months.

To make the custard crumb
In a stand mixer, whip the butter, sugar and egg yolks for 3 minutes until aerated. In a separate bowl, mix together the custard powder, milk powder, flour and salt, then add these dry ingredients to the whipped yolks. Beat the mixture briefly until it comes together.

Bring the dough together into a ball and then roll between 2 sheets of greaseproof paper to a thickness of 5 mm (¼ in). Leave the dough to chill in the fridge for 2 hours, then preheat the oven to 130°C/Gas Mark ¾ and bake for 20 minutes. Once cooled, slice the cookie by hand into small brunoise. Store the crumb in an airtight container in the freezer for up to 1 month.

continued overleaf

**brown butter apples, cinnamon berries,
custard & rhubarb**

For the rhubarb gel
1 kg rhubarb, peeled and diced
300 g honey
5 g citric acid
200 g beetroot (beet) juice
5 g gola peppercorns
10 g pink peppercorns
20 g hibiscus
2 g xanthan gum
3 g agar agar
10 g lemon juice

To make the rhubarb gel
Place the rhubarb into a blender with the honey, citric acid and beetroot (beet) juice and blend for 2 minutes to combine.

Toast the spices in a wide frying pan until fragrant, then blitz to a fine powder in a spice grinder, along with the hibiscus.

Transfer the rhubarb mixture to a saucepan, along with the ground spice mixture, and cook until the liquid has reduced by half. Add the xanthan gum and agar agar and use a hand-blender to combine, then cook for 1 minute more.

Leave the gel to set in the fridge for 2 hours, then transfer to a blender and blend for 1 minute with the lemon juice. Store the rhubarb gel in squeezy bottles in the fridge and use within 1 week.

To finish
Churn 250 g of the ice cream 2 hours before serving, then keep at -11°C (12°F) until ready to serve.

Take out 4 pre-chilled bowls and place a spoonful of the custard crumb in each one. Top with a generous quenelle of the ice cream, then immediately glaze each quenelle with 10 g of the rhubarb gel. Allow the gel to set on the cold ice cream in the chiller for 2 minutes before serving.

benne seed miso cookie

The recipe for this benne seed miso cookie came about during the first Covid-19 lockdown in the UK in 2020. With Ikoyi closed for the first time since its opening, the future of the business was worryingly uncertain, and I suddenly had ample time for anxious reflection. I kept myself busy during those long and listless groundhog days by running around my parents' garden, the same way I had as an overly energetic kid. My friend Hee-Won sent me a workout programme designed around kettlebells and free weights equipment, but as I didn't have any to hand, I found a decently hefty rock in one of my mother's flowerbeds and used that as my instrument of self-castigation. I stood in the backyard every day, lifting the stone high above my head, across my body and over my shoulders. It felt like a self-imposed prison-labour experience – not that being at home was anything like being in prison, but losing the freedom of mobility certainly came close. I guess I was filling the void of my daily working existence; cycling back and forth to the restaurant every day and living out the physically demanding hours of kitchen life had created in me a dependency on struggle and exhaustion.

After these workouts, the only kind of food I wanted to cook was for comfort. One particularly dark and rainy day, I thought about making some cookies for my family. With no time constraints, I dreamed into the early hours of the morning about the best cookies I had ever eaten, using memory to inform my recipe. Back in college, my friend Chris's mother had delivered a particularly good batch when dropping him off at his dorm during the beginning of fall semester. The cookies had been light, slightly greasy, crispy on the outside with a soft, melt-in-the-mouth chewy inside. They'd had a large diameter – as wide as my hand – but they were paper thin. I remember holding one in my hand, bending it in half so that I could fit more of it into my mouth, the same way I would a slice of pizza.

The Ikoyi version of this cookie, much like the other lockdown-inspired items that made their way on to our menu, is an ode to sublime comfort and deliciousness. We season the cookies with benne seed miso, benne seeds, smoked salt and chunks of fruity dark (semisweet) chocolate. To ensure the cookies are as thin as possible but retain their shape, we blast-chill them as soon as they come out of the oven, which halts the baking process and solidifies the fat and structure of the cookie. We mostly serve them plain, but sometimes we shave white or black truffle on to them to intensify their earthy flavours. We warm the cookies very gently to order, so they are just soft enough to bend but don't fall apart.

For the cookies
480 g butter, softened
400 g light brown sugar
240 g caster (superfine) sugar
4 eggs
80 g Benne Miso (page 236)
380 g plain (all-purpose) flour
60 g benne seeds
7 g bicarbonate of soda (baking soda)
12 g smoked salt
440 g dark (semisweet) chocolate

To finish
smoked salt
80 g black or white truffles, sliced

To make the cookies
In a stand mixer, whip the butter with the sugars until very fluffy. Beat in 1 egg at a time until fully incorporated, then add the miso, continuing to whip until a smooth batter is formed.

Add all the dry ingredients and beat until just combined, then add the chocolate. Chill the dough in the fridge for 1 hour, and then roll into a log 7.5 cm (3 in) in diameter. Freeze the cookie dough overnight.

The next day, slice the log into 65 g pieces, and then roll each piece into tight balls, making sure there are no air pockets. Place the cookie dough balls on a sheet of baking parchment over a gastronorm, positioning them 5 cm (2 in) apart. Leave at room temperature for 30 minutes to temper, then flatten each ball gently to form a patty shape.

Preheat the oven to 160°C/325°F/Gas Mark 3 on a low fan speed.

Bake the cookies for 6 minutes, then turn them over and bake for another 5–7 minutes until they are golden brown, crispy on the edges but slightly raw in the centre. When they are fresh from the oven, the cookies will be so soft they will disintegrate if handled, so blast-chill them immediately or leave to cool in the freezer until fully set.

To finish
Remove the cookies from the chiller or freezer and temper for 15–30 minutes. Preheat the oven to 110°C/230°F/Gas Mark ¼ and gently warm the cookies through until bendable. Serve immediately with smoked salt and slices of black or white truffle.

pistachio, muscat grape & grains of peace

The first time I ate pistachio with fruit was in 2009 at Thomas Keller's New York restaurant Per Se. It was a Hudson Valley 'gateau' of foie gras, sandwiched between a pistachio cookie base and rhubarb jelly topping. Served alongside warm slices of brioche, the duck liver on bread tasted like the best peanut butter and jelly sandwich I had ever eaten. This epiphanic moment made me realize how playful food could be even at such a serious and refined level.

After that, I began searching for the highest-quality nuts and seeds I could find, from Italy to Iran and beyond, with the aim of creating my own playful version of a dish inspired by the combination of peanut butter and jelly, but one that would focus more than anything on the deliciousness of pistachios. I had spent years looking for the right press to extract oil from nuts at low temperatures, and I finally got my hands on the right piece of equipment just as I began using Bronte pistachios from Mount Etna, Sicily. Harvested every other year and collected by hand on steep, volcanic slopes rich with nutrients, the Bronte is an incomparably floral and green kind of pistachio.

We roast the nuts so that they release their essential oils before we pass them through our press, then churn another round of nuts over several hours to make pistachio butter. We combine the two, then enhance the fruity notes by emulsifying the pistachio base with fresh Muscat grape juice. To give the dish texture, we top the ice cream with a cookie seasoned with grains of peace. This fruity spice, eaten in Cameroon like candy, brings with it flavours of liquorice, bubble gum and citrus rind, acting as a supporting role to the pistachio, augmenting the sense of intrigue.

I often think about how the creative process at Ikoyi shares similarities with wine-making. Through my cooking, I want to express something true to the ingredient that I am working with, giving it room to raise its own voice, while honouring elements of its flavour with delicate intervention.

**For the pistachio and Muscat grape ice
   cream**
510 g Pistachio Oil (see Nut & Seed Oils,
   page 232)
1.05 kg Pistachio Butter (made using
   peanut butter method on page 81)
550 g caster (superfine) sugar
125 g tapioca starch
75 g ice cream stabilizer
35 g smoked salt
2 kg Muscat grapes
1.9 kg filtered water

For the grape soup
2 g passion berries
5 g grains of peace
480 g grape juice (left over from the ice
   cream recipe above)
45 g honey
80 g Shiso Vinegar (see Herb Vinegar,
   page 231)
2.4 g agar agar

For the hibiscus and oolong tea glaze
5 g green Sichuan peppercorns
10 g long peppercorns
1 kg filtered water
500 g caster (superfine) sugar
60 g hibiscus
15 g oolong tea
30 g Shiso Vinegar (see Herb Vinegar,
   page 231)

For the caramelized white chocolate
500 g white chocolate, broken into
   small chunks

To make the pistachio and Muscat grape ice cream
Whisk the pistachio oil into the pistachio butter and set aside.

In a blender, blend all the dry ingredients together for 30 seconds.

In a separate blender, blitz the grapes for 3 minutes, then pass
through a chinois. Weigh out 1.4 kg of the juice, keeping the rest
for the grape soup. Add the water and grape juice to the dry
ingredients and blitz for a further 2 minutes.

Transfer this mixture to a saucepan and cook at 100°C (212°F) for
5 minutes, or until it thickens enough to coat the back of a spoon.
Cool the mixture in a gastronorm over ice, then add the pistachio
oil and butter and hand-blend to combine. Leave the ice cream
mixture to mature overnight before freezing. Store in an airtight
container in the freezer and use within 6 months.

To make the grape soup
Blitz the passion berries and grains of peace in a spice grinder to
a fine powder.

In a saucepan, combine the grape juice with the honey, ground
spices, shiso vinegar and agar agar and bring to the boil for
1 minute. Leave the soup to set in the fridge before blitzing for
a further 1 minute. Store the soup in an airtight container in the
fridge and use within 1 week.

To make the hibiscus and oolong tea glaze
Toast the spices in a wide frying pan until fragrant, then blitz to a
fine powder in a spice grinder.

Mix all the ingredients except the vinegar together in a medium
pot and reduce slowly to a strained weight of 360 g. Remove from
the heat and stir in the shiso vinegar. Store the glaze in an airtight
container and use within 1 month.

To make the caramelized white chocolate
Preheat the oven to 120°C/250°F/Gas Mark ½.

Place the chocolate chunks in a baking tray and bake for 45 minutes,
stirring every 15 minutes, until lightly browned. Freeze the chocolate,
then blitz to a fine powder in a blender. Store in an airtight
container in the freezer and use within 1 month.

For the grains of peace cookie
10 g grains of peace
160 g egg whites
195 g caster (superfine) sugar
10 g Roasted Miso Powder (page 238)
18 g matcha powder

To make the grains of peace cookie
Blitz the grains of peace to a fine powder in a spice grinder.

In a bowl, whisk the egg whites to soft peaks, then add the sugar, a spoonful at a time, whisking between each addition until you have a stiff, glossy meringue. Fold in the roasted miso, grains of peace and matcha.

Using a flat, circular mould with a 5 cm (2 in) diameter as a stencil, spread circles of meringue over silicone baking mats on a flat gastronorm. Leave to rest at room temperature for 1 hour.

Preheat the oven to 85°C/185°F.

Bake the meringues for 3 hours. Store in an airtight container and use within 1 month.

To finish
Churn 250 g of the ice cream 2 hours before serving, then keep at -11°C (12°F) until ready to serve.

Take out 4 pre-chilled bowls and place a spoonful of the caramelized white chocolate in each one. Top with a generous quenelle of the ice cream, then immediately glaze each quenelle with 10 g of the grape soup. Glaze 4 of the cookies with the hibiscus and oolong tea glaze then place the cookies on top of the ice cream.

improvisations

Sometimes I like to plunder the depths of childhood for imagery, flavour, texture and events in order to create a recipe. My memory seems to be a limitless resource for an extremely specific set of sensory impressions, fantasies and myths. None of these improvised dishes ever make it back on to the menu. For me, the beauty of recreating specific mementos lies in making them as ephemeral as the experiences on which they're based. We've had hundreds of these improvised dishes on our menu over the last few years, but I have picked a few of my favourites, perhaps the most fun ones, for you to reimagine.

plantain, smoked scotch
bonnet & raspberry

see p. 206

the breakfast sandwich **see p. 208**

aromatic nigerian uda pods see p. 211

199   **chicken fried in aromatic beef fat,
sansho berries & winter truffles**   **see p. 211**

**fried landes chicken &
chicken offal hot sauce** see p. 213

201
aged sheep kebab, green goddess &
brittany seaweed
see p. 216

202   **sweetbreads, schrenckii caviar &**
freshly dug potatoes   **see p. 219**

creamed spinach see p. 222

overripe plantain caramelized in
ginger & kelp with uziza jam

see p. 224

205 **tiger nut custard &**
mount etna pistachio   **see p. 226**

plantain, smoked scotch bonnet & raspberry

I had never eaten plantain before we opened Ikoyi, but I'd learned a few things about it during my initial readings about the produce of Sub-Saharan West Africa. In this early stage of development, the Scotch bonnet chilli symbolized the essence of flavour for a cuisine I could neither understand nor relate to. I couldn't figure out how to connect my passion for deliciousness to a food culture I hadn't grown up eating. So I began to look at the plantain and the chilli as abstract, artistic forms when creating dishes. What did their colours signify? How could I manipulate their geometry? How could I elicit emotions in combining the ingredients? How could I reflect my sense of forced alienation towards these ingredients back to the guests eating them through their form?

During my adolescence, I was fascinated by British film director Ridley Scott's *Alien* film saga. From a very early age, I was deeply obsessed with the morbid, cyborg forms of the mechanical space design and the terrifying but visceral curves of the aliens themselves. I loved the purity and coherence of this nihilistic aesthetic: the conflict of man mastering outer space against unstoppable, intelligent life. In creating the plantain dish, my fascination with death and outer space re-emerged with a newfound association. As the first dish on the menu, I wanted it to capture each element of taste: salty, sour, bitter, sweet and umami. But my first thought was of colour. I wanted the dish to be red, to act as a kind of warning for the heat to come, so I came up with the recipe for the spiced raspberry salt, which would coat the fried plantains with an almost synthetic-looking fur of dust, calling to mind the surface of Mars.

I wanted to harness the intensity of the chillies but also to present them subtly, catching the diner off guard. So I burned and smoked the chillies with shallots and infused them into oil, which would later be made into an emulsion with eggs, aromatic pickles and sweet condiments. In slicing the plantain, I trimmed as little as possible to attain a futurist ideal of plantain, a kind of Platonic plantain form, more plantain-like than before it was cut, as if it were some kind of hyperbolic graphic art. The dish is ultimately playful, because its redness actually relates to the tart sourness of the raspberry, while it's the yellow of the emulsion that contains the elements of burning and heat. Guests often dip the plantain in this sauce to lessen the heat, only to find that it's the innocent-looking sauce that contains the spice, not the potent red salt. The sleek curvature of the emulsion, synthetic in appearance yet totally organic, combined with the rusty-hued fleece of the razor-sharp plantain, became the blueprint of how I would create at Ikoyi.

For the smoked Scotch bonnet oil
700 g red chillies, pierced
75 g Scotch bonnet chillies, pierced
900 g shallots, halved
grapeseed oil, for coating
100 g smoked paprika
1.5 kg rapeseed (canola) oil

**For the smoked Scotch bonnet
     emulsion**
6 g fine salt
65 g egg yolks
8 g Dijon mustard
30 g apple cider vinegar
100 g House Pickle (page 230)

For the raspberry salt
600 g freeze-dried raspberry powder
50 g ground cinnamon
20 g ground cloves
100 g paprika
20 g fine salt

For the plantain flour
300 g coarse white corn grits
75 g sorghum flour
112 g tapioca starch
37 g rice flour
8 g fine salt
3 g ground cloves
5 g paprika
3 g Cameroon chilli powder

To finish
1 ripe yellow plantain
50 g buttermilk
2 kg grapeseed oil, for deep-frying
fine salt

To make the smoked Scotch bonnet oil
Lightly coat the chillies and shallots in grapeseed oil, then place in an even layer over a very hot grill. Leave them to heavily char, turning once to cook on both sides. Transfer the charred chillies and shallots into a deep gastronorm, cover the container with cling film, then leave to soften for 2 hours.

Once softened and cooled, finely chop the chillies and shallots, then transfer into a vacuum-seal bag with the smoked paprika and rapeseed (canola) oil. Cold-infuse the oil for 48 hours in the fridge before straining through a muslin cloth. Store the oil in an airtight container in the fridge and use within 1 month.

To make the smoked Scotch bonnet emulsion
Blitz the salt, egg yolks, mustard and vinegar in a food processor until a coherent paste forms. Emulsify the egg mixture by slowly adding 375 g of the smoked Scotch bonnet chilli oil. Scrape down the sides of the blender, then add half of the house pickle. Continue emulsifying with another 375 g of the smoked Scotch bonnet chilli oil, followed by the second half of the house pickle.

Store the emulsion in an airtight container in the fridge and use within 1 week.

To make the raspberry salt
Blend all the ingredients together in a spice grinder to form a fine power. Pass the powder through a fine sieve, then store in an airtight container and use within 6 months.

To make the plantain flour
Place all the ingredients in a blender and blitz for 2 minutes. Store the powder in an airtight container and use within 1 month.

To finish
Peel the plantain and slice the tips at a sharp angle. Lay the plantain curved side up and slice into 4 horizontal portions, each 1 cm (½ in) thick. Trim the plantain portions to 13 cm (5 in) long and carve so that each edge of the plantain is clean.

Brush the plantain slices with the buttermilk and place into the plantain flour. Carefully spread a layer of flour over the exposed side of plantain, making sure not to create clumps with the buttermilk. Remove the plantain slices from the flour and set aside on a piece of greaseproof paper.

Heat the oil to 170°C (338°F) in a deep pot and fry the plantain slices for 4 minutes until golden. Season with fine salt, then scatter 5 g raspberry salt over each piece. Take out 4 room-temperature plates and place a plantain slice in the centre of each. To the left of the plantain, make a quenelle of the smoked Scotch bonnet emulsion, then serve.

the breakfast sandwich

During the first few months of opening Ikoyi, I developed a bit of a fast-food addiction. After a long day at work conceptualizing tasting menus and obsessing over the organization, cleaning and structure of our kitchen, I'd saunter off to a fast-food place at one o'clock in the morning to grab myself a blissful hit of instant gratification. In my delirium, I'd observe the rapidity of burgers wrapped, milkshakes poured and fries scooped. The sterile light exposed the creepy food mechanizations as I watched in fixated silence, fetishizing the consistency of their kitchen system. I felt numb from an exhausting, over-active brain. At the time, it seemed that the only antidote to overthinking the formulas for food creativity was to imbibe the extreme opposite.

There is some irony in what makes ambitious chefs feel good. It makes me wonder whether we are really cooking for ourselves or for some kind of socially constructed ideal of excellence. If I look to the food memories with the most constancy in my life, I'd be lying if I said that sausage and egg sandwiches weren't in my top three. It's funny to think of all the business meetings Iré and I had while eating these, later having to answer journalists' questions about our top places to eat in London. I can't deny my childhood excitement at sneaking some fast-food breakfast before school. I always knew there was something disturbingly decadent but synthetic about the perfectly seasoned, springy meat and rubbery egg. While I managed to kick the late-night after-work addiction, it's not uncommon for our small kitchen team to huddle around a greasy bag before a busy day of prep.

After much research, I found a recipe for the sausage patty. For our version, we use cuts of aged Mangalitza pork pressed into moulds with a handful of questionable seasonings. For the egg, we steam an omelette with chunks of Taleggio, then slice it into neat rectangles. We top the patty with a slice of cheese infused with beef stock and spiced Guinness. These three dripping layers sit between a light bun brushed with a crunchy glaze to add another textural element. I wanted to celebrate the artificiality of the fast-food breakfast sandwich by perversely exaggerating each of the components that I'd come to love.

For the white pepper sausage patty
30 g white peppercorns
20 g black Urfa biber chilli
30 g garlic powder
30 g onion powder
2 kg Mangalitza sausage meat
25 g rosemary, finely chopped
40 g dextrose
8 g fish sauce
30 g smoked salt

For the spiced Guinness cheese slice
10 g white Penja peppercorns
20 g Aleppo chilli flakes
500 g Guinness
200 g Aged Beef Stock (page 231)
5 g Worcestershire sauce
10 g Suya Pea Reduction (page 237)
30 g lemon thyme, picked
60 g garlic, finely sliced
16 g sodium citrate
850 g Montgomery Cheddar, grated

For the Taleggio omelette
200 g whipping cream
14 eggs, lightly beaten
400 g Taleggio, torn into chunks
6 g smoked salt

For the milk bread dough
236 g filtered water
9 g dried fast-action yeast
60 g honey
45 g whole milk
550 g strong white bread flour
7 g salt
2 eggs
80 g Rendered Aged Beef Fat (page 230)

To make the white pepper sausage patty
Toast the spices in a wide frying pan until fragrant, then blitz to a fine powder in a spice grinder.

Place all the ingredients into a bowl and mix together very well. Leave to set overnight in the fridge. Roll into 40 g balls and then set each one in a burger patty press or shape to a patty 10 cm (4 in) in diameter. Store the patties between sheets of baking parchment in an airtight container in the fridge and use within 2 days.

To make the spiced Guinness cheese slice
Toast the spices in a wide frying pan until fragrant, then blitz to a fine powder in a spice grinder.

In a saucepan, bring the beer, stock, Worcestershire sauce, suya pea reduction and spices to a simmer. Remove from the heat and add the lemon thyme and garlic. Infuse for 1 hour, then strain through a chinois.

Pour 500 g of the infused liquid into a pan and whisk in the sodium citrate. Place the pan over a low heat and slowly add the cheese, in batches, until you have a fondue-like texture. Pour the cheese sauce into a gastronorm lined with baking parchment – it should be about 2 mm (1/16 in) deep. Leave the cheese to cool, then slice into 7.5 cm (3 in) squares. Store the cheese slices between baking parchment in an airtight container in the fridge and use within 5 days.

To make the Taleggio omelette
Preheat the oven to 90°C/195°F/Gas Mark ¼.

Lightly whip the cream, then fold in the beaten eggs. Pour this mixture into a large gastronorm, then scatter over the Taleggio chunks and season with the smoked salt. Wrap the gastronorm in cling film, then steam the omelette for 4 minutes in the oven. Cool to room temperature, then slice the omelette into 7.5 cm (3 in) squares. Store in an airtight container in the fridge and use within 1 day.

To make the milk bread dough
Heat the water to 42°C (108°F). Add the yeast and honey and prove for 20 minutes.

In a stand mixer, combine the yeast water with the milk, flour, salt and eggs and knead for 20 minutes. Add the beef fat and mix for a further 10 minutes. Prove for 2 hours at room temperature, then punch out the air and leave in the fridge overnight.

The next morning, shape the bread into 85 g balls, making sure they are very tight and smooth. Flatten and prove on a baking tray for several hours until very well risen.

For the crunch topping
210 g rice flour
14 g dried fast-action yeast
30 g rapeseed (canola) oil
30 g smoked rapeseed (canola) oil
30 g soft brown sugar

To finish
Buffalo Sauce (page 234), for brushing
unsalted butter

To make the crunch topping
Preheat the oven to 180°C/350°F/Gas Mark 4.

In a bowl, mix together all the crunch topping ingredients
with 250 g water until well combined. Add more water if
necessary so the mixture is just pourable. Brush the mixture
on to the proved milk bread rolls.

Bake the rolls for 15 minutes and use immediately.

To finish
Sear 4 sausage patties on either side for 45 seconds–1 minute
or until well-browned. Brush the patties with buffalo sauce
and grill very quickly to create a sticky, caramelized surface.
Place a cheese slice on top of each patty, then transfer to
the top rack of the grill to slowly melt and keep warm.

Slice the milk bread rolls in half and butter the insides. Toast
the buttered side in a hot pan until golden.

Preheat the oven to 60°C/140°F, then steam 4 omelettes in
the oven for 3 minutes to reheat.

To build the sandwiches, start with the bottom half of each
roll, followed by the egg, then the cheese-coated patty and
finally the top half of the bread. Serve with more buffalo
sauce, if you like.

chicken fried in aromatic beef fat, sansho berries & winter truffles

Our first version of fried chicken was born out of an excess supply of aged beef fat, left over from the ribs we'd been receiving from our butchers. Consequently, many of our recipes ended up with beef fat in them; it replaced butter in our sauces, and even ended up in many of our desserts. The most delicious application, however, turned out to be using aromatic beef fat to baste perfectly cooked fried chicken.

I'd never eaten juicy fried chicken breast before, and took it as a personal challenge to use this part of the bird. Since it has very little connective tissue or fat, even a flawlessly cooked piece of chicken breast can be bland if the seasonings or brine aren't on point. Though the skin and fat can taste sublime, chicken breast itself still seems to be lacking. I was happy to discover pasture chickens from a farm in Yorkshire that are plump enough to take on an intense brine and an injection of seasoned beef fat.

We blast the chicken in the fryer twice to ensure a crisp coating, and also so that we can monitor the internal temperature in between cooking. The second fry takes the bird up to 55°C (131°F), at which point we carve it in half to expose the flesh, basting it with the aromatic beef fat. We serve the chicken with winter truffles and a reduction of roasted chicken wings, smearing the flavour compounds of caramelized collagen into the innocuous white flesh.

For the brined chicken
10 g dried Scotch bonnet chillies
20 g Sichuan peppercorns
20 g black peppercorns
20 g ground cumin
10 g coriander seeds
8 cloves
1 kg filtered water
100 g fine salt
2 × 300 g herb-fed chicken breasts
30 g grated lemon zest
40 g fresh root ginger, peeled and sliced
40 g garlic, sliced

For the garri fried chicken coating
15 g black peppercorns
10 g gola peppercorns
20 g ground ginger
20 g madras curry powder
30 g smoked paprika
600 g plain (all-purpose) flour
50 g tapioca flour
200 g garri
15 g bicarbonate of soda (baking soda)
30 g garlic powder
20 g fine salt

For the aromatic beef fat
20 g uda pods
2 kg Rendered Aged Beef Fat (page 230)
50 g garlic, sliced
bunch of lemon thyme
20 g Suya Powder (page 233)

To finish
100 g buttermilk
3 kg grapeseed oil, for deep-frying
Roasted Chicken Wing Jus (page 231–2)
black Urfa biber chilli
20 g Salted Sansho Berries (page 231)
strawberry mint
winter truffles

To brine the chicken
Toast the spices in a wide frying pan until fragrant.

In a saucepan, bring the water to the boil and add the salt, stirring until dissolved. Take off the heat and pour into a deep gastronorm, then add all the remaining ingredients, including the toasted spices. Wrap the gastronorm in cling film and cool to room temperature, then place in the fridge to infuse overnight.

The next day, strain and place the chicken breasts in a vacuum-seal bag with 150 g of the brine. Leave to cure for 3 hours in the fridge. Rinse the chicken by soaking it in a bowl of water for 30 minutes, changing the water halfway through. Store the chicken on wire racks in the fridge and use within 3 days.

To make the garri fried chicken coating
Toast the peppercorns in a wide frying pan until fragrant, then blitz to a fine powder in a spice grinder.

Sift the flours, then combine all the ingredients and stir very well with a whisk. Store the coating in an airtight container and use within 1 month.

To make the aromatic beef fat
Preheat the oven to 80°C/175°F.

Toast the uda pods in a wide frying pan until fragrant.

In an ovenproof pan, melt the rendered aged beef fat and heat to 80°C (175°F), then add the remaining ingredients, including the uda pods. Transfer to the oven and leave to infuse for 2 hours.

Strain the infused fat and leave to cool. Store the fat in an airtight container in the fridge and use within 2 weeks.

To finish
Place the buttermilk in a bowl. Lightly dust each chicken breast in the garri coating, then dip in the buttermilk. Return the chicken to the garri coating once more, ensuring the breasts are fully coated by pressing the flour mixture gently on to the chicken. Shake each piece and place on a sheet of baking parchment. Rest in the fridge for 2 hours, then take out and rest for 30 minutes at room temperature.

Gently warm the aromatic beef fat in a saucepan.

Heat the oil to 190°C (374°F) in a deep pot. Fry the chicken for 3 minutes, then rest on a wire rack for 10 minutes under a warm salamander or on the top rack of the grill. Once the internal temperature has reached 40°C (104°F), fry the chicken once more.

Rest the chicken until it reaches 55°C (131°F), then carve lengthways, turning each piece breast side up. Spoon the beef fat over the chicken flesh and coating and allow the excess to drip through the wire rack.

Place a chicken breast half in the centre of each of 4 plates. Bring the roasted chicken wing jus to a simmer, season with the black Urfa biber chilli and sansho berries, then glaze each breast with the hot jus. Garnish with strawberry mint and slices of winter truffle and serve.

fried landes chicken & chicken offal hot sauce

The original Ikoyi fried chicken had been off the menu for some time before we brought it back in a new guise. The pandemic had forced us to close the restaurant for some months, and when we returned, it didn't feel right to jump straight back into a conceptual tasting menu. There was a sense that we all needed some healing after our futures were thrown into jeopardy, and the prolonged anxiety had left us broken and searching for purpose. As I contemplated the meaning of comfort food, I reimagined how I'd like to cook and eat fried chicken.

For this second iteration, I wanted to serve half a chicken, this time including the breast, leg, oyster, parson's nose and foot. In contrast to the first style, which was perhaps more elegant, this version of our fried chicken displays more of a medieval morbidity, with the crisped chicken foot extending beyond the plate. I felt there would be more of a sense of theatre in eating the bird with the hands, picking up the gnarled claw and dipping the melting flesh into a hot sauce made of the chicken's offal.

After salting the chicken overnight, we steam each part individually at differing temperatures and for different times; the breast is steamed at a lower temperature in order to retain some of its moisture, while the dark meat is steamed at a higher temperature to soften the tougher tissues and muscles. The Landes chicken has a layer of exceptional yellow fat under the skin due to slow outdoor rearing and its diet of maize. We decided not to batter the chicken but to fry it naked instead, dusting it in a salt of fermented onions, hen-of-the-woods mushrooms and dried corn miso.

fried landes chicken & chicken offal hot sauce

serves 4 — pictured on p. 200

For the chicken finishing salt
1 kg Tropea onions, halved
40 g fine salt
1 kg hen-of-the-woods mushrooms
10 g cumin seeds
150 g Suya Pea Miso (page 236)
30 g smoked salt
7 g red chilli powder
25 g caster (superfine) sugar

For the 7082 pickles
200 g chardonnay vinegar
100 g honey
5 g yellow mustard seeds
100 g fermented Tropea onion juice, left over from the finishing salt
30 g dill
600 g 7082 cucumbers, halved lengthways
20 g smoked salt

For curing the chicken
25 g fennel seeds
15 g coriander seeds
15 g black peppercorns
15 g cubeb peppercorns
5 g star anise
200 g sea salt flakes
2 × 1.2 kg Landes chickens
200 g Rendered Aged Beef Fat (page 230)
iced water

To make the chicken finishing salt
Place the onions into a large vacuum-seal bag. Add 20 g of the fine salt to the bag and toss well. Spread the onions out into an even layer and seal on full. Leave to ferment for 7 days at 24–28°C (75–82°F). Repeat the same process for the mushrooms. If the bags expand too much, 'burp' out the air by making a small incision and then reseal. Taste the onions and mushrooms after 1 week: they should be sour, with complex, tart flavours. You can ferment them for several more days if required to achieve the desired flavour profile.

Preheat the oven to 55°C/130°F, and line 2 baking trays with silicone baking mats.

Strain the fermented onions and mushrooms, reserving the fermented onion juices to use in the pickle later. Place both the fermented onions and mushrooms on the prepared baking trays and dehydrate in the oven overnight.

The next day, toast the cumin in a wide frying pan until fragrant, then transfer to a spice grinder, along with the dried vegetables, suya pea miso, sugar and other spices. Blitz to a fine powder. Store the powder in an airtight container and use within 6 months.

To make the 7082 pickles
In a saucepan, bring the vinegar, honey and mustard seeds to a simmer. Leave to cool, then blend the liquid with the fermented onion juices and dill.

Season the cut sides of the cucumbers with the smoked salt. Place in a vacuum-seal bag with the pickling liquid, seal on full and marinate for at least 3 days in the fridge before using. Store the pickles in an airtight container in the fridge and use within 3 months.

To cure the chicken
Toast the spices in a wide frying pan until fragrant. Transfer to a blender, along with the salt, and blend until it forms a rough powder.

Cut through the back of each chicken with heavy-duty scissors to remove the backbone and chop off the neck and head with a cleaver. Reserve these off-cuts for stock. Remove the heart and liver and reserve for the offal hot sauce. Discard the gall bladder and keep the gizzard for another use. Remove the wishbone and slice the chicken in half through the breastbone.

Place some of the curing salt in a tea strainer and dust generously over the skin and flesh of the chickens. Leave them to marinate overnight.

For the chicken offal hot sauce
300 g chicken hearts and livers, taken
  from the chickens above
250 g whole milk
2 eggs
45 g rum
200 g whipping cream
400 g Ikoyi Hot Sauce (page 234)
30 g Citrus Kosho (page 236)
10 g smoked salt

To finish
3 kg grapeseed oil, for deep-frying

The next day, preheat a water bath to 75°C (167°F). Remove the legs from the breasts. Place in a vacuum-seal bag with 100 g of the beef fat and cook in the water bath for 3 hours.

Reduce the water bath heat to 55°C (131°F). Place the breasts in a vacuum-seal bag with the remaining 100 g of beef fat and cook for 2 hours in the water bath. Shock the chicken in iced water and reserve. Store in an airtight container in the fridge and use within 5 days.

To make the chicken offal hot sauce
Soak the chicken hearts and livers overnight in 100 g of the milk. If the chickens haven't yielded the amount you need for the recipe, you can order extra livers for the recipe.

The next day, strain the offal and discard the soaking milk. Place the hearts and livers in a blender and add the eggs, rum, cream and the remaining 150 g milk. Blend for 1 hour until the mixture reaches 60°C (140°F).

Chill the mixture, then blend with the hot sauce and citrus kosho for 5 minutes until very glossy. Season well with smoked salt. Store the offal hot sauce in an airtight container in the fridge and use within 1 week.

To finish
Heat the oil to 170°C (340°F) in a deep pot and fry the chicken legs for 6 minutes and the breasts for 3 minutes, then rest on a wire rack for 10 minutes under a warm salamander or on the top rack of the grill. Once the chicken reaches 55°C (131°F), transfer it to a mixing bowl. Dust the chicken generously with the finishing salt, then arrange the pieces on 4 serving plates. Serve with small bowls of the offal hot sauce and 4 of the 7082 pickles, cut into slices.

aged sheep kebab, green goddess & brittany seaweed

During my adolescence, I lived in the northwest of England, just outside Manchester. There wasn't a great number of restaurants near me, but as a special treat, my mother used to take me to Papa's, a local takeaway in a nearby town called Tytherington. The small business was run by a friendly Greek family, who supplied the community with fish and chips, kebabs and saveloys, a kind of bright red, deep-fried sausage made up of mysterious flavourings, pork, beef and unknown meat trimmings.

I remember standing in line with my £5 note – at the time, that was enough for a large kebab, large chips and a fizzy drink – dwarfed by the dusty workmen, teenagers and early evening socializers. I stood shyly in my dorky red school uniform, fascinated by the boundless, malt-coloured bathtub of oil from which 'Papa' would fish out haddock and soggy chips. I'd perch on the acrylic cabinet containing the fresh condiments and peer through to the back, where one of the sons was removing a frozen and deathly grey cylinder of meat from blue plastic wrapping. With one confident thrust, the young man impaled the meat on a blunt-looking spear and left it out to thaw in the humid back kitchen.

At the age of eight, sourcing and traceability weren't of much concern to me, so the fake-style meat and grisly vision of the cleaved kebab did not stop me from salivating as I watched slices of fatty, ovine gristle get shoved into a pitta along with chilli, garlic sauce and a salad of pickles and onions. The depth of seasoning and the bouncy texture of the meat, cut through with spicy-sour condiments, was an addictive sensation that became a lifelong craving.

Our kebab is unquestionably a homage to the ones I ate as a youngster. The meat is composed of the seven-week aged shoulder and belly of a retired mothering sheep from our friend Matt Chatfield, who runs The Cornwall Project. We mince the mutton with 40 per cent of its weight in fat, along with spices and onions squeezed of their juices. In search of that bouncy, resistant texture, I spoke with Kian Samyani of Berenjak restaurant in London, where he makes Iranian-style *koobideh*, a black-peppered lamb kebab with that characteristic bounce. He recommended a pinch of bicarbonate of soda (baking soda) thrown in the spice mix, which gives our kebabs that faux-meat springiness. With the fresh acidity of the green goddess and crunchy, pickled seaweed, the outcome undoubtedly has a cleaner taste than Papa's version.

**aged sheep kebab, green goddess &
brittany seaweed**

serves 4

pictured on p. 201

For the kebab spice base
30 g black peppercorns
30 g Sichuan peppercorns
60 g sumac
40 g hibiscus powder
40 g black Urfa biber chilli
25 g red chilli powder
120 g fine salt
40 g bicarbonate of soda (baking soda)

For the sheep kebab
500 g white onions, peeled
25 g garlic, sliced
1 kg sheep mince (60:40 meat-to-fat
    ratio)

For the brassica mustard salt
2 kg collard greens, any thick stems
    removed
500 g spinach, any thick stems
    removed
fine salt
yellow mustard seeds

For the green goddess sauce
80 g white onions, chopped
30 g chardonnay vinegar
30 g wild garlic
30 g tarragon, picked
40 g lovage, picked
20 g chives
20 g capers
20 g green chillies
80 g avocado
150 g plain yogurt
100 g Simple Mayonnaise (page 230)
30 g Green Oil (page 232)

For the pickled Brittany seaweed
50 g honey
60 g apple cider vinegar
200 g fresh wakame, rinsed

To make the kebab spice base
Toast the peppercorns in a wide frying pan until fragrant, then transfer to a spice grinder with the other spices, salt and bicarbonate of soda (baking soda). Blitz to a fine powder. Store the spice base in an airtight container and use within 1 month.

To make the sheep kebab
Place the onions into a food processor and blend to a fine paste. Squeeze the onion paste through a chinois, keeping the juices to use in another recipe.

In a large bowl, mix together the garlic, sheep mince and onion paste with 50 g of the spice base. Place in a blast-chiller set to -1°C (30°F) for 30 minutes. Pass the mixture through a mincer on medium setting twice, then roll into 50 g balls. Store the kebab balls on a wire rack in the fridge and use within 1 day.

To make the brassica mustard salt
Arrange the greens and spinach on a silicone baking mat in a flat layer and dehydrate for 1 hour at 75°C (167°F).

Weigh the dried greens then calculate 5 per cent of the weight to get your salt measurement, and 4 per cent to get your mustard seed measurement. Blend all the ingredients in a spice grinder to a fine powder. Store the powder in a sealed container with silica gel and use within 1 month.

To make the green goddess sauce
Place all the ingredients, except the simple mayonnaise and green oil, in a blender and blend for 3 minutes until glossy and smooth. Fold in the mayonnaise, followed by the green oil. Store the sauce in an airtight container in the fridge and use within 3 days.

To make the pickled Brittany seaweed
In a saucepan, combine the honey and vinegar with 80 g water. Bring to the boil, then pour over the wakame in a bowl. Leave to marinate overnight. Drain, reserving the pickling liquid, and slice the wakame into 1 mm-thick strips. Place the strips in an airtight container with the pickling liquid. Store in the fridge and use within 1 month.

improvisations

continued overleaf

aged sheep kebab, green goddess & brittany seaweed

For the blood orange marmalade
1.2 kg blood oranges
100 g blood orange juice
15 g pectin
150 g caster (superfine) sugar
30 g pasilla chillies, ground to a powder
10 g sumac
80 g honey
100 g Ikoyi Hot Sauce (page 234)
filtered water
20 g smoked salt

To finish
Suya Butter (page 230), melted, for
    basting
nasturtium leaves

To make the blood orange marmalade
Slice the oranges in half and remove the pith, seeds and outer stem. Remove the flesh from the skins and keep aside. Finely slice the skins and reserve.

Place the orange flesh into a blender with the extra blood orange juice and pectin and blend for 1 minute. Transfer the mixture to a saucepan and add the sugar and sliced skins. Bring to the boil, and once just thickened, take it off the heat. Stir in the ground pasilla chillies and sumac, along with the honey and hot sauce.

Return to the blender and blend with just enough filtered water to create a smooth, light texture. Season well with smoked salt. Store the marmalade in an airtight container in the fridge and use within 6 months.

To finish
Flatten 4 of the sheep kebabs and shape each one into an oval. Cook over the grill on high heat for 30 seconds on each side, basting with suya butter. Leave to rest on a higher part of your grill until the internal temperature reaches 58°C (136°F), then caramelize the kebabs on a hot plancha to create a crispy exterior.

Slice the kebabs while still quite hot: the meat should be fairly tense. As there is so much fat, it's preferable to eat the kebab at a higher temperature, so work quickly. Take out 4 plates. Brush some of the blood orange marmalade over the meat and place a kebab in the centre of each plate. Dress the plates with green goddess sauce and cover the kebabs with slices of the seaweed, followed by nasturtium leaves. Finish with a dusting of the brassica mustard salt and serve.

sweetbreads, schrenckii caviar & freshly dug potatoes

Sweetbreads are the thymus gland from veal or lamb. At Ikoyi, we prefer the bovine kind, since they're thicker and can sustain greater caramelization when cooked in foaming butter. We first brine our sweetbreads in salted milk before confiting them in fat. Once cooked, the sweetbreads rest in the chiller with a weighted press to create an even cooking surface, so that we can achieve a slightly denser consistency. We dust the delicate lobes in cornflour (cornstarch) prior to pan-roasting them in a golden fat infused with dried fruits and spices. The bronzed nuggets coated in bubbles of agitated browned butter emit aromas of butterscotch, roasted meat and smoked peppers. The outermost layer is brittle, cracking open to reveal the creamy, rose-tinted core.

While there is something quite debauched about the metallic spheres of caviar cloaking the sumptuous offal, the processing technique of the caviar itself gives the dish an even greater sense of personality. This caviar comes from pure schrenckii sturgeon, an extremely rare breed of fish grown in clear spring water in the mountainous regions of China. Our producer there, Hermes from N25 Caviar, hand-selects fish of the correct maturity that hold eggs worthy of ageing. Working almost like a chef himself, he tailors the salting and ageing period to the attributes of each given fish. Their eggs are reminiscent of custardy egg yolk and hazelnut, flavours that give the schrenckii its distinct character.

For the sweetbread preparation
30 g fine salt
100 g filtered water
900 g whole milk
2 kg veal sweetbreads
200 g Rendered Aged Beef Fat (page 230)
iced water

For the hazelnut black trumpet sauce
600 g red onions, sliced
70 g butter
36 g garlic, sliced
36 g Scotch bonnet chillies, sliced
15 g Malabar peppercorns
25 g sweet paprika
3 cloves
500 g black trumpet mushrooms
200 g chanterelle mushrooms
rapeseed (canola) oil, for coating
1.6 kg Cold-Brew Dashi (page 231)
450 g whipping cream
175 g Hazelnut Butter (made using peanut butter method on page 81)

For the freshly dug potatoes
1 kg Violetta or Yellow Nicola potatoes, scrubbed and sliced into 2.5 cm (1 in)-thick rounds
50 g extra virgin olive oil
10 g smoked salt

To prepare the sweetbreads
In a saucepan, quickly bring the salt and water to the boil and stir to dissolve. Pour into a bowl with the milk and whisk well. Add the sweetbreads to the milk brine, ensuring they are covered, and leave in the fridge for 24 hours.

The next day, drain the sweetbreads and place in a vacuum-seal bag with the beef fat. Confit for 90 minutes at 65°C (149°F). Shock in iced water, then transfer to a flat gastronorm. Place another gastronorm on top with a weight to press them down, and transfer to the fridge for at least 6 hours to set.

Once set, carefully remove all the membranes and then slice the sweetbreads into 50 g portions. Store the sweetbreads on a wire rack in the fridge and use within 3 days.

To make the hazelnut black trumpet sauce
In a large pan, slowly caramelize the onions in the butter until they are very sweet and dark. Add the garlic and Scotch bonnets towards the end.

Toast the spices in a wide frying pan until fragrant. Blitz in a spice grinder to a fine powder, then add to the onion mix.

Wash the mushrooms to remove dirt and debris, then lay them out on a kitchen cloth to dry in a warm place. Heat a frying pan until searing hot and toss handfuls of the mushrooms lightly in rapeseed (canola) oil. Fry the mushrooms in small batches so they don't overcrowd the pan. Leave them to char on their sides, moving them as little as possible, as doing so will cool down the pan and cause the mushrooms to release moisture.

Transfer to a blender, along with the onions and all the remaining ingredients. Blend for 5 minutes (you may need to work in batches). The final consistency should be an aerated nutty cream, totally smooth. Pass through a chinois. Store the sauce in an airtight container in the fridge and use within 1 week.

To cook the freshly dug potatoes
Preheat the oven to 90°C/195°F.

Toss the potato slices in the extra virgin olive oil and smoked salt. Place in a gastronorm and wrap with cling film, then steam in the oven for 45 minutes until just tender. Leave the potatoes to cool to room temperature, then store in an airtight container in the fridge and use within 3 days.

For the charred scallion vinaigrette
600 g spring onions
50 g garlic chives
rapeseed (canola) oil, for coating
5 g cubeb peppercorns
2 g Sichuan peppercorns
600 g extra virgin olive oil
300 g apple cider vinegar
20 g Worcestershire sauce
20 g smoked salt
15 g Roasted Kelp Paste (from Roasted
   Kelp Oil, page 233)

To finish
50 g cornflour (cornstarch)
rapeseed (canola) oil, for frying
Baobab Butter (page 230)
60 g N25 schrenckii caviar
smoked salt
Roasted Hazelnut Oil (see Nut & Seed
   Oils, page 232)

To make the charred scallion vinaigrette
Toss the spring onions and garlic chives in some rapeseed (canola) oil, then place in an even layer over a hot grill until blackened and smoky. Transfer the charred spring onions and chives to a gastronorm and wrap with cling film. Leave to continue cooking in the residual heat for 1 hour.

Toast the peppercorns in a wide frying pan until fragrant, then blitz to a fine powder in a spice grinder.

Place the spring onions and chives in a blender, along with the spice mix and all the other ingredients. Blend for 3 minutes. Leave to marinate overnight, then strain the next day. Store the vinaigrette in an airtight container in the fridge and use within 2 weeks.

To finish
Pat 4 sweetbread portions dry and roll in the cornflour (cornstarch). Heat a generous amount of rapeseed (canola) oil in a frying pan until lightly smoking. Place the sweetbreads into the pan and leave to caramelize until golden and crispy, adjusting the heat so they don't burn. Continue to cook the sweetbreads on all sides until evenly browned. Remove the sweetbreads from the pan and drain the fat.

Wipe the pan with a paper towel, then place it back over a medium–high heat. Add a large spoonful of baobab butter, along with the sweetbreads, and baste them without burning the butter. Remove the sweetbreads and set aside. Add 4 tablespoons of the potatoes to the same pan and warm through, dressing lightly with the charred scallion vinaigrette.

Warm 4 large spoonfuls of the hazelnut black trumpet sauce until barely hot – if you allow it to boil, it will thicken and ruin the smooth texture. Divide the sauce between 4 plates, pouring it into the centre of each one, and tap the undersides to flatten the sauce. Place a mound of potatoes in the centre of each plate, then top each with a sweetbread, followed by a quenelle of caviar. Season the dish with smoked salt and drizzle with hazelnut oil and some of the leftover juices from the pan before serving.

creamed spinach

The first time I ate in a steakhouse was with my father in San Francisco, at a place called John's Grill. The only thing I can really remember is the fresh creamed spinach, a simple bowl of well-seasoned greens cooked down with garlic and mascarpone. Since then, I've had the idea in my mind that creamed spinach is the ultimate comforting side dish, easily capable of taking centre stage on a menu as it's so deliciously satisfying to eat.

Although this is a short recipe, it's probably one of my most versatile. The base of part-chopped, part-blended spinach has a consistency similar to that of a risotto, and it goes well with almost anything: grilled meat, fish or a few shavings of truffle.

We work with the seasonal spinach from NamaYasai Farm in East Sussex, a verdant county south of London. Each variety contributes its own unique characteristic to the dish: the fat hen spinach is delicate, breaking down into the cooked cream base, whereas the New Zealand spinach adds an earthy, textural crunch. We split the spinach with oils of roasted mushrooms and garlic, lubricating its consistency and giving it an appealing sheen.

For the creamed spinach
25 g black peppercorns
10 g cayenne pepper
10 g ehuru
1.5 kg New Zealand spinach
1.5 kg fat hen spinach
iced water
250 g butter
70 g garlic, roughly chopped
500 g mascarpone
30 g Dijon mustard
15 g smoked salt

To finish
25 g benne seeds
25 g Roasted Garlic Oil (page 232)
40 g Roasted Mushroom Oil (page 232)

To make the creamed spinach
Toast the spices in a wide frying pan until fragrant, then blitz to a fine powder in a spice grinder.

Blanch both varieties of spinach separately for 30 seconds, then shock in iced water. Squeeze out all the moisture, then roughly chop the spinach.

Melt the butter in a wide pan, then add the garlic and spices. Stir in the fat hen spinach, mascarpone and Dijon mustard, stirring to combine and simmering to thicken slightly.

Transfer to a blender and blend for 1 minute, then fold in the chopped New Zealand spinach and season with the smoked salt. Pour the creamed spinach into a large, flat gastronorm and blast-chill to cool quickly. Store in an airtight container in the fridge and use within 5 days.

To finish
Preheat the oven to 160°C/325°F/Gas Mark 3.

Toast the benne seeds for 15 minutes, then set aside.

Warm 240 g of the creamed spinach in a pan until it begins to steam. Take off the heat and stir in the roasted garlic oil. Divide the spinach between 4 bowls and cover generously with the toasted benne seeds, then drizzle with the roasted mushroom oil before serving.

overripe plantain caramelized in ginger & kelp with uziza jam

We try to sit down and eat together as a team in the early afternoons before dinner service. We take it in turns to cook for the others, and we usually make vegetable-focused food using by-products from the main menu preparations as well as any excess from the farm deliveries. Some of the team find the regular appearances of fried rice with daikon or lentil and root vegetable stew slightly spartan at times, but in the end a heavy meal will only weigh us down and make our minds cloudy before a busy service ahead.

But there is one addictive treat that always makes its way into our day. One of our team members, Emmanuel, has a daily ritual of surreptitiously gathering all the over-ripe plantain trimmings and frying them for a staff snack. The slightly burned, chewy bits of warped and blackened plantain thrash about in a giant mixing bowl, along with ginger, garlic and spices. The recipe comes from his Ghanaian family, and he swears by it as the only real way to eat plantain. I always watch in amusement as every single piece gets gobbled up by the chefs and servers racing in and around the kitchen in anticipation of dinner service.

When it's used in this way, the plantain becomes so sweet, with just a hint of bitterness, and the sour zing of fresh ginger balances out the palate with a subtle savouriness from the garlic and caramelizing sugars. This merging of tastes is so unbeatably moreish that we couldn't not put it on the menu. It has since replaced the original Plantain, Smoked Scotch Bonnet & Raspberry (page 206), until we come across an even more delicious alternative.

To ensure the plantains cook to the right sweetness and texture, it's important to ripen your plantains in a warm room for up to five days. The fruit should be almost entirely black, with small streaks of yellow, and it should be soft to the touch. There is nothing worse than using underripe plantain, which has a papery feel and an acerbic bite. The aim is to caramelize the plantains until the point that they are almost molten and golden brown with aromas of muscovado sugar.

For the plantains
2 overripe plantains

For the ginger coating
3 g cloves
150 g fresh root ginger, peeled and
  roughly chopped
40 g garlic, roughly chopped
250 g rapeseed (canola) oil
20 g lemon juice
20 g Worcestershire sauce
10 g Suya Pea Reduction (page 237)
15 g grated lemon zest
30 g sweet paprika
15 g garlic powder
10 g ground ginger
10 g red chilli powder
8 g salt

For the uziza jam
10 g uziza peppercorns
550 g Cabernet Sauvignon vinegar
120 g honey
120 g filtered water
80 g caster (superfine) sugar
400 g raspberries
1.5 g agar agar
150 g maple verjus

To finish
Rendered Aged Sheep Fat (see
  Rendered Aged Beef Fat, page 230)
2 kg grapeseed oil, for deep-frying
chives, sliced into small rounds
4 pieces of Ikoyi Kimchi (page 234–6),
  sliced to the same width as the
  plantains
Roasted Kelp Oil (page 233)
smoked salt

To prepare the plantains
Slice the plantain skins lengthways and peel to remove. Square off the top ends of the plantains at an angle. Cut each plantain in half horizontally, then slice each piece in half lengthways, to a thickness of 3 mm (⅛ in). Store the plantain on sheets of baking parchment in the fridge and use within 1 day.

To make the ginger coating
Toast the cloves in a wide frying pan until fragrant, then blitz to a fine powder in a spice grinder.

Place all the ingredients in a blender, including the ground cloves. Add 100 g water and blitz together to form a smooth paste. Store the ginger coating in an airtight container in the fridge and use within 1 week.

To make the uziza jam
Toast the uziza peppercorns in a wide frying pan until fragrant, then blitz to a fine powder in a spice grinder.

In a saucepan, heat 400 g of the vinegar with the honey, water and sugar to 103°C (217°F), then add the raspberries and uziza powder. Transfer to a blender and blend for 1 minute. Leave to marinate for 2 hours, then strain.

Transfer the strained liquid to a saucepan. Add the agar agar and hand-blend to combine, then bring to the boil for 30 seconds. Chill until set completely, then return to the blender and blend with the verjus and the remaining 150 g vinegar for 5 minutes. Pass the jam through a chinois, then place in a vacuum-seal bag and seal to remove the air bubbles. Store the jam in an airtight container in the fridge and use within 1 month.

To finish
In a saucepan, gently warm the aged sheep fat.

Heat the oil to 170°C (340°F) in a deep pot and fry the plantains for 4–5 minutes until caramelized and soft. Remove from the pot and immediately brush with the hot sheep fat. Leave to cool for 30 seconds, then brush the ginger coating on top with a wide brush in long, uninterrupted motions.

Cover the plantains with a carpet of chopped chives and place a piece of kimchi at the top end of each piece of plantain. Take out 4 plates and place a piece of plantain in the centre of each one. Drizzle generously with roasted kelp oil and season with smoked salt. Place a spoonful of the jam to the left of each piece of plantain and serve.

tiger nut custard &
mount etna pistachio

Some of the most memorable servings I've made have been dishes that falter precariously between sweet and savoury. The combined flavours of burned sugar, silken cream, roasted nuts and grilled meats can quickly go from being a sublime experience to one that is disturbing and misjudged if not balanced properly. I enjoy pushing the diner to this extreme point of instability, where the balance of satisfying their palate could easily swing in or out of favour.

When we reopened Ikoyi after the UK's second Covid-19 lockdown in 2021, I wanted to serve something refreshing, light-textured but intensely flavoured mid-way or perhaps towards the end of the meal, at some point before the main savoury course. The idea of serving something dessert-like in appearance came to mind. I'd always loved the minimalist simplicity of crème Catalan and so used the concept of a set cream as the base for our tiger nut custard. Inspired by the Catalan version's dark-tinted cream, which is stained by liquid caramel, I decided to encase our custard in an obscure substance. Instead of introducing sugar into the recipe, I was intrigued to play with the toasted notes of caramel that you often find in nuts.

We achieve the creaminess of custard using a technique similar to Japanese steamed *chawanmushi*. Instead of adding dairy, we soak and blend the tiger nuts with a light dashi, leaving the mixture to macerate, allowing the sugars and starches of the tiger nuts to seep well into the infusion. Once strained through muslin cloth and seasoned, we mix the tuber milk with eggs and steam until just set. While the custard looks simple, understanding when to stop the steaming process is, in fact, quite complex and requires careful observation. We cook the custard to about 80 per cent of its final doneness, leaving the bowls to rest at room temperature as the residual heat continues the cooking and setting of the base.

The purest expression of roasted nuts we could find for this serving was the Bronte pistachio from Mount Etna. We roast the nuts very gently, careful to loosen the oils without over-caramelizing them. While still hot, we press the nuts through our nut press, extracting verdant, plankton-like sap as the husks fall to the side like shed skins. The chilled oil transforms into a fluid, gel-like texture, glazing the surface of the custard and sitting on it like jelly. We serve the custard at room temperature, so the tiger nuts can release their flavour more easily.

The first spoonful of the dish comes off quite mild because of the temperature. As the pistachio oil warms, sweet and roasted flavours enter the palate, with an underlying, subtle umami from the caviar and dashi, rendering the addition of salt unnecessary.

For the tiger nut custard base
500 g peeled tiger nuts
3 kg filtered water
100 g kombu
20 g dried porcini mushrooms (ceps)
20 g dried shiitake mushrooms
160 g white soy sauce
120 g honey

To finish
40 g eggs
80 g tiger nut custard base (see above)
Pistachio Oil (see Nut & Seed Oils, page 232)
80 g N25 kaluga caviar

To make the tiger nut custard base
Soak the tiger nuts in 1 kg of the filtered water overnight. At the same time, pour the remaining 2 kg filtered water into a vacuum-seal bag and add the kombu, porcini and shiitake. Seal and leave to infuse overnight in the fridge.

The next day, strain the tiger nuts and transfer to a blender. Add the contents of the vacuum-seal bag and blend for 5 minutes (you may need to do this in batches). Leave to infuse for 2 hours, then strain through a chinois, pressing the solids to release all the liquid. Strain the liquid again, this time through a muslin cloth, this time not using any pressure. This will ensure the custard base is free of any particles.

Season with the white soy sauce and honey and store in an airtight container in the fridge. Use within 3 days.

To finish
In a bowl, gently whisk the eggs with a fork, making sure not to over-aerate them. Add 80 g of the custard base to the bowl and stir gently. Pass through a chinois, then transfer to a vacuum-seal bag. Seal until there are no air bubbles.

Preheat the oven to 85°C/185°F.

Take out 4 custard bowls and add 30 g custard to each, being careful not to disturb or shake the liquid. Place the bowls in a flat gastronorm. Cover with cling film, then steam in the oven for 25–30 minutes. Allow to cool in the gastronorm to room temperature for 10 minutes, then place in a blast-chiller at -5°C (23°F) until completely set.

Glaze the custard bowls with fresh pistachio oil, placing a 20 g spoonful of caviar to the left of each one, then serve.

base recipes

Butters

Anchovy Butter
Makes approx. 500 g

50 g Scotch bonnet chillies
10 g black peppercorns
500 g butter, cubed
75 g Ortiz anchovies, chopped
25 g grated lemon zest
30 g garlic, finely chopped
30 g fresh root ginger, finely chopped

Scorch the chillies with a blowtorch, then deseed and chop.

Toast the black peppercorn in a wide frying pan until fragrant, then blitz to a fine powder in a spice grinder.

Put half the butter into the base of a Pacojet container, then top with the anchovies, lemon zest, chillies, garlic and ginger. Scatter over the peppercorn powder, then top with the remaining butter. Compact the butter and make sure the surface is smooth. Freeze overnight.

The next day, process the butter in the Pacojet and refreeze. Repeat the process 3 more times.

Store the butter in an airtight container in the fridge and use within 1 week.

Baobab Butter
Makes approx. 1 kg

5 g black peppercorns
10 g Madagascan peppercorns
10 g red chilli powder
3 g ground cloves
10 g smoked paprika
20 g baobab powder
5 g garlic powder
1 kg butter, at room temperature

Toast the black and Madagascan peppercorns in a wide frying pan until fragrant. Blitz to a fine powder in a spice grinder, then mix with the other powdered spices and garlic powder.

Beat the butter and spices together in a stand mixer for 3 minutes until well combined.

Store in an airtight container in the fridge and use within 1 week.

Honey Butter
Makes approx. 1.5 kg

500 g butter, at room temperature
1 kg honey
12 g smoked salt

In a stand mixer, beat together the butter, honey and salt for 3 minutes until well combined. Store in an airtight container in the fridge and use within 1 week.

Suya Butter
Makes 1.8 kg

For the brown butter
2 kg butter

For the suya butter
1 quantity Suya Powder (page 233)
250 g garlic, finely minced

To make the brown butter
Heat the butter slowly in a heavy-based pot until the butter reaches 170°C (338°F), stirring frequently to disperse the caramelized solids and create an evenly browned butter.

To make the suya butter
Preheat the oven to 80°C/175°F.

Cool the butter to 80°C (175°F) in a deep square gastronorm, then add all the suya powder and minced garlic. Whisk well to combine, then wrap the container in cling film and leave in the oven for 2 hours.

Decant the melted butter through a muslin cloth-lined chinois to remove the solids.

Store the butter in an airtight container in the fridge and use within 1 week.

Rendered Aged Beef Fat
Makes approx. 1.6 kg

5 kg beef rib-cap fat*, diced into small chunks

Preheat the oven to 115°C/240°F/Gas Mark ½.

Put the beef fat chunks into a large gastronorm and bake for 12 hours, then strain the fat through a muslin cloth-lined chinois.

Store the rendered fat in an airtight container in the fridge and use within 2 weeks.

*This recipe also works for other animal fats, such as sheep or pork.

Condiments, Pickles & Vinegars

House Pickle
Makes 4 kg

1.1 kg apple cider vinegar
2 kg filtered water
900 g honey
25 g black peppercorns
10 g ehuru
10 g uda pods
10 g ancho chillies
10 g lavender
10 g thyme
20 g bay leaves

In a large pot, bring the vinegar, water and honey to the boil, then set aside.

Toast the peppercorns, ehuru and uda pods in a wide frying pan until fragrant, then add to the pickle liquid, along with the chillies, lavender, thyme and bay leaves. Cool the pickle to room temperature and leave to infuse overnight in the fridge.

Strain the pickle the next day and store in an airtight container in the fridge. Use within 3 months.

Simple Mayonnaise
Makes 2 kg

500 g olive oil
1 kg grapeseed oil
130 g egg yolks
30 g Dijon mustard
14 g smoked salt
40 g lemon juice
200 g House Pickle (see above)
70 g filtered water (if needed)

In a jug, mix together the olive and grapeseed oils.

In a food processor, blitz the egg yolks, mustard, salt and lemon juice until a cohesive paste forms. Emulsify the egg mixture by slowly adding half of the mixed oil. Scrape down the sides of the blender, then add half of the house pickle. Continue emulsifying with the remaining the oil, followed by the remaining house pickle. Add the filtered water to loosen if necessary.

Store the mayonnaise in an airtight container in the fridge and use within 1 week.

Pickled Wild Garlic Capers
Makes 500 g

500 g wild garlic capers
150 g fine salt
100 g honey
500 g apple cider vinegar
20 g ancho chillies

Mix the capers with the salt in a vacuum-seal bag. Seal and leave to rest in the fridge for 1 month.

After a month, remove the capers from the bag and rinse well.

In a saucepan, combine the honey, cider vinegar and chillies with 100 g water. Bring to the boil, then remove from the heat and cool to room temperature.

Transfer to a vacuum-seal bag with the rinsed capers. Seal and marinate for 1 month before using.

Store the capers in an airtight container in the fridge and use within 1 year.

Salted Sansho Berries
Makes 1 kg

1 kg fresh sansho berries
80 g fine salt

Mix the sansho berries with the salt in a vacuum-seal bag. Seal and allow the salted sansho berries to rest in the fridge for 3 months before using them. Store the sansho berries in an airtight container in the fridge and use within 1 year.

Smoked Vinaigrette
Makes 1.2 kg

330 g maple verjus
765 g extra virgin olive oil
90 g Roasted Garlic Oil (page 232)
24 g cayenne pepper
30 g smoked paprika
24 g garlic powder

Whisk all the ingredients together until fully emulsified.

Prepare a handheld smoker filled with oak chips. Spread the mixture on to a thin layer in a large gastronorm and wrap in cling film. Make a small incision in the cling film and insert the tip of the smoker. Smoke the vinaigrette for 30 seconds, then seal the hole with another piece of cling film.

Leave to infuse for 1 hour, then repeat the smoking process 4 times.

Store the vinaigrette in an airtight container in the fridge and use within 1 month.

Fruit Vinegar
Makes 1.8 kg

1 kg fruit, such as strawberries, plums, cherries and mango, chopped
100 g honey
1.5 kg white wine vinegar

Mix the fruit with the honey and vinegar in a vacuum-seal bag. Seal and leave to age for 4 months in the fridge.

Strain through a muslin cloth-lined chinois. Store the fruit vinegar in an airtight container in the fridge and use within 1 year.

Herb Vinegar
Makes 1 kg

300 g herbs, such as shiso, lovage, parsley and dill, chopped
1 kg white wine vinegar

Mix the herbs with the vinegar in a vacuum-seal bag. Seal and age for 4 months in the fridge.

Strain through a muslin cloth-lined chinois. Store the herb vinegar in an airtight container in the fridge and use within 1 year.

Dashi & Stocks

Cold-Brew Dashi
Makes 1.4 kg

50 g kombu
20 g dried shiitake mushrooms
20 g dried porcini mushrooms (ceps)
1.5 kg filtered water

Soak the kombu and mushrooms in the water for 12 hours at room temperature, then strain. Use by the next day.

Aged Beef Stock
Makes 5 kg

5 kg beef rib trim and bones*, chopped into small pieces
rapeseed (canola) oil
7 kg filtered water

Preheat the oven to 160°C/325°F/Gas Mark 3.

Lightly coat the meat and bones in rapeseed (canola) oil and roast for 90 minutes.

Place the roasted trimming and bones into a deep stock pot and cover with the filtered water. If there is any meat stuck to the roasting trays, deglaze with some of the water and add to the stock pot.

Bring to a very low simmer and cook for 12 hours, keeping it below boiling, as if you were infusing the stock like a tea.

Strain the stock through a muslin cloth-lined chinois into a pan and reduce to the desired intensity, at which point you can season the stock or jus with vinegars and infusions.

Store in an airtight container in the fridge and use within 1 week.

*This recipe also works well for sheep and pork stocks.

Roasted Chicken Wing Stock
Makes 8 kg

8 kg chicken wings
10 kg filtered water

Preheat the oven to 170°C/340°F/Gas Mark 3½.

Roast 8 kg of the wings for 2 hours, then transfer into a large stock pot and cover with the water. Deglaze any of the meat stuck to the roasting trays with some of the water and add to the stock pot.

Bring to a very low simmer and cook for 12 hours, keeping it below boiling, as if you were infusing the stock like a tea.

Strain the stock through a muslin cloth-lined chinois. At this point, you can use the stock as it is, reduce it to your desired intensity, or continue with the instructions below to make a jus.

Roasted Chicken Wing Jus
Makes 1 kg

3 kg chicken wings
125 g butter
200 g shallots, peeled and quartered
20 g lemon juice
30 g lemon thyme

Place the extra 3 kg chicken wings in a deep stock pot with the butter. Once they are caramelized, remove the chicken wings from the pot and set aside.

continued overleaf

Add the shallots to the residual fat in the pot and cook. Once the shallots are also deeply caramelized, return the chicken wings to the pot, along with the strained stock. Simmer for 3 hours, then strain through a muslin cloth-lined chinois once more into a pan.

Reduce the jus to a glaze-like consistency and season with the lemon juice. Allow to cool to 80°C (175°F), then add the lemon thyme. Infuse for 30 minutes, then strain.

Store the jus in an airtight container in the fridge and use within 1 week.

Roasted Fish Bone Stock
Makes 4 kg

5 kg turbot bones
rapeseed (canola) oil
6 kg filtered water

Preheat the oven to 140°C/275°F/Gas Mark 1 and line 2 gastronorms with baking parchment.

Dry the bones and rub with rapeseed (canola) oil. Place the bones in the lined gastronorms and roast for 1 hour, then transfer to a deep stock pot and cover with the water.

Bring to the boil, then reduce to a very low simmer, so the stock is barely bubbling, almost as if you were infusing the bones like a tea. Cook for 1 hour, then strain through a muslin cloth-lined chinois into a pan.

Reduce the stock to 4 kg, or to your desired intensity.

Store in an airtight container in the fridge and use within 1 week.

Octopus Stock

The octopus gelatine gleaned from the octopus recipes on pages 83 and 111 is a useful ingredient and should be reserved. It contains a lot of salinity and savoury flavour from the black garlic and uda pods, and can be let down to make a useful seasoning stock. Because the exact quantities vary depending on how much gelatine you are able to glean, I have given ratios rather than quantities for this recipe.

reserved octopus cooking gelatine
filtered water
kombu
lemon juice

Weigh the octopus gelatine and multiply the weight by 2.5 to work out the required weight of water. Calculate 2.5 per cent of the gelatine weight: this is the required weight for the kombu.

Combine the gelatine and water in a large stock pot and heat until it reaches 70°C (158°F).

Take off the heat and add the kombu. Leave to infuse for 1 hour, then strain and season to taste with lemon juice.

Store in an airtight container in the fridge and use within 1 week.

Oils

Nut & Seed Oils

At Ikoyi, we make all our nut and seed oils in our nut press. First we roast the nuts as below to loosen the fats, then we pass them through the press. To make a nut oil without a nut press, just follow the steps below.

1 part nuts or seeds
4 parts grapeseed oil (optional)

Preheat the oven to 150°C/300°F/Gas Mark 2.

Roast the nuts or seeds for 8 minutes, then transfer to a high-powered blender along with the grapeseed oil, if using. Blend for 7 minutes. Cool the blended oil and leave it to marinate in the fridge overnight.

The next day, strain the oil through a muslin cloth-lined chinois.

Store the nut oil in an airtight container in the fridge and use within 1 month.

Green Oil
Makes 500 g

200 g parsley leaves
200 g lovage leaves
50 g chive leaves
100 g chervil leaves
900 g grapeseed oil

In a blender, blend the leaves with the oil for 7 minutes, working in batches if needed. Blast-chill the oil very quickly, then leave to marinate in the fridge overnight.

The next day, strain the oil through a muslin cloth-lined chinois.

Store the oil in an airtight container in the fridge and use within 2 weeks.

Roasted Mushroom Oil
Makes 1.8 kg

2 kg grapeseed oil
100 g dried porcini mushrooms (ceps)
100 g dried shiitake mushrooms
100 g dried hen-of-the-woods mushrooms
100 g dried black trumpet mushrooms
100 g dried chanterelle mushrooms

Preheat the oven to 85°C/185°F.

Pour the oil over the mushrooms in a large, flat gastronorm. Wrap the container in cling film, then bake for 15 hours. Strain the hot oil through a muslin cloth-lined chinois.

Store in an airtight container in the fridge and use within 1 month.

Roasted Garlic Oil
Makes 1.5 kg

500 g whole garlic bulbs
1.5 kg grapeseed oil

Preheat the oven to 140°C/275°F/Gas Mark 1.

Wrap the garlic bulbs in foil and roast for 1 hour.

Remove the foil and transfer the whole roasted garlic bulbs to a blender with the oil. Blitz for 2 minutes.

Transfer the garlic oil mixture to a vacuum-seal bag. Seal and leave to infuse for 2 days in the fridge.

After 2 days, pass the oil through a muslin cloth-lined chinois.

Store in airtight container in the fridge and use within 1 month.

Gola Peppercorn Oil
Makes 200 g

50 g gola peppercorns*
200 g grapeseed oil

Preheat a water bath to 75°C (167°F).

Toast the peppercorns in a wide frying pan until fragrant, then blitz to a fine powder in a spice grinder. Mix the peppercorns with the oil in a vacuum-seal bag. Seal and cook for 1 hour in the water bath, then leave to infuse overnight.

The next day, pass the oil through a muslin cloth-lined chinois. Store in an airtight container in the fridge and use within 1 month.

*This recipe can be applied to a variety of peppercorns.

Roasted Kelp Oil & Roasted Kelp Paste
Makes 500 g

200 g kombu
500 g grapeseed oil

Preheat the oven to 220°C/425°F/Gas Mark 7.

Roast the kombu on a baking tray for 15 minutes, then transfer to a blender and blitz to a fine powder. Add the oil and blend for a further 7 minutes.

Transfer the mixture to the fridge and leave to marinate for 2 days.

Once the sediment has fully settled, decant the roasted kelp oil off the top and keep the paste for another use.

Store the oil in an airtight container in the fridge and use within 1 month.

Cures & Salts

Fish Cure
Makes 1 kg

500 g caster (superfine) sugar
500 g fine salt

Mix together the sugar and the salt. Store in an airtight container and use within 6 months.

Citrus Fish Cure
Makes 600 g

10 g green Sichuan peppercorns
20 g uziza peppercorns
20 g grains of paradise
10 g fennel seeds
300 g fine salt
200 g caster (superfine) sugar
15 g grated lime zest
15 g grated yuzu zest

Toast the peppercorns, grains of paradise and fennel seeds in a wide frying pan until fragrant, then blitz to a fine powder in a spice grinder.

Mix together the salt, sugar, spices and citrus zest.

Store the cure in an airtight container in the fridge and use within 1 week.

Katsuobushi Salt
Makes 400 g

25 g cumin seeds
25 g coriander seeds
10 g black peppercorns
5 g uda pods
5 g star anise
5 g ehuru
160 g katsuobushi
200 g smoked salt

Toast the spices in a wide frying pan until fragrant, then blitz to a fine powder in a spice grinder.

Toast the katsuobushi in a large frying pan until browned and very smoky. Transfer to a blender, along with the salt and the spice mixture. Blend all the ingredients to a fine powder.

Store the katsuobushi salt in an airtight container and use within 6 months.

Spices & Hot Sauces

Suya Powder
Makes 325 g

10 g uda pods
20 g black peppercorns
10 g gola peppercorns
5 g Sichuan peppercorns
5 g grains of paradise
3 g cloves
10 g cumin seeds
5 g fennel seeds
40 g smoked paprika
35 g cayenne pepper
15 g Cameroon chilli powder
15 g madras curry powder
5 g ground cinnamon
10 g ground ginger
10 g onion powder
5 g garlic powder
10 g dried oregano
80 g peanuts
10 g katsuobushi
20 g crayfish powder

Preheat the oven to 200°C/400°F/Gas Mark 6.

Toast the whole spices in a wide frying pan until fragrant. Blitz to a fine powder in a spice grinder. Sift into a bowl with the ground spices, along with the onion and garlic powder and the oregano. Set aside.

Place the peanuts into a roasting tray and roast for 12 minutes, then cool to room temperature. Freeze the peanuts, then pulse in a blender until a fine powder is achieved.

Reduce the oven temperature to 150°C/300°F/Gas Mark 2. Place the katsuobushi and crayfish powder on a baking tray and bake for 15 minutes until lightly browned, then blitz to a fine powder in a spice grinder.

Mix all the ingredients together and store in an airtight container for up to 2 months.

Ren's Iru Vadouvan

Our vadouvan blend is made by our spice supplier, Ren, using her mix of madras curry powder, curry leaves and black sesame. In this recipe, we dehydrate and pulverize fermented locust beans, also known as *iru*, to give the blend extra depth. This recipe is a simplified version of the original, which can take 3–4 hours to make.

Makes 150 g

20 g iru
60 g sunflower oil
400 g red onions, very finely diced
30 g fresh curry leaves
50 g madras curry powder
25 g black sesame seeds
fine salt

Preheat the oven to 55°C/130°F.

Spread out the iru on a baking tray and place in the oven for 12 hours to dry out, then blitz in a spice grinder to a fine powder.

Pour the oil into a frying pan and fry the onions until very golden brown and crispy, stirring constantly. Dry the onions out well on paper towels and leave to cool.

Transfer the onions to a food processor and blend with the curry leaves until well combined. Add the curry powder, ground iru and black sesame. Mix with a whisk and season to taste with fine salt.

Store the vadouvan in an airtight container and use within 10 days.

Lacto-Fermented Scotch Bonnet Chillies
Makes 400 g

500 g Scotch bonnet chillies, halved and deseeded
10 g fine salt

Mix the chillies and salt in a large vacuum-seal bag and toss well to distribute the salt. Make sure the chillies are evenly spaced out in a single layer. Seal the bag on full and leave to ferment for 7 days at 24–28°C (75–82°F). If the bag has expanded too far, 'burp' out the air by making a small incision and then reseal.

Once the chillies have reached a sour, fragrant and meaty flavour profile, store them in an airtight container in the fridge and use within 2 months.

Ikoyi Hot Sauce
Makes 4 kg

2.9 kg red chillies, stems removed
150 g garlic, peeled
93 g fine salt
350 g light brown sugar
350 g honey
70 g rice vinegar
25 g fish sauce
100 g Lacto-Fermented Scotch Bonnet Chillies (page 234)
15 g white Penja peppercorns
10 g gola peppercorns
5 g cubeb peppercorns
50 g grated lemon zest

Place the chillies, garlic and fine salt into a blender and blend to form the paste. Divide the mixture equally between 2 vacuum-seal bags. Seal on full and ferment for 7 days at 24–28°C (75–82°F). If the bags expand too much, 'burp' out the air by making a small incision and then reseal.

Remove the contents of one of the bags and place in a new vacuum-seal bag with the sugar, honey, vinegar and fish sauce. Seal, and reserve this mixed bag (bag A) for 1 week in the fridge, while continuing to ferment the other bag (bag B).

After the second week, empty the contents of bag A into a saucepan. Bring to the boil, then simmer for 15 minutes. Remove from the heat and cool to room temperature.

Toast the spices in a wide frying pan until fragrant, then blitz to a fine powder in a spice grinder.

Transfer the cooled, cooked contents of bag A to a blender, along with the contents of bag B. Blend for 4 minutes. Add the fermented Scotch bonnets and the toasted ground spices and blend for a further 2 minutes.

Pass the hot sauce through a muslin cloth-lined chinois and mix in the lemon zest, then age for 1 month.

Store the hot sauce in an airtight container in the fridge and use within 3 months.

Buffalo Sauce
Makes 1.8 kg

260 g Aged Beef Stock (page 231)
1 kg Ikoyi Hot Sauce (page 234)
100 g Coffee Buckwheat Shoyu (page 237–8)
150 g honey
300 g butter, cut into cubes

Reduce the aged beef stock to a glaze consistency, then transfer to a blender. Add the hot sauce, shoyu and honey and blend for 2 minutes. Add the butter piece by piece, emulsifying it into the mixture between additions.

Store the buffalo sauce in an airtight container in the fridge and use within 2 weeks.

Roasted Malted Barley Bread Spice Glaze
Makes 2.5 kg

1 kg Roasted Malted Barley Bread Miso (page 237)
7 kg filtered water
150 g dried porcini mushrooms (ceps)
150 g dried black trumpet mushrooms
300 g kombu
100 g black garlic
30 g pasilla chillies
8 star anise
4 cloves
20 g long peppercorns
agar agar

In a blender, blend the roasted malted barley bread miso with the filtered water. Transfer to a large pot over a very low heat and add the remaining ingredients, except the agar agar. Simmer for 3 hours, then strain through a muslin cloth-lined chinois.

Calculate 0.02 per cent of the strained weight: this is the weight for your agar agar. Remove 200 g of the liquid from the pot and transfer to a blender with the agar agar. Blend to combine, then transfer back into the remaining liquid and hand-blend to incorporate. Freeze overnight.

The next day, hang the frozen miso water in a muslin cloth, allowing the melting liquid to strain through as it thaws. Reduce the clarified tamari very slowly on the stove until it coats the back of a spoon.

Store the reduction in an airtight container in the fridge and use within 3 months.

Ikoyi Kimchi
Makes 2 kg

1 kg kohlrabi, sliced into eighths*
500 g baby leeks, sliced into rounds*
300 g pears, sliced into eighths*
60 g fine salt
100 g benne seeds
10 g cubeb peppercorns
5 g Malabar peppercorns
5 g black peppercorns
25 g smoked paprika
10 g ancho chillies
25 g red chilli powder
80 g garlic, roughly chopped
80 g fresh root ginger, roughly chopped
100 g Lacto-Fermented Scotch Bonnet Chillies (page 234)
25 g Benne Miso (page 236)
50 g dried shrimps
50 g tamari
50 g honey
100 g Cold-Brew Dashi (page 231)
45 g smoked salt

In a large bowl, toss the kohlrabi, leeks and pears with the fine salt and leave overnight or for at least 6 hours at room temperature, then lightly rinse.

Toast the benne seeds and spices in a wide frying pan until fragrant, then blitz to a fine powder in a spice grinder.

Place the garlic, ginger, chillies, benne miso, shrimps, tamari, honey, cold-brew dashi and smoked salt in a blender, and add the spice mix. Blend for 2 minutes to form a paste.

In a large, deep gastronorm, mix the paste well with the kohlrabi, leeks and pears until well combined. Pack the mixture tightly into large vacuum-seal

opposite: coffee buckwheat shoyu

see p. 237

continued overleaf

bags and seal on full. Leave the kimchi to ferment for 5 days at 24–28°C (75–82°F), then transfer to the fridge for 1 month before using.

Store the kimchi in an airtight container in the fridge and use within 3 months, or age for up to 1 year.

*This recipe can be applied to a variety of fruits and vegetables, such as apples, cabbage, daikon and beetroots (beets).

Citrus Kosho
Makes 1 kg

We produce our citrus kosho during the prime season for citrus during winter. We select a mixture of blood orange, yuzu, Buddha's hand lemon, makrut lime and green chillies.

300 g green chillies, deseeded and finely chopped
50 g Scotch bonnet chillies, deseeded and finely chopped
75 g fine salt
650 g grated citrus zest
100 g citrus juice

Mix together the chillies, salt and citrus zest and juice. Place in an airtight container and age in the fridge for 1 month before using.

It will keep for up to 6 months in the fridge.

Misos

I developed our misos in conjunction with our fermentation chef, Ed Welby, during his time at Ikoyi. We use the misos and their reductions as flavour-intensifiers in many of our recipes. While they may not be the star of a given dish, they play an important role in laying the foundations for deep, savoury taste.

Jasmine Rice Koji
Makes 1 kg
pictured on p. 235

1 kg jasmine rice
filtered water, for soaking
koji spores

Soak the rice in filtered water overnight.

The next day, preheat the oven to 100°C/210°F/Gas Mark ¼. Steam the rice for 20 minutes in the oven until cooked but not mushy.

Line a square gastronorm with a clean kitchen cloth. Cool the rice in the gastronorm to 30°C (86°F) and break the grains apart to ensure they are well separated and not sticking together. Use a tea strainer to apply a layer of koji spores to the rice. Turn the grains and coat once more time with another layer of spores to make sure all the grains are well inoculated.

Preheat a water bath to 38°C (100°F). Place the gastronorm into the water bath and cover with a slightly dampened kitchen cloth. Leave to ferment for 24 hours, then break up the grains and rearrange into rows a few inches apart. Ferment for a further 24 hours, making sure to monitor the temperature so that it does not exceed 42°C (108°F). Reduce the temperature of the water bath or fan the grains if the temperature begins to approach that limit.

After 48 hours, the grains should smell fruity, almost like peaches.

Store the koji in an airtight container in the fridge and use within 3 days.

Caramelized Jerusalem Artichoke Miso
Makes 1.2 kg

1 kg Jerusalem artichokes, halved lengthways
rapeseed (canola) oil
400 g Jasmine Rice Koji (see above)
340 g sea salt flakes
1 kg filtered water

Preheat the oven to 170°C/340°F/Gas Mark 3½ and line a gastronorm with foil.

Coat the artichoke pieces in the oil and place in an even layer in the prepared gastronorm. Roast for 1 hour until the artichokes are caramelized and soft in the centre, then leave to cool.

Weigh out 600 g of the artichokes and transfer to a food processor. Add the jasmine koji and 70 g of the sea salt flakes and blitz to form a smooth miso paste.

Dissolve another 70 g of the sea salt flakes in the filtered water and use the resulting brine to adjust the consistency of the paste to ensure it is smooth and not too thick.

Pack the miso tightly into a sterilized fermentation vessel and cover with the remaining 200 g sea salt flakes. Place a layer of cling film on top of the salt, followed by some weights. Leave to ferment at room temperature for 1 year.

Once it's ready, store the miso in an airtight container in the fridge and use within 1 year.

Benne Miso
Makes 1 kg
pictured on p. 239

600 g benne seeds
400 g Jasmine Rice Koji (see above)
280 g sea salt flakes
1 kg filtered water

Preheat the oven to 160°C/325°F/Gas Mark 3.

Toast the benne seeds for 15 minutes.

Allow the seeds to cool, then transfer to a food processor, along with the jasmine koji and 40 g of the sea salt flakes. Blitz to form a smooth miso paste.

Dissolve another 40 g of the sea salt flakes in the filtered water and use the resulting brine to adjust the consistency of the paste to ensure it is smooth and not too thick.

Pack the miso tightly into a sterilized fermentation vessel and cover with the remaining 200 g sea salt flakes. Place a layer of cling film on top of the salt, followed by some weights. Leave to ferment at room temperature for 3 weeks, and then for a further 3 months in the fridge.

Once it's ready, store the miso in an airtight container in the fridge and use within 1 year.

Suya Pea Miso
Makes 1 kg

200 g dried red peas, soaked overnight
400 g Jasmine Rice Koji (see above)
100 g Suya Powder (page 233)
280 g sea salt flakes
1 kg filtered water

Preheat the oven to 160°C/325°F/Gas Mark 3. Steam the soaked peas in the oven until tender but not mushy. They should be just soft enough to crush between thumb and forefinger. Leave to cool completely.

Once cooled, weight out 500 g of the cooked peas and transfer to a food processor. Add the jasmine koji, suya powder and 40 g of the sea salt flakes. Blitz to form a smooth miso paste.

Dissolve another 40 g of the sea salt flakes in the filtered water and use the resulting brine to adjust the consistency of the paste to ensure it is smooth and not too thick.

Pack the miso tightly into a sterilized fermentation vessel and cover with the remaining 200 g sea salt flakes. Place a layer of cling film on top of the salt, followed by some weights. Leave to ferment at room temperature for 3 weeks, and then for a further 3 months in the fridge.

Once it's ready, store the miso in an airtight container in the fridge and use within 1 year.

Note: To make a plain pea miso, replace the suya powder with another 100 g of cooked red peas.

Suya Pea Reduction
Makes 2.5 kg

1 kg Suya Pea Miso (see above)
7 kg filtered water
300 g kombu
100 g black garlic
150 g dried porcini mushrooms (ceps)
150 g dried black trumpet mushrooms
agar agar

In a blender, blend the suya pea miso with the filtered water. Transfer to a large pot over a very low heat and add the kombu, black garlic and dried mushrooms. Simmer for 3 hours then strain through a muslin cloth-lined chinois.

Calculate 0.02 per cent of the strained weight: this is the weight for your agar agar. Remove 200 g of the liquid from the pot and transfer to a blender with the agar agar. Blend to combine, then transfer back into the remaining liquid and hand-blend to incorporate. Freeze overnight.

The next day, hang the frozen miso water in a muslin cloth, allowing the melting liquid to strain through as it thaws. Reduce the clarified tamari very slowly on the stove until it coats the back of a spoon.

Store the reduction in an airtight container in the fridge and use within 3 months.

Pumpkin Seed Miso
Makes 1kg

600 g pumpkin seeds
400 g Jasmine Rice Koji (see opposite)
280 g sea salt flakes
1 kg filtered water

Preheat the oven to 160°C/325°F/Gas Mark 3.

Toast the pumpkin seeds for 15 minutes. Allow the seeds to cool, then transfer to a food processor with the jasmine koji and 40 g of the sea salt flakes. Blitz to form a smooth miso paste.

Dissolve another 40 g of the sea salt flakes in the filtered water and use the resulting brine to adjust the consistency of the paste to ensure it is smooth and not too thick.

Pack the miso tightly into a sterilized fermentation vessel and cover with the remaining 200 g of sea salt flakes. Place a layer of cling film on top of the salt and then add some weights.

Leave to ferment at room temperature for 3 weeks, and then for a further 3 months in the fridge.

Once it's ready, store the miso in an airtight container in the fridge and use within 1 year.

Pumpkin Seed Miso Butter
Makes 600 g

250 g pumpkin seeds
60 g Pumpkin Seed Miso (page 237)
40 g honey
20 g baobab powder
250 g Brown Butter (see Suya Butter, page 230)
10 g smoked salt

Preheat the oven to 170°C/340°F/Gas Mark 3½ and roast the pumpkin seeds for 15 minutes.

Allow the seeds to cool, then blend in a food processor with all the other ingredients for 8 minutes.

Store the pumpkin seed miso butter in an airtight container in the fridge and use within 1 month.

Roasted Malted Barley Bread Miso
Makes 1 kg

600 g Roasted Malted Barley Bread (page 81)
400 g Jasmine Rice Koji (see opposite)
280 g sea salt flakes
1 kg filtered water

Preheat the oven to 140°C/275°F/Gas Mark 1.

Roast the bread for 15 minutes. Allow to cool, then shred into small pieces and place in a food processor with the jasmine koji and 40 g of the sea salt flakes. Blitz to form a smooth miso paste.

Dissolve another 40 g of the sea salt flakes with the filtered water and use the resulting brine to adjust the consistency of the paste to ensure it is smooth and not too thick.

Pack the miso tightly into a sterilized fermentation vessel and cover with the remaining 200 g of sea salt flakes. Place a layer of cling film on top of the salt, and then top with some weights. Leave to ferment at room temperature for 3 weeks, and then for a further 3 months in the fridge.

Once it's ready, store the miso in an airtight container in the fridge and use within 1 year.

Coffee Buckwheat Shoyu
Makes 1.8 kg

600 g dried red peas, soaked overnight
600 g buckwheat
koji spores
1.9 kg filtered water
365 g sea salt flakes
200 g ground coffee

Preheat the oven to 100°C/210°F/Gas Mark ¼. Steam the soaked peas in the oven until tender but not mushy. They should be just soft enough to crush between thumb and forefinger. Leave to cool completely.

Adjust the oven to 170°C/340°F/Gas Mark 3½ and roast the buckwheat for 45 minutes until very dark and nutty. Transfer to a food processor and blitz to form a rough powdered grain.

continued overleaf

Weigh out 1.25 kg of the cooked red peas and mix well with the toasted buckwheat. Make sure the mixture has cooled to 30°C (86°F), then line a square gastronorm with a clean kitchen cloth and fill it with the red pea and buckwheat mixture. Use a tea strainer to apply a layer of koji spores to the red peas and buckwheat. Turn the mixture over, then cover with another coat of spores to make sure the whole thing is well inoculated.

Preheat a water bath to 38°C (100°F). Place the gastronorm into the water bath and cover with a slightly dampened kitchen cloth. Leave to ferment for 24 hours.

Break up the koji mixture and rearrange into rows a few inches apart. Ferment for a further 24 hours, making sure to monitor the temperature so that it does not exceed 42°C (108°F). If it does approach this limit, reduce the temperature of the water bath or fan the mixture.

After 48 hours, the koji mixture should have changed dramatically and should smell of caramelized fruit.

Bring 500 g of the filtered water to the boil and dissolve the salt. Whisk this brine into the remaining filtered water. Crumble the koji mixture into a sterilized fermentation vessel, along with the ground coffee.

Make sure that the brine has cooled to below 35°C (95°F), then pour it over the koji mixture and coffee and stir well. Place a layer of cling film on top of the mixture, making sure it is in direct contact with its surface, then cover the container with a breathable towel attached with a rubber band to ensure the mixture can vent.

Let the shoyu ferment for 4 months at room temperature. For the first 2 weeks, stir the shoyu well with a whisk once a day. After this time, stir the shoyu once a week. Once the shoyu has achieved an intense level of umami and complexity, strain and press through a muslin cloth-lined chinois. It should taste deeply savoury, with notes of coffee and toasted grains.

Store the shoyu in an airtight container in the fridge and use within 1 year.

Roasted Miso Powder
Makes 200 g

1 kg miso (any of the previous recipes or store-bought)
filtered water (for adjustment)

Preheat the oven to 60°C/140°F.

Hand-blend your miso of choice with just enough filtered water that it becomes spreadable. Use a palette knife to spread the miso over silicone baking mats and dehydrate for 12 hours in the oven.

Remove from the oven and leave to cool to room temperature. Break up the dried sheets of miso and transfer to a blender. Blend for 2 minutes to form a fine powder: it should be totally pulverized.

Sift through a fine sieve. Store the roasted miso powder in an airtight container and use within 6 months.

opposite: benne miso see p. 236

notes

glossary

Terms

bloom (in terms of gelatine)
Blooming gelatine is the process of soaking gelatine in water to soften before using it.

brunoise
Brunoise is a term for finely quartered vegetables producing fine, equally sized cubes.

cold-smoke
The process of smoking ingredients at cold or low temperatures so as to not cook the target ingredient.

seal on full (relating to vacuum-sealing)
A means of sealing food in a vacuum-pack bag on full pressure to remove all air in the environment.

Equipment

blast-chiller
An adjustable fridge/freezer that can quickly cool food items to a precise, chilled temperature. Blast chillers are used to quickly chill sauces, purées or ice cream bases to retain maximum freshness. We also use blast chillers to dry meat or fish for short periods of time.

blowtorch
A handheld device that with an adjustable flame used to cook or burn food and enhance flavour.

chinois
A cone-shaped sieve used to filter liquids or strain stocks and sauces to create a smooth consistency.

dehydrator
A low temperature oven or box that dries food so that it can be blitzed to a powder or used for a crisp consistency.

fermentation vessel
A jar or tub made of glass or plastic with a sealable lid used to store and ferment ingredients.

gastronorm
A flat metal container of varying sizes used to hold food products or finished dishes.

handheld smoker
A portable device that can be filled with woodchips used to smoke ingredients or dishes.

pacojet
A commercial machine used for churning ice creams, purées and sauces.

plancha
A flat-top griddle used for caramelizing and searing meat, fish or vegetables with a minimal amount of smoking.

salamander
A specialized grill used to quickly warm, brown or finish dishes.

vacuum-seal bag
A plastic, food-grade and heat-safe bag that can be airtight sealed to store or cook food.

vacuum-sealer
A device that removes air from the space around food within a sealed bag.

water bath / sous vide
A controlled bath that maintains water at a consistent temperature to cook food slowly for extended periods of time in a controlled environment.

index

Photographs are indicated by page numbers in *italics*.

recipe notes

All menu recipes serve four.

The recipes within were developed in a working professional kitchen and so menu sub-recipes may produce extra quantities than those required to make up a four-person serving. Storage instructions are given for all sub-recipes.

All butter is unsalted, all milk is whole (full-fat) and all herbs are fresh, unless otherwise specified. Eggs are assumed to be large (US extra-large) and preferably organic and free-range.

When using the zest of citrus fruit, buy unwaxed or organic.

Cooking and preparation times are for guidance only, as individual ovens vary. If using a convection (fan) oven, follow the manufacturer's instructions concerning oven temperatures.

Some of the recipes require advanced techniques, specialist equipment and professional experience to achieve good results.

Exercise a high level of caution when following recipes involving any potentially hazardous activity including the use of high temperatures and open flames and when deep-frying. In particular, when deep-frying, add food carefully to avoid splashing, wear long sleeves, and never leave the pan unattended.

Some recipes include raw or very lightly cooked eggs, meat or fish, and fermented products. These should be avoided by the elderly, infants, pregnant women, convalescents and anyone who has an impaired immune system.

As some species of mushrooms have been known to cause allergic reaction and illness, do take extra care when cooking and eating mushrooms and do seek immediate medical help if you experience a reaction after preparing or eating them.

When sterilizing jars for preserves and ferments, wash the jars in clean, hot water and rinse thoroughly. Heat the oven to 140°C/275°F/Gas Mark 1. Place the jars on a baking sheet and place in the oven to dry.

When no quantity is specified – for example of oils, salts and herbs used for finishing dishes or for deep-frying – quantities are discretionary and flexible.

about the author

Jeremy Chan is the chef and co-founder of Ikoyi in London. After studying languages and philosophy at university, he went on to work in the field of renewable energy before embarking on his career in cooking. Jeremy opened Ikoyi with his best friend, Iré Hassan-Odukale, in 2017 and earned a Michelin star a year after opening, followed by a second star three years later. Ikoyi was named one of the World's 50 Best Restaurants in 2022 and is known to be one of the most original, flavour-driven restaurants of its time. The foundation for the restaurant's menu is a vast collection of spices from Sub-Saharan West Africa and produce from local farms and artisan producers, with fish, beef and vegetables sourced from the British Isles to create a cuisine based on the islands' micro-seasonality. All of Jeremy Chan's dishes touch on personal memories to do with spice and flavour, many of them relating to his childhood in Hong Kong.

acknowledgements

Thank you to Alia for your continual support, encouragement and advice while writing this book. Thank you to my family, Lorna, Roy and Julia, for letting me write this book in your dining room and for believing in me. Thank you to my kitchen and management team, who supported me through the whole process: Christian Faulkner, Max Coen, Riccardo 'Bibo' Manca, Cedric Campbell-Carter, Sean Singco, Ed Welby, Edward Moore, Paulina Bartecka, Manny, Father Boateng, Dominik Jurasz and Kostas Chiotelis. Thank you to Uncle Segun, Aunty Abi, Nana, Oye Hassan-Odukale and Uncle Adrian for your wisdom and willingness to always support us. Thank you to Maureen Evans for the beautiful photography. Thank you to Ian Warren, Matt Chatfield, Dan Cox, Robin, Ikuko, Oli and Calixta for sharing your farms with us. Thank you to Shola Olunloyo for inspiring us to work with African umami. Thank you to Emily Takoudes and Emilia Terragni for your guidance and for giving me the opportunity to create this book. Thank you to Iré for creating Ikoyi with me and for your perpetual kindness, which forms the context in which all of our work comes to life.

Phaidon Press Limited
2 Cooperage Yard
London E15 2QR

Phaidon Press Inc.
65 Bleecker Street
New York, NY 10012

phaidon.com

First published 2023
© 2023 Phaidon Press Limited

ISBN:
978 1 83866 630 9 (trade edition)
978 1 83866 684 2 (signed edition)

A CIP catalogue record for this book is available from the
British Library and the Library of Congress.

Commissioning Editor: Emily Takoudes
Project Editor: Claire Rogers
Production Controller: Adela Cory
Design: Associate Studio
Photos: Maureen Evans

The publisher would like to thank Ruth Ellis, Laura Nickoll,
Tara O'Sullivan and Ellie Smith.

Printed in China